Researching Collocations in Another Language

Also by Andy Barfield

AUTONOMY YOU ASK! (*co-edited with M. Nix*)

LEXICAL PROCESSING IN SECOND LANGUAGE LEARNERS: PAPERS AND PERSPECTIVES IN HONOUR OF PAUL MEARA (*co-edited with T. Fitzpatrick*)

MAINTAINING CONTROL: AUTONOMY AND LANGUAGE LEARNING (*co-edited with R. Pemberton and S. Toogood*)

RECONSTRUCTING AUTONOMY IN LANGUAGE EDUCATION: INQUIRY AND INNOVATION (*co-edited with S. Brown*)

Also by Henrik Gyllstad

TESTING ENGLISH COLLOCATIONS: DEVELOPING RECEPTIVE TESTS FOR USE WITH ADVANCED SWEDISH LEARNERS

Researching Collocations in Another Language

Multiple Interpretations

Edited by

Andy Barfield
Chuo University, Tokyo, Japan

Henrik Gyllstad
Lund University, Sweden

palgrave
macmillan

First published 2009 by
PALGRAVE MACMILLAN

Palgrave Macmillan in the UK is an imprint of Macmillan Publishers Limited, registered in England, company number 785998, of Houndmills, Basingstoke, Hampshire RG21 6XS.

Palgrave Macmillan in the US is a division of St Martin's Press LLC, 175 Fifth Avenue, New York, NY 10010.

Palgrave Macmillan is the global academic imprint of the above companies and has companies and representatives throughout the world.

Palgrave® and Macmillan® are registered trademarks in the United States, the United Kingdom, Europe and other countries

ISBN-13: 978-0-230-20348-8 hardback

This book is printed on paper suitable for recycling and made from fully managed and sustained forest sources. Logging, pulping and manufacturing processes are expected to conform to the environmental regulations of the country of origin.

A catalogue record for this book is available from the British Library.

A catalog record for this book is available from the Library of Congress.

10 9 8 7 6 5 4 3 2 1
18 17 16 15 14 13 12 11 10 09

Printed and bound in Great Britain by
CPI Antony Rowe, Chippenham and Eastbourne

Andrew
dedicates this publication
to the love and memory
of his parents,

John (1923–2008) and Muriel (1925–2009) Barfield.

Henrik dedicates this publication to

Magdalena.

Contents

List of Figures

List of Tables

Acknowledgements

The cover design is based on work by Henrik Gyllstad, and the cover photo of the Windrush River by Minster Lovell Hall, Oxfordshire is courtesy of Andrew Barfield.

Notes on Contributors

Svenja Adolphs is Associate Professor in Applied Linguistics in the School of English Studies at the University of Nottingham. Her interests are in the areas of discourse analysis and corpus linguistics, and she been involved in a range of spoken corpus development projects, including both native and non-native varieties. She has published widely on pragmatic aspects of multiword expressions and is currently overseeing a project on the description of such expressions in spoken learner English.

Andy Barfield teaches in the Faculty of Law at Chuo University, Tokyo. His research interests include collaborative curriculum development, learners' collocation development, and learner autonomy in second language education. Andy's book publications include *Reconstructing Autonomy in Language Education: Inquiry and Innovation* (2007; co-edited with S. Brown; Palgrave Macmillan) and *Lexical Processing in Second Language Learners: Papers and Perspectives in Honour of Paul Meara* (2009; co-edited with T. Fitzpatrick; Multilingual Matters).

June Eyckmans teaches at the Erasmus University College Brussels and the Vrije Universiteit Brussels. Her research interests include the development of tests to measure L2 phrasal knowledge. Recent publications include *Measuring Receptive Vocabulary Size: Reliability and Validity of the Yes/No Vocabulary Test* (2004; Utrecht: LOT); Formulaic sequences and perceived oral proficiency: putting a lexical approach to the test (2006; co-authored with F. Boers, J. Kappel, H. Stengers and M. Demecheleer: *Language Teaching Research* 10/3: 245–61); Learners' response behaviour in Yes/No Vocabulary Tests (2007; co-authored with H. Van de Velde, R. Van Hout, and F. Boers: in H. Daller, J. Milton and J. Treffers-Daller (eds), *Modelling and Assessing Vocabulary Knowledge*, 59–76; Cambridge University Press.)

Sylviane Granger is Professor of English Language and Linguistics and Director of the Centre for English Corpus Linguistics at the University of Louvain (Belgium). In 1990 she launched the *International Corpus of Learner English* project, which has grown to contain writing by EFL learners from 19 different mother tongue backgrounds. Her main research interests centre on the compilation and exploitation of learner and bilingual corpora, second language acquisition, phraseology and lexicography. Sylviane's publications include *Computer Learner Corpora, Second Language Acquisition and Foreign Language Teaching* (2002; co-edited with J. Hung and S. Petch-Tyson; John Benjamins), *Phraseology: An Interdisciplinary Perspective* (2008; co-edited with F. Meunier; John Benjamins), and *Phraseology in Foreign Language Learning and Teaching* (2008; co-edited with F. Meunier; John Benjamins).

Nicholas Groom is a Lecturer in Applied Linguistics at the Centre for English Language Studies, University of Birmingham, UK. His research focuses on developing and applying corpus linguistic approaches to issues in second language acquisition, English language teaching and discourse analysis, and his recent publications span all three of these areas.

Henrik Gyllstad is Senior Lecturer in English Linguistics at the Centre for Languages and Literature, Lund University, Sweden. His main research interests range across language testing and general second language vocabulary and phraseology acquisition. He is also interested in vocabulary acquisition within English for Specific Purposes, and the processes involved in the storage and activation of words in the bilingual lexicon. Henrik's publications include: Testing L2 Vocabulary: Current test formats in English as an L2 used at Swedish Universities (2004; *The Department of English in Lund: Working Papers in Linguistics* 4: 21–40), The Word Doctor (2005; *Essential Teacher Compleat Links* 2/3) and *Testing English Collocations: Developing Receptive Tests for Use with Advanced Swedish Learners* (2007; Lund: Lund University).

Susanne Handl is a full-time Linguistics lecturer at Munich University. Her main research interests, besides collocations and lexicography, are lexicology, semantics and text linguistics with a strong affinity to corpus linguistics. Publications include: Essential collocations for learners of English: The role of collocational direction and weight (2008; in S. Granger and F. Meunier (eds), *Phraseology in Foreign Language Learning and Teaching*, 43–65; John Benjamins); Collocation, anchoring and the mental lexicon – an ontogenetic perspective (2009; co-authored with E. Graf; in H.-J. Schmid and S. Handl (eds), *Cognitive Foundations of Linguistic Usage Patterns*; de Gruyter); in preparation; *Collocation – Convenience Food for the Learner* (John Benjamins).

Birgit Henriksen is Senior Lecturer at the Department of English, Germanic and Romance Studies at the University of Copenhagen. Her main research interests are the acquisition of adjectives, the construct of network knowledge, and vocabulary learning tasks. She recently co-authored an anthology of vocabulary learning tasks, and her latest project dealt with the acquisition of network knowledge, lexical inferencing and writing. Birgit's publications include: Three dimensions of vocabulary development (1999; *Studies in Second Language Acquisition* 21/2: 303–17); Teaching collocations: Pedagogical implications based on a cross-sectional study of Danish EFL learners' written production of English collocations (2006; co-authored with R. Revier; in M. Bendtsen, M. Björklund, C. Fant and L. Forsman (eds), *Språk, lärende och utbildning i sikte: festskrift tillägnad professor Kaj Sjöholm* (173–89); Pedagogiska fakulteten Åbo Akademi, Vasa) and *Vocabulary and Writing in the First and Second Language: Processes and Development* (2008; co-authored with D. Albrechtsen and K. Haastrup; Palgrave Macmillan).

Jingyi Jiang is Associate Professor at the School of Foreign Languages, South China University of Technology, Guangzhou, China, where she teaches Advanced English and Extensive Reading to undergraduate students and Second Language Acquisition to graduate students. Her research interests are second language acquisition, teaching pedagogy, as well as materials development. Jingyi's recent publications include *Zooming In: An Integrated English Course* (2007; Shanghai: Shanghai Foreign Language Education Press) and *Reading to Develop Your Ideas* (2005; Shanghai: Shanghai Foreign Language Education Press), for both of which she was chief editor, and Textbooks and learners (2006; *Foreign Language World* 2: 53–6).

Yuri Komuro teaches English at Chuo University, Tokyo. She specializes in lexicography, and her main research interests have been centred on the treatment of collocation in learners' dictionaries and on the development of phraseological dictionaries. As a lexicographer, she has worked on the English learners' dictionary *Luminous English–Japanese Dictionary* (2001, 1st edn; 2005, 2nd edn) and the *Longman English–Japanese Dictionary* (2006).

Phoebe Ming-sum Lin is working on her PhD thesis in Applied Linguistics in the School of English Studies, University of Nottingham. Her thesis is on the prosody of formulaic sequences, and her main research interests include formulaic language, prosody, corpus linguistics, psycholinguistics and second language acquisition. She has presented widely on the issue of formulaic sequences.

Hilary Nesi is Professor in English Language at Coventry University, UK. She has led projects to create the BASE corpus of British Academic

Spoken English, and the BAWE corpus of British Academic Written English, and she is a member of the advisory panel for Macmillan English Dictionaries. She is the author of *The Use and Abuse of Learners' Dictionaries* (2000; Max Niemeyer) and has published a number of articles on the design and use of learners' dictionaries, as well as many papers relating to the teaching of English for Academic Purposes. Hilary recently wrote a chapter on the history of electronic dictionaries for the *Oxford History of English Lexicography* (2008; Oxford University Press).

Marnie O'Neill is an Associate Professor at The University of Western Australia and coordinates the professional doctoral programme in the Graduate School of Education. She teaches and supervises in both the on-shore programs and the transnational programs in Singapore and Hong Kong. Her doctoral thesis focused on cultural variation in reading comprehension, particularly of literary texts. Marnie supervises qualitative interpretivist studies in fields such as gender studies, curriculum theory, policy and practice, classroom interaction, teacher induction and professional development, and social discourse theory. Her professional publications include three sets of resource books for teaching literature.

Elke Peters completed her PhD at the University of Leuven (Belgium) in 2006. Her PhD project centred on L2 vocabulary acquisition through reading. She investigated the effect of three potential enhancement techniques on L2 learners' use of an online dictionary and on their word retention. Elke works as Assistant Professor of German at the Department of Applied Language Studies at the Lessius University College (Antwerp). She is also a research fellow at the University of Leuven. Her research interests focus on L2 vocabulary acquisition, CALL and language testing. She has, among others, published in *Language Learning, Language Learning & Technology*, and *ITL* (*International Journal of Applied Linguistics*).

Randi Reppen is Professor of Applied Linguistics in the English Department of Northern Arizona University. Her research interests include the use of corpora for materials development and language teaching and also how corpus linguistics can be used to inform our knowledge of how young students acquire writing. Randi's publications include articles in *Applied Linguistics, TESOL Quarterly, Language Awareness,* and *The ELT Journal*. She recently co-edited with Annelie Ädel *Corpora and Discourse: The Challenges of Different Settings* (2008; John Benjamins).

Robert Lee Revier is a PhD fellow at Aarhus University (Denmark), where he is conducting research in foreign language learning and teaching. A major aim of his PhD project is to develop a test for measuring productive knowledge of English collocations. Robert's graduate work is summarized in Revier and Henriksen (2006): Teaching collocations: Pedagogical implications based on a cross-sectional study of Danish EFL learners' written production of English collocations (in M. Bendtsen, M. Björklund, C. Fant and L. Forsman (eds), *Språk, lärende och utbilding i sikte* (173–89), Pedagogiska fakulteten Åbo Akademi, Vasa).

John Shillaw is Professor of English Language Education at Nanzan University, Japan. His interest in using corpora to develop vocabulary tests later led John to research the validity of checklist (Yes/No) tests. His research and publications include: Using a corpus to develop vocabulary tests (1994; in L. Flowerdew and A.K.K. Tong (eds), *Entering Text*, 166–82, Hong Kong University of Science and Technology); The application of the Rasch model to Yes/No vocabulary tests (1999; unpublished PhD thesis; University of Wales Swansea); Putting Yes/No tests in context (2009; in T. Fitzpatrick and A. Barfield (eds), *Lexical Processing in Language Learners: Papers and Perspectives in Honour of Paul Meara*; Multilingual Matters).

Lars Stenius Stæhr is Senior Lecturer at the Centre for Internationalisation and Parallel Language Use at the University of Copenhagen. His PhD research aimed to define and operationalise the multidimensional construct of vocabulary knowledge and empirically investigate the relationship between vocabulary knowledge and listening comprehension in English as a foreign language. This involved exploring the role of collocation knowledge in achieving successful listening comprehension. Lars' research interests lie in the field of second language acquisition and language testing and focus on the relationship between lexical competence and language proficiency. His publications include: Vocabulary size and the skills of listening, reading and writing (2008; L.S. Stæhr, *Language Learning Journal* 36/2: 139–52) and *Vocabulary Knowledge and Listening Comprehension in English as a Foreign Language: An Empirical Study Employing Data Elicited from Danish EFL Learners* (2005; L.S. Jensen, Copenhagen: Copenhagen Business School/Samfundslitteratur).

Alison Wray is a Research Professor in the Centre for Language and Communication Research at Cardiff University, UK, and is the Director of Research in the Cardiff School of English, Communication and Philosophy. She has extensively researched the phenomenon of formulaic language, publishing many articles and two books (2002, *Formulaic Language and the Lexicon*, Cambridge University Press; 2008, *Formulaic Language: Pushing the Boundaries*, Oxford University Press). She has also contributed to debates on the evolutionary origins of language and edited *The Transition to Language* (2002; Oxford University Press). She is co-author of two research method books (2006, *Projects in Linguistics*, 2nd edn, Hodder Arnold, with Bloomer; 2006, *Critical Reading and Writing for Postgraduates*, with Wallace, Sage).

Yang Ying is a lecturer at the National University of Singapore, coordinating and teaching English proficiency and writing skills courses and taking charge of SELF (an Independent Learning Facility) at the Centre for English Language Communication. Her current research interest is in English language programme and course design, learner autonomy, textbook writing and L2 collocation knowledge and development. Yang has worked as an associate editor for a number of national textbook projects in mainland China. Her major publications include three sets of reading textbooks, a book on creative college writing, and papers mainly on collocation learning and collocation awareness.

1

Introduction: Researching L2 Collocation Knowledge and Development

Andy Barfield and Henrik Gyllstad

The collocation gap in second language acquisition research

For anyone learning or teaching a second language, collocation is undoubtedly one of the most fascinating (and at times frustrating) challenges that they will face. Equally, for those interested in researching second language (L2) collocation knowledge and development, the challenges are both fascinating and frustrating, but for different reasons. Although several wide-ranging volumes of research in L2 vocabulary acquisition have been published in the last 15 years or so (Arnaud and Béjoint, 1992; Coady and Huckin, 1997; Schmitt and McCarthy, 1997; Read, 2000; Schmitt, 2000; Nation, 2001; Schmitt, 2004; Bogaards and Laufer, 2004; Daller et al., 2007; Fitzpatrick and Barfield, 2009), they have rarely included dedicated studies of L2 collocation knowledge and development. In fact, in the last decade, only five book-length publications in English stand out for the more specific focus that they take on L2 collocation knowledge and use (Cowie, 1998c; Lewis, 2000; Nesselhauf, 2005; Schmitt, 2004; Meunier and Granger, 2008). The first situates collocation within the broader field of phraseology and provides a far-ranging exposition of corpus-based studies, some of which are collocation-focused. *Teaching Collocation*, edited by Lewis, is also multi-authored and is directed towards the pedagogic treatment of collocations in the classroom. Nesselhauf's solo-authored volume provides an in-depth analysis of the Verb + Noun collocations in a corpus of essays written by advanced German L1 learners of English. The two other edited volumes (Schmitt, 2004) and (Meunier and Granger, 2008) go beyond collocation itself by taking a generally wider view of the formulaic and phraseological patterning of language. Until now, then, there has been no single volume of work focused solely on researching L2 collocation knowledge and development within different local contexts.

To address this gap, *Researching Collocations in Another Language* is an international collection of L2 collocation studies that, for the first time, brings together dedicated research from Asia, Europe, and North America in the following four areas:

- using learner corpora to identify patterns of L2 collocation use (Part I, Chapters 2–5)
- developing appropriate L2 collocation lexicographic and classroom materials (Part II, Chapters 6–9)
- investigating how learners' L2 collocation knowledge can be assessed (Part III, Chapters 10–13)
- exploring the processes and practices by which learners develop their L2 collocation knowledge and use (Part IV, Chapters 14–17).

Each part includes three research chapters and a critical commentary. Written by experts in the respective field (Part I: Sylviane Granger; Part II: Hilary Nesi; Part III: John Shillaw; Part IV: Birgit Henriksen and Lars Stenius Stæhr), the commentary chapters identify and take up issues of interest across each set of research studies and constructively re-frame them within a broader critical view. While Alison Wray looks back, in Chapter 18, the closing chapter, at the whole collection to draw out further connections and potential contradictions in researching collocations in another language, it is our wish, in this opening chapter, to lay out the general contours for the work that follows in the rest of this book. We will first consider differing interpretations of the concept of collocation and how these lead into varying research priorities. We will then highlight some of the major issues that previous research has addressed in the four distinct areas of focus of this book, and outline the particular research studies and commentaries in each of the four parts of *Researching Collocations in Another Language*.

Two major conceptual underpinnings of L2 collocation research

Research on collocation has commonly been carried out within two different but sometimes somewhat overlapping traditions, which we can refer to as the *frequency-based* and the *phraseological* traditions. In the former, frequency and statistics are intrinsic ingredients in the analysis of textual instantiations of collocation. In the phraseological tradition, work on collocation is guided by syntactic and semantic analyses, largely inspired by Russian and continental European work on phraseology.

The frequency-based view of collocation

In the frequency-based tradition, collocations are, in general, seen as units consisting of co-occurring words within a certain distance of each other, and a distinction is often made between frequently and infrequently co-occurring words. Pioneering work within this tradition was carried out by Firth (1952/3, 1956, 1957a, 1957b),[1] Halliday (1961, 1966) and Sinclair (1966, 1987a, 1987b, 1991; Sinclair et al., 1970). Firth was concerned with theorizing how meaning was produced at 'mutually congruent series of levels' (Firth, 1957a: 176) within language (context of situation, collocation, syntax, phonology, and phonetics). Although each level of the system is interdependent with the others, Firth was careful to distinguish 'colligation' (Firth, 1956: 113; 1957a: 181–3) within the syntactic level from collocation. Arguing that one of the meanings of 'night' is established through its collocability with the word 'dark', Firth suggested that part of the meaning of a word could be established by collocation. He summed this up in his famous exclamation 'You shall know a word by the company it keeps' (1957a: 179), and was dismissive of an essentialist semantic view where individual words have intrinsic core meanings. Rather, collocation was for Firth a central dimension in understanding how meaning and functional value are created through use: 'The distribution of the collocations in larger texts will probably provide a basis for functional values or meanings for words of all types' (Firth, 1952/3: 23). Firth saw collocations as sequences of co-occurring words, where the length of sequences varied greatly from two words up to 15. He envisioned different types of collocations such as 'habitual', 'more restricted technical', 'unique', and 'a-normal' (Firth, 1957b), but did not specifically define them or distinguish them clearly from one another.

Building on the sometimes rather vague writing of Firth, Halliday took a slightly different conceptual view of collocation as a syntagmatic association of lexical items that could be quantified textually in terms of their probability of occurrence at a certain distance from one another (1961: 276). Halliday posited, alongside the paradigmatic category of 'set', the syntagmatic category of 'collocation' for understanding lexis in language. The interaction of these two axes allows analysis of 'a very simple set of relations into which enter a large number of items'

(Halliday, 1966: 153). According to Halliday, collocation restricts the co-occurrence of particular lexical items and may allow for prediction of items that co-occur 'with a probability greater than chance' (Halliday, 1966: 156). He used 'lexical item' to mean a lexeme in all its derivative forms. Halliday also introduced the terms 'node', 'collocate', and 'span' to refer to the item under study (*node*), the co-occurring item (*collocate*), and the specified environment in which the node and the collocate may co-occur (*span*), respectively. These terms have proven fundamental to the operationalization of collocation and have served as indispensable tools for subsequent research.

Sinclair's innovative and far-reaching contributions to the work on collocation originate from his attempts to solve some of the practical problems concomitant with a Firthian view of collocation. He applied in practice Firth's original ideas to the Office of Scientific and Technical Information (OSTI) project (Krishnamurthy, 2004), and later also to one of the largest (for its time) and most ambitious research projects in computational lexicography ever carried out: the COBUILD project (Carter, 1998: 167). On the one hand, Sinclair expanded on Halliday's notion of probability of co-occurrence within a certain distance by calculating that a span of ±4, that is, four locations (number of orthographic words) to the left and to the right, respectively, of the node, constitutes the optimal environment within which 95 per cent of that node's collocational influence occurs (Jones and Sinclair, 1974: 21). On the other, the COBUILD project revealed that the most frequent of words of English tend to be collocated in delexical senses rather than in a full lexical sense so that they 'function as elements of structure' (Renouf, 1987: 177). Collocation itself was now becoming more clearly understood as a level of language use or 'lexical realisation of the situational context' (Moon, 1987: 92) – as Firth had originally claimed. For example, the differing textual collocates of 'skate' – 'ice', 'roller,' and 'winter' for sporting activity, and 'fish', 'ray', 'shark', and 'water' for fish (Moon, 1987: 91–2) – uncovered the distinct contextually bound meanings of the item. Another major insight from the COBUILD project was that the different senses of lexical items had such constrained typical phrasal patternings that few frequent words could be thought 'to have a residue of patterning that can be used independently' (Sinclair, 1987b: 158).

Two principles of interpretation were proposed by Sinclair (1987a: 318–19; 1991: 109–21) for how meaning is produced in text: *the open-choice principle* and *the idiom principle*. The former envisages language text as the result of a very large number of complex choices to do with individual lexical items (the 'slot-and-filler' model). Texts are then seen as a number of slots that are filled item by item from a lexicon, if various local constraints are satisfied. The latter principle – the idiom principle – is an important complement to the open-choice principle. One of its central claims holds that 'a language user has available to him or her a large number of semi-preconstructed phrases that constitute single choices, even though they might appear to be analysable into segments' (Sinclair, 1991: 110). Sinclair's view is that the idiom principle takes precedence over the open-choice principle and that text production is constantly constrained by the collocational restrictions that words (and multiword phrases) carry in relation to other words (and multiword phrases).

A fairly recent extension of the pioneering frequency-based work outlined above can be seen in 'lexical bundle analysis'. Lexical bundles are loosely defined as 'recurrent expressions, regardless of their idiomaticity, and regardless of their structural status' (Biber et al., 1999a: 990). Used predominantly in corpus-based analyses of recurrent sequences of words widely distributed across texts in specific registers, the lexical bundle approach allows researchers to search for identical instantiations of *n*-word bundles (e.g. 2-word, 3-word, 4-word, 5-word bundles, and so on). Lexical bundles are seen by some as having a pre-fabricated or formulaic status (see, for example, Biber and Barbieri, 2007: 265). They are also considered to display non-idiomatic or transparent meanings (Biber and Barbieri, 2007: 269) and to occur more often in spoken than written discourse.

The phraseological view of collocation

In contrast to the frequency-based tradition, the common ground for those working within the phraseological tradition lies in the treatment of collocation as a word combination, displaying various degrees of fixedness, and in the preoccupation with collocation typology, that is, the decontextualized classification of collocations. The approach is heavily influenced by work carried out primarily in Russia in the 1940s (Cowie, 1998a, 1998b), but a close connection between a phraseological view of collocation and lexicography and pedagogy dates back further at least to the work of Bally[2] in Geneva and Palmer[3] in Tokyo in the early twentieth century. Bally worked on developing various phrase-based (Hausmann, 1979: 189; Siepmann, 2006: 9) French learning materials for foreign students at Geneva University in 1909, whereas Palmer collaborated with A. S. Hornby (Smith, 1998; Cowie, 1999; Smith, 1999) to categorize and meticulously codify the lists of collocations they had drawn up for the development of appropriate English language materials in the pre-war period in Japan. Their innovative treatment of multiword units saw the light of day in general-purpose English dictionaries for learners (Hornby et al., 1942, 1948) and is detailed by Cowie (1998b: 210–13; 1999: 52–81).

Other more theoretical views of the variability of multiword units emerged from the work of Vinogradov and Amosova in the Soviet Union (Cowie, 1998b: 213–18) and were taken up in the West from the 1970s onwards, in particular with regard to 'collocation restriction' (Aisenstadt, 1979; 1981). Seminal work within the phraseological tradition can be found in Aisenstadt (1979, 1981), Cowie (1981, 1988, 1991, 1994, 1998c), Benson (1989), Howarth (1996), Benson et al. (1986a, 1986b, 1997), Cowie and Howarth (1996), Howarth (1996, 1998a, 1998b), Mel'čuk (1998) and Nesselhauf (2005). The phraseological school has been rather less concerned with frequencies and statistical significance per se, and rather more interested in word combinations, their degree of opacity, and the commutability (also called substitutability) of the word elements in these combinations. Frequency-based approaches alone do not suffice: '... phraseological significance means something more than what any computer algorithm can reveal' (Howarth, 1998a: 27).

Cowie (1981, 1988, 1991, 1994, 1998a) has argued that collocations are associations of two or more lexemes (or roots) occurring in a specific range of grammatical constructions. Restricted collocations have been further defined by Cowie as 'word-combinations in which one element (usually the verb) [has] a technical sense, or a long-established figurative sense which [has] lost most of its analogical force' (Cowie, 1991: 102). On the whole, Cowie (1981, 1998a), followed by Howarth (1996, 1998a, 1998b) and Nesselhauf (2005), presents the case for a scalar analysis of word combination categories, ranging in the form of a continuum from transparent, freely recombinable collocations at one end to unmotivated and formally invariable idioms at the other. A straightforward illustration of this can be seen in Howarth's (1998b: 164) examples of 'free combination' (*blow a trumpet*), 'restricted collocation' (*blow a fuse*), 'figurative idioms' (*blow your own trumpet*), and 'pure idioms' (*blow the gaff*). An interesting feature of the scalar view is that, while collocations are in most cases lexically variable, they are also characterized by arbitrary limitations of choice at one or more points. Cowie exemplifies this with combinations like *cut one's throat* and *slash one's wrist*, which are appropriate in English, but where substitution of the verb creates infelicitous variants such as **slash one's throat* and ?*cut one's wrist* (see also Howarth, 1996; 1998a; 1998b).

A somewhat different typology of collocation within the phraseological tradition has been developed by Benson et al. (1986b, 1997) in distinguishing between grammatical and lexical collocations (cf. Firth's distinction between collocation and colligation). In a grammatical collocation, a dominant word (noun, adjective or verb) is combined with a preposition or grammatical structure. Eight major types of grammatical collocations (G1–G8) are identified, such as Noun + Preposition, Noun + *to* + Infinitive, Adjective + Preposition, with each consisting of a varying number of subtypes. Type G8, for example, comprises no fewer than 19 different English verb patterns. The seven main categories of lexical collocation represent word combinations consisting of nouns, adjectives, verbs, and adverbs only, but without any function words (Verb + Noun, Adj + Noun, Noun + Verb, Adj + Adv and Verb + Adv).

In stark contrast to the Benson, Benson and Ilson dictionary, radically different forms of phraseological dictionary are currently being developed, where collocation entries are first organized by key themes or concepts (see, for example, Siepmann, 2005, 2006, 2008; Pecman, 2008) and the user is then guided from conceptual frames to phrase-based collocational encodings. The first generation of such electronic 'onomasiological' collocation dictionaries, once completed, will probably enable interactivity within and between entries through bilingual displays, hyperlinked access points, and semantic query functions (Pecman, 2008) – and may well help to reconcile some of the differences between the two traditions presented here.

Summing up

In presenting the evolution of two major conceptual views of collocation, it has been our intention to summarize some of the major issues that have concerned researchers working within these two traditions. The picture we have painted is by necessity somewhat partial and incomplete,[4] but it serves, we hope, to illustrate how different conceptualizations can lead into quite distinct research agendas. Against this notably complicated set of background issues, we will now introduce the L2 collocation research in this volume.

L2 collocation research in this volume

Each of the sections that follow in this introduction is separated into two parts: *Setting the scene*, and *Research and commentary*. In *Setting the scene*, we give a general overview of previous research in each area and draw out various questions that L2 collocation research has tried to address. In *Research and commentary*, we introduce the three research studies and the respective commentary chapter in each of the four parts of this book.

Part I: L2 collocation learner corpus research

Setting the scene

Since the creation of the first computer-readable, written English corpus – the Brown corpus (Kucera and Francis, 1967) – over 40 years ago, we have witnessed, over the last two decades, the development of a number of different 'learner corpora'. These corpora, either ready-made for generic use or especially compiled for a specific study (aka do-it- yourself corpora), are collections of cross-sectional or longitudinal data, in the form of L2 users' written or spoken language productions. One of the more well-known computerized learner corpora is the International Corpus of Learner English (ICLE) (see Granger, 1998a, 2003), which now enables researchers to investigate the language use of advanced students of English coming from as many as 16 L1 backgrounds (Granger et al., 2009). Despite technological advances in corpus analysis, the number of corpus-based studies devoted to L2 collocation research has been fairly modest until now. In particular, research investigating spoken L2 collocation use (including the phonological realization of collocation) is conspicuously absent (see, though, De Cock, 2000, 2004), but a handful of L2 collocation corpus studies have investigated written L2 collocation production (Dechert and Lennon, 1989; Zhang, 1993; Chi, Wong and Wong, 1994; Howarth, 1996, 1998a, 1998b; Granger, 1998b; Gitsaki, 1999; Nesselhauf, 2005).

A common methodological denominator of these studies is the adoption of a typological and more phraseologically oriented approach to collocation. Zhang (1993) analysed English essays written by 30 non-native speaker and 30 native speaker first-year university students in terms of their use of no fewer than 66 types of lexical and grammatical collocations. Similarly, Gitsaki (1999), who looked at English essays written by Greek L1 secondary school students, classified her subjects' collocations into 37 types. On the whole, the close attention to a precise lexicographic description of phraseological units and their varying degree of fixedness and idiomaticity has largely been extended into L2 collocation research with learner corpora. Yet, given the dominance of frequency-based studies in L1 corpus studies, it is perhaps surprising that this kind of phraseologically oriented approach has been so dominant in L2 collocation corpus studies to date.

A second point of interest in previous studies is the object of analysis. Some studies (Zhang, 1993; Gitsaki, 1999) have cast a very wide net indeed by using a highly comprehensive classification system for collocations. This may be problematic, especially in comparisons of relatively small data sets of native speaker and learner data, because some types of collocations may occur only once or twice in a data set, if at all. Other studies (Howarth, 1996, 1998a, 1998b; Granger, 1998b; Nesselhauf, 2005) have concentrated their analysis on one or, at most, two types of collocation. Granger (1998b) analysed French L1 learners' use of English Adv + Adj combinations, whereas both Howarth (1996) and Nesselhauf (2005) aimed at mapping out L2 learners' use of restricted Verb + Noun collocations. Howarth examined essays written by postgraduates coming from a large number of L1 backgrounds, and Nesselhauf analysed essays written by advanced undergraduate German L1 learners of English. The assumption behind the focus on restricted collocations is that it is precisely these word combinations that form the very large repository of phrases between free combinations and idioms, and which pose the greatest collocation challenge to learners. The advantage of limiting the focus to fewer types of collocation is that it is much more likely that a data set taken from a corpus – even a smaller one – will contain sufficient tokens for a clear comparative analysis.

Research and commentary

The three studies in this section make use of methods and techniques not commonly seen in mainstream L2 collocation research. In Chapter 2 Groom uses a lexical bundle analysis, and a more traditional node and collocate analysis, on corpus data from Swedish undergraduate learners of English to examine whether increased, immersion-based L2 exposure leads to significant improvements in terms of the number of correctly produced collocations. In Chapter 3, Lin and Adolphs explore uncharted waters by investigating whether holistic storage of collocations can be phonologically analysed. This chapter provides a rare example of L2 collocation research based on a corpus of spoken language. In Chapter 4, Reppen applies a lexical bundle analysis to the writing of primary school children across a whole school year. By using a corpus of written English essays from young L1 English and L1 Navajo users, Reppen explores variation by age and language group in the production of 3-word bundles. The results point to a number of interesting language and sociocultural questions worthy of further investigation. All three studies break with the phraseologically oriented approach to L2 collocation prevalent in previous studies. Granger's commentary in Chapter 5 highlights how conflicting results from phraseological studies may emerge as an effect of different operationalizations of collocation, and how previously perceived weaknesses in learner output can be reinterpreted in a different light. Granger particularly welcomes research involving spoken corpora, and she also emphasizes the need for small-scale exploratory research to try out and evaluate new research methodologies.

Part II: L2 collocation lexicographic and classroom materials research

Setting the scene

In addition to the *The BBI Combinatory Dictionary* (Benson, Benson and Ilson, 1986; 1997) mentioned earlier, there are two other English print[5] monolingual collocation dictionaries commonly available to researchers, teachers, and learners: Kozlowska and Dzieržanowska's (1982) *Selected English Collocations* (SEC), later republished as *The Dictionary of Selected Collocations* (DOSC) (Hill and Lewis, 1997), and *The Oxford Collocations Dictionary for Students of English* (OCDSE) (2002). The microstructure of entries varies in these dictionaries as regards the display of possible collocate ranges for headwords and the degree of syntactic and semantic information. This variation bears direct relationship to the conceptual view of collocation taken. The BBI comes from within the phraseological/word combination tradition, while the SEC/DOSC and the OCDSE adhere to the lexical frequency/co-occurrence view of collocation. '(C)ompiled without any sort of computer assistance whatsoever' (Knowles, 1993: 300), SEC/DOSC organizes entries for adverbs and nouns by listing possible lexical collocates in separate subentries (Cowie, 1998b: 222–4) for each of its 3200 headwords. Unlike the SEC/DOSC (and the BBI), the OCDSE draws on corpus data – the British National Corpus (BNC; Oxford University, 2005) – for the selection of collocates under its 9000 or so headwords. It targets collocations that should be useful for upper-intermediate+ learners dealing with a moderately formal register. The OCDSE divides polysemous words into different senses. It also groups collocates for each sense into distinct word classes and typographically separates sets of similar collocates within each word class. Many of the collocate groupings also have an example sentence to illustrate the contextualized use of a specific collocation.

The three print dictionaries mentioned above have been positively received (Gold, 1988; Herbst, 1988; Cueto, 1998; Appleby, 2000; Howarth, 2000; Klotz, 2003), but, in contrast to the wealth of user-related investigations for general-purpose dictionaries (for comprehensive overviews, see Béjoint, 2000; Cowie, 1999; Hartmann, 2001), there have been few dedicated studies of monolingual collocation dictionary L2 users. Benson (1989) reported how, under controlled conditions, advanced learners (Russian teachers of English) can improve their use of collocation with the aid of a collocation dictionary (the BBI). Studies by Béjoint (1981) and Bogaards (1990) pointed to variation in users' look-up strategies for multiword combinations in general-purpose dictionaries, whereas Atkins and Varantola (1997) discovered that non-native speakers often looked for collocation information in dictionaries to be reassured about their L2 collocation knowledge. An investigation by Frankenberg-Garcia (2005) required her fourth-year translation majors to translate a newspaper text. Although only 16 per cent of their 146 look-ups were concerned with finding a suitable collocate, students rated their collocation searches as highly successful and helpful.

As Rundell (1999) observes, identifying suitable collocations and understanding collocation restrictions is one of the most important productive needs of learners. Yet, the overall picture we have of what learners do, and how they do it and why, when they use lexicographic collocation resources for their production, can be described as extremely sketchy at best. The same may be said for our understanding of how learners use pedagogic materials specifically designed for developing their L2 collocation ability. Following Lewis's (Lewis, 1993, 1997) groundbreaking 'popularist' (Thornbury, 1998: 13) works on a lexical approach to language learning and teaching collocation (Lewis, 2000), learner resources aimed at the global ELT market have been produced (for example, McCarthy and O'Dell, 2005; for a review, see Pulverness, 2007). However, research has yet to explore how learners use and evaluate these kinds of materials in local contexts.

Research and commentary

The three studies in Part II directly address the telling gaps just noted. In Chapter 6, Handl explores a new multi-dimensional classification for elaborating the criteria by which collocations can be selected for advanced learners' dictionaries. This leads to an alternative microstructure for print and electronic collocation dictionaries that helps learners identify more easily the collocations they need. Komuro examines in Chapter 7 what problems learners encounter in using specific OCDSE entries in order to identify improvements for the design of more user-friendly collocation entry structures in the future. In the final study of this section, Jiang (Chapter 8) takes a critical look at how English textbooks in China present vocabulary to learners. Noting an almost complete lack of focus on collocation, Jiang reports on a series of quantitative and qualitative interventions informing the design, use, and evaluation of pilot collocation classroom materials with Chinese university students. In her commentary on these three studies (Chapter 9), Nesi considers the wider implications of the detailed description of collocational relations that these chapters present. Nesi also discusses the methodological implications of these studies for future research, as well as the insightful critiques of existing practices that they offer for further improving lexicographic and pedagogic materials.

Part III: L2 collocation knowledge assessment research

Setting the scene

Assessment of learners' acquisition, knowledge and use of L2 collocations forms an essential part of furthering our understanding of how learners cope with these challenges. Broadly speaking, previous studies fall into those that focus on the development process of an assessment instrument itself (Schmitt, 1998, 1999; Bonk, 2000; Gyllstad, 2007), and those that develop assessment instruments predominantly for the purpose of a particular research project (Biskup, 1992; Bahns and Eldaw, 1993; Farghal and Obiedat, 1995; Granger, 1998b; Gitsaki, 1999; Mochizuki, 2002; Barfield, 2006; Keshavarz and Salimi, 2007; Laufer and Girsai, 2008).

Earlier studies tended to use a relatively small number of items in the assessment of L2 collocation knowledge. Farghal and Obiedat (1995) tested Arabic L1 learners' knowledge of 11 Noun + Noun collocation-pairs and 10 Adjectival + Noun collocation-pairs, and Bahns and Eldaw (1993) examined German L1 learners' knowledge of 15 English lexical Verb + Noun collocations, whereas Gitsaki (1999), in one of her questionnaires, investigated Greek L1 learners' knowledge of just ten English collocations. With so few items, drawing well-founded and generalizable conclusions is difficult, and the content validity as well as the reliability may be compromised. In recognition of these threats, more recent studies have used a larger number of items: Bonk (2000): 50; Mochizuki (2002): 70; Barfield (2006): 120; Gyllstad (2007): 50 and 100; Keshavarz and Salimi (2007): 50.

There has also been great variation in item selection for different assessment measures. Gitsaki (1999) drew on English textbooks used in Greek schools for her test items, and Bahns and Eldaw (1993) took target collocations from textbooks and dictionaries. Farghal and Obiedat (1995), on the other hand, used collocations from the domains of food, clothes, colours, and weather. In some cases, researchers have not reported how their items were chosen (Biskup, 1992; Keshavarz and Salimi, 2007), which hinders proper evaluation of their findings. Several studies have used either corpora or corpus-based frequency lists to sample items for assessment (for example, Mochizuki, 2002; Gyllstad, 2007). A growing trend in current research is to cross-check selected items against information available in mega-corpora like the BNC (Oxford University, 2005) or the Bank of English (HarperCollins, 2007).

With the exception of Gitsaki (1999), Bonk (2000), and Keshavarz and Salimi (2007), most previous studies have involved assessment of lexical collocations. One of the more popular ways of assessing knowledge of lexical collocations has been L1–L2 translation (Biskup, 1992; Bahns and Eldaw, 1993; Farghal and Obiedat, 1995; Laufer and Girsai,[6] 2008), either through the translation of sentences, or isolated items. Some researchers have used short, decontextualized prompts in a 'stimulus-response' manner (Schmitt, 1998, 1999; Barfield, 2009). Other measures, including assessment of either grammatical or lexical collocations, have involved L2 sentence cloze items (Bahns and Eldaw, 1993; Farghal and Obiedat, 1995; Gitsaki, 1999; Bonk, 2000), and discrete receptive tasks of different kinds (Granger, 1998b; Bonk, 2000; Mochizuki, 2002; Gyllstad, 2007).

A common question in previous research has been whether L2 collocation knowledge develops alongside general L2 proficiency. Gitsaki (1999), Bonk (2000), and Gyllstad (2007) all claim a positive correlation, whereas Howarth (1996, 1998a, 1998b) and Barfield (2006) did not find support for such a position. Other more disparate findings include Farghal and Obiedat's (1995) assertion that paraphrasing as a type of lexical simplification strategy is used extensively among learners to compensate for a lack of well-developed collocation knowledge, Howarth's (1996, 1998a, 1998b) finding that learners' use of infelicitous collocations often involves blends of two or more acceptable nativelike collocations from overlapping collocation clusters, and Granger's (1998b) claim that learners have a weak sense of salience and that they overuse certain word elements in combinations as 'safe bets'.

Research and commentary

The three studies in Part III are all concerned with defining and operationalizing the construct they are assessing, and creating inherently reliable and valid measures. In Chapter 10, Revier reports on the initial development process of a discrete test of productive collocation knowledge called CONTRIX. This is designed to assess learners' knowledge of *whole* collocations, where potentially required function words such as determiners and prepositions are considered as important as the lexical elements. Revier also takes great pains to separate the degree of transparency of a collocation as a factor in the assessment. In Chapter 11, Eyckmans traces the development of a reliable, corpus-based test of receptive phrasal knowledge called DISCO. Combining techniques both from the frequency-based and the phraseological traditions, Eyckmans sets up a longitudinal, experimental design where receptive L2 collocation knowledge is mapped in relation to spoken L2 proficiency. Gyllstad reports, in Chapter 12, on the development of two tests of receptive collocation knowledge, called COLLEX and COLLMATCH. The research is focused on arriving at reliable and valid measures of receptive collocation knowledge as a construct, and investigating the relationship between this construct and vocabulary size. In his commentary in Chapter 13, Shillaw draws out a number of common themes in the three studies, including how to define collocation knowledge as a construct and operationalize such a construct in a test. He also looks at the underlying assumptions of the tests featured and addresses the different validation techniques used.

Part IV: L2 collocation learner process and practice research

Setting the scene

As Willis notes (2003: 219), 'Many learners ... are not consciously aware of collocation, or of the importance of fixed phrases.' For this reason, advocates of specific approaches to collocation learning (for example, Sinclair and Renouf, 1988; Baigent, 1999; Lewis, 2000) emphasize noticing language chunks as a crucial initial process in dealing with comprehended input, but also point out that noticing alone is not sufficient. Learners need to be guided to notice 'similarities, differences, restrictions and examples arbitrarily blocked by usage' (Michael Lewis, 2000: 184) if they are to transform input into uptake; such hypothesizing should be constantly encouraged as learners record and experiment with collocation examples and continually readjust their changing awareness and use of collocation. This, the argument goes, will help them build systematic L2 collocation awareness and knowledge.

System building in L2 vocabulary acquisition is often seen in terms of lexical network building (Meara, 1990, 1992, 1996; Vermeer, 2001; Read, 2004; Meara and Wolter, 2004; Wilks and Meara, 2007). How such network building *may* apply to L2 collocation development is illustrated in an experimental study by Haastrup and Henriksen (2000). They identify the three major phases of noticing, analysing, and integrating whereby learners incorporate new words into their L2 lexical networks. Haastrup and Henriksen's position is that the analysing phase is where learners can create syntagmatic links between L2 words, which arguably suggests that learners tend to analyse and segment, before resynthesizing collocations as they become part of their developing L2 lexical networks. Haastrup and Henriksen further characterize such network building as 'a very slow process' (2000: 235). As to potential theoretical reasons for this slowness, Wolter (2006) suggests, particularly with regard to non-equivalent L2-L1 collocations, that successful acquisition of such multiword units first requires changes in learners' conceptual worlds, which makes learners less adept at mastering non-equivalent L2–L1 collocations. These different claims about collocations raise fundamental questions about whether collocations are stored holistically or not, as has been argued for formulaic sequences (see, for example, Schmitt and Carter, 2004: 4–6). Although the jury is still out on resolving such crucial issues, there is now some specific empirical evidence that collocations enable greater speed of processing (Ellis, 2008: 6) and that non-native speakers process collocations less quickly than native speakers do (Siyanova and Schmitt, 2008).

Although such theoretical positions have been advanced, very little research has been completed into learners' actual practices of L2 collocation development (Coxhead, 2008: 159). At a general level, Hunt and Beglar (2005: 35) observe: 'Although little is known about the acquisition of L2 collocational knowledge, ultimately most EFL learners probably develop it through processing large quantities of written input in which most of the vocabulary is known.' Hunt and Beglar further suggest that such rich exposure can be enhanced through conscious attention to, and recycling of, frequent collocations and the collocates of words that learners already know well. A few studies shed more specific light on learner practices and processes of L2 collocation development. Yang and Hendricks (2004) explored how collocation-awareness-raising (CAR) tasks helped postgraduate students improve their collocation use in drafting and redrafting essays. Their students also reported that the CAR approach made them more aware of collocations in their out-of-class reading and that they were keen to continue developing their use of collocation in other language tasks. In a smaller scale pilot study, Coxhead (2008) found that students could become sensitized to noticing and retrieving multiword combinations from reading texts, but their motivation to reproduce newly retrieved phrases was hindered by a sense of risk and fear of negative evaluation within the particular institutional setting. Coxhead's investigation reminds us that, in addition to metacognitive awareness and active involvement, other influential factors clustering around learners' changing L2 collocation processes and practices need to be considered too, such as previous learning experiences, awareness of collocation, institutional and sociocultural contexts of exposure and use, not to mention learners' short-term and longer-term goals in learning English.

Research and commentary

In Chapter 14, Yang and O'Neill investigate how a group of adult EFL learners develop their collocation learning over a five-month period on an intensive English course. The authors interviewed the students at the beginning and end of the language programme, and also analysed the students' reflective learning journals. This qualitative longitudinal investigation illuminates different problems that learners face, the great variety of strategies they use, and important adjustments they may make, in becoming more collocationally aware and proficient. The research by Peters in Chapter 15 explores the effects of an attention-drawing technique on the recall of individual words and collocations with two groups of advanced EFL learners. Finding no significant quantitative difference between groups in their recall of individual vocabulary items and collocations, Peters takes a detailed qualitative look at the students' strategy use and their perceptions of the task and test in order to probe further learners' positions and decision making about collocation learning. In his narrative reconstruction of key processes in learners' emerging L2 collocation awareness and development, Barfield (Chapter 16) follows learners' decision making in great depth over a nine-month period. Examining how learners interpret their collocation practices in relation to their changing sense of who they are in terms of their own understandings of the world, this study identifies both lexical and sociocultural reorganization as overarching characteristics of learners' L2 collocation development. In their commentary on these three studies, Henriksen and Stenius Stæhr address central processes in the development of L2 collocational knowledge. They also discuss the challenges that learners experience in acquiring such knowledge, as well as the challenges that researchers face in identifying and interpreting the processes at play. Henriksen and Stenius Stæhr conclude by briefly considering different pedagogic implications for teachers wishing to help their learners develop L2 collocational knowledge.

Closing remarks

We began this chapter by noting the collocation gap in L2 acquisition research, and we then presented two major traditions in collocation research, the frequency-based tradition and the phraseological-typological school. In the second half of the chapter, we set the scene for each of the four areas that this volume covers. Here, we briefly reviewed previous L2 collocation research in each area, before we highlighted the particular focus of the research studies and respective commentary chapter in each part of this volume. This was all done by way of giving a general introduction and re-interpretation of the field, where we could signpost important background issues and highlight some of the major conceptual positions, practices and priorities that run through the L2 collocation research that follows. How these become further developed and re-constructed is at the heart of the research chapters and commentaries, as well as the final conclusion chapter by Alison Wray, in *Researching Collocations in Another Language: Multiple Interpretations*. We hope that many different interesting spaces for further developments in practice and theory will continue to be produced in the interplay between the work that researchers do and the multiple interpretations that others make of the research done.

Notes

1. We have dated Firth's publications here according to the indication given by F. R. Palmer (Palmer, 1957) and Firth (1957c).
2. Bally differentiated between 'les associations libres et occasionnelles, les séries phraséologiques ou groupements usuels et les unités indissolubles' in developing these materials (Hausmann (1979: 189). He did not however use the term 'collocation'.
3. Harold Palmer taught at University College London from 1915 to 1922 before taking a specially created position as linguistic adviser to the Japanese Department (= Ministry) of Education in 1922 (Cowie, 1999: 4–5; Smith, 1999: 57–67), where the Institute for Research in English Teaching (IRET) was established in 1923. In 1933, Palmer published the *Second Interim Report on English Collocations* (Palmer, 1933b); this was also the year that he and A. S. Hornby started working together on collocations (Smith, 1999: 131). Palmer (1931, 1933a, 1933b, 1934) coined the term collocation, noting, for example,

in a 1934 report for the IRET (Palmer, 1934: 20): 'In 1930 … we presented in mimeographed form a rough draft of a collection of collocations (culled for the most part from Saito's *Idiomological Dictionary*).'
4. For a more comprehensive review of how the phenomenon of collocation has been treated in the literature, see Nesselhauf (2004, 2005).
5. We have not included the *COBUILD English Collocations on CD-ROM* (1995) as it is no longer being produced and so will probably be unavailable for future students, teachers, and researchers.
6. This study also includes L2–L1 translation.

Acknowledgement

We would like to thank Elke Peters, Jingyi Jiang, Marnie O'Neill, Randi Reppen, Robert Revier, Sylviane Granger, and Ying Yang for their helpful feedback on earlier drafts of this chapter.

Part I

L2 Collocation Learner Corpus Research

2

Effects of Second Language Immersion on Second Language Collocational Development

Nicholas Groom

Introduction

Traditionally, language learners, teachers and researchers have assumed that the best – indeed, perhaps the only – way to develop a nativelike command of second language (L2) collocations is to spend an extended period of time living and working or studying in an L2 environment, thereby providing maximum opportunities for repeated exposure to these combinations, in much the same way that knowledge of L1 collocational patterning is acquired. Recently, however, doubts about the efficacy of even this immersion-based approach to L2 collocational development have begun to emerge, with the publication of a large-scale study of collocation usage among advanced-level German EFL students by Nadja Nesselhauf (2005). Focusing on Verb + Object structures such as *make money*, *follow a trend* or *do the washing up*, Nesselhauf (2005: 236) found that 'increased exposure to English in English-speaking countries leads to [only] a slight improvement' in terms of the number of correct collocations produced by the learner. More worryingly still, Nesselhauf also found that 'the length of stays in English-speaking countries does not seem to lead to an increased use of collocations; instead, there even seems to be a slight trend in the opposite direction' (Nesselhauf, 2005: 236). That is, learners who have spent time in an L2 environment seem to produce fewer collocations than do their peers who have not.

These are startling findings, which fly in the face of received wisdom among lay and expert observers of L2 collocational development alike. However, Nesselhauf's conclusions are restricted to a particular type of collocation, which is itself rooted in a particular – and by no means universally accepted – theoretical model of phraseology (see, for example, Cowie, 1994, 1998c; Howarth, 1996, 1998a; for discussion,

Gledhill, 2000; Frath and Gledhill, 2005; Granger and Meunier, 2008). It is also worth noting that Nesselhauf did not subject her data to rigorous statistical analyses, but interpreted them rather impressionistically (Cobb, 2006). The question thus arises as to whether the same findings would still be obtained if the concept of collocation were theorized and operationalized in an entirely different way. It is this question that forms the central focus of this chapter. My general approach to this issue will be from the theoretical and methodological standpoint of corpus linguistics (Sinclair, 1991, 2003, 2004; Biber, Conrad and Reppen, 1998; Granger, 1998a; Hunston, 2002; Barnbrook, 2007). That is to say, I will define collocation not as a qualitative category but as a quantitative phenomenon, which can only be observed systematically though the computational analysis of large, electronically stored corpora of authentic language data. I will test Nesselhauf's claims by comparing the number of collocations found in two corpora of essays written by Swedish undergraduate students of English as a foreign language. One corpus consists of texts written by students who have never immersed themselves in an English L1 environment, and the other consists of comparable data written by students who have spent at least one year living in an English L1 country. Two very different frequency-based measures of collocation will be applied to both corpora, each of which I will now introduce in turn.

The lexical bundle approach

As mentioned previously, I will use the term 'collocation' in this chapter not to refer to a particular ontological category of word combination, as in Nesselhauf (2005), but rather as 'a general term for two or more words occurring near each other in a text' (Sinclair, 2003: 173). One way of operationalizing this deceptively simple definition is to treat collocations very literally as co-locations, that is, as exact repetitions of contiguous multiword sequences such as *you know what, on the other hand* or *in the context of the*. These strings are variously referred to in the literature as n-grams (Manning and Schütze, 1999), chains (Stubbs, 2003), clusters (Scott, 2001; Scott and Tribble, 2006), formulaic sequences (Schmitt, 2004) and lexical bundles (Biber and Conrad, 1999; Biber et al., 1999b; Biber, Conrad and Cortes, 2003). The latter term will be preferred here.

Lexical bundle analysis is now very well established as a general research procedure (see Reppen this volume for a more detailed presentation). Although lexical bundles as objects of analysis have been criticized for being under-theorized (Sinclair, 2001), and for being insensitive to constituency and positional variation (Cheng, Greaves and Warren, 2006), they have proved effective as indicators of register and genre (for example, Biber et al., 1999b; Stubbs and Barth, 2003; Biber, 2006; Hyland, 2008), and as indicators of qualitative differences between apprentice and expert texts, particularly in the field of academic writing (Conrad, 2001; Cortes, 2004). They are also now widely regarded as 'an important component of fluent linguistic production and a key factor in successful language learning' (Hyland, 2008: 4; see also Pawley and Syder, 1983; Nattinger and DeCarrico, 1992; Lewis, 1997, 2000; Wray, 2002; Oakey, 2002; Schmitt, 2004; Conklin and Schmitt, 2007), and thus as constituting direct evidence in support of the claim that much of the language produced by native speakers and writers is not generated from scratch, but is assembled according to what Sinclair (1991: 110) has termed the *idiom principle*. Accordingly, it would seem reasonable to propose these extended collocational sequences as a possible quantitative measure of L2 collocational development.

However, it is important to note that we cannot make a simple 'more-is-better' assumption about the relationship between the number of lexical bundle types and/or tokens found in a corpus on the one hand, and the level of collocational development achieved by the writers of the texts in that corpus on the other. While such an assumption would probably be valid at very low levels of L2 proficiency, it is not supported by corpus-based studies of higher-level learners. On the contrary, intermediate- to advanced-level L2 corpora have consistently been found to contain even more lexical bundle types and tokens than comparable L1 corpora do (see De Cock et al., 1998; Milton, 1998; Cobb, 2003; Leńko-Szymańska, 2008). While the reasons for this are not yet fully understood, it is often suggested that intermediate and advanced learners may be 'overusing' the stock of multiword units that they do know in comparison to native-speaker levels of usage. This invites the hypothesis that L2 collocation development at advanced proficiency levels may involve a process of gradual downwards adjustment from overuse towards native-speaker norms.

Although intuitively appealing, this hypothesis is offset by the fact that there are also many lexical bundles that seem to be *under*used in learner corpora when compared against native-speaker data. Milton (1998), for example, found that while Cantonese L1 students at an English-medium university overused explicitly taught stock phrases such as *in my opinion*, *as we all know* and *in a nutshell* in their writing, they typically underused lexical bundles that impersonalize evaluative statements (e.g. *it can be seen*; *this is not to*) or effect transitions between general and specific levels of argumentation (e.g. *in this case the*; *an example of this*).

Another possibility is that native speakers *do* actually know and use more lexical bundles than L2 learners do, and that the observation of more lexical bundles occurring in an L2 learner corpus than in an L1 corpus may be an artefact of the lexical bundle analysis procedure itself. In more detail, the argument runs as follows. If L1 speakers and writers have a larger stock of lexical bundles upon which to draw than do their L2 counterparts, it is reasonable to assume that many of these lexical bundles will constitute alternative ways of making essentially the same meaning (e.g. *it is unclear whether* or *I haven't a clue whether* instead of *I don't know whether*). Expanding this point a little further, it is also likely that native (and nativelike) speakers will embellish and adapt canonical forms of bundles more frequently than L2 learners will (e.g. ***I really do honestly** think that*; *it is not* ***remotely*** *clear whether*; ***I haven't the foggiest/faintest idea** how*). Access to this variety means that each particular lexical bundle type is used much less frequently than it would be by an L2 speaker, and thus may not even appear above the cut-off point set for a particular piece of corpus research. This would therefore lead to the misleading impression that L2 learners use more lexical bundle types and tokens than do their L1 counterparts.

My position is that this latter explanation is more persuasive than is the overuse hypothesis in broad terms, although I accept that overuse effects may also have a substantial role to play. In either case, the practical upshot is the same: if we want to use a lexical bundle approach to compare the levels of collocational development in two advanced-level L2 corpora, it turns out that we will have to adopt the somewhat counterintuitive premise that fewer may actually mean better.

The node and collocates approach

The other frequency-based measure of collocational development that I will employ in this chapter is associated most strongly with the work of Sinclair (1966, 1991, 2003, 2004). Like the lexical bundle approach, this approach is entirely dependent upon computer algorithms in order to identify its objects of analysis. However, instead of requiring the computer to search for repeated strings of orthographic wordforms, it involves identifying single wordforms that occur significantly frequently within a short span of a pre-specified 'node' word or phrase:

> We may use the term *node* to refer to an item whose collocations we are studying, and we may then define a *span* as the number of lexical

> items on each side of a node that we consider relevant to that node. Items in the environment set by the span we will call *collocates*.
>
> (Sinclair, 1966: 415)

Three questions about this 'node and collocates' (N&C) approach need to be addressed here. The first concerns how we are to judge when or whether a word is occurring 'significantly frequently' within the span of any given node word; the second concerns how wide the span itself should be; and the third concerns how node words are selected for analysis. The first two of these questions will be discussed in turn below; I will return to the third question later in this chapter.

As is well known, lists of collocates ranked according to raw frequency figures tend to be dominated by words from closed grammatical classes such as determiners, prepositions, conjunctions and pronouns. As these words occur frequently in the environment of almost every node word or phrase, it is difficult to establish on the basis of raw frequency data alone whether the co-occurrence of these items with any given node is phraseologically significant, or merely indicative of the general grammatical properties of the language. It is for this reason that I will perform two statistical tests on each dataset: t-score and Mutual Information (MI). Essentially, t-score is a measure of how *certain* we can be in claiming a collocational relationship between two items in a corpus, while MI is a measure of how *strong* the collocational bond between two items is (Clear, 1993; Barnbrook, 1996; Oakes, 1998; Hunston, 2002).

Turning now to the question of span width, I will follow the standard practice of setting a default span of four words to the left and to the right of the node term. Restricting the analysis to such a short span of text in this way has attracted criticism from advocates of the category-based approach to collocation adopted by Nesselhauf (2005). Howarth (1996), for example, points out that it will miss instances featuring long-range dependencies such as that illustrated in Example 1 below:

Example 1

> the **impact** that opening up Heathrow to more foreign carriers, including American and United Airlines, and the Government's decision to hand some of its Tokyo slots to virgin Atlantic would **have** on BA's profits.

This is certainly true, but these critics have not established that such long-range dependencies are the norm, or even that they occur in sufficiently large numbers to cast serious doubt on the quantitative findings of studies based on smaller spans. (In the Bank of English (HarperCollins, 2007), for instance, *have* remains one of the most frequent and statistically significant collocates within a 4-word span of *impact* despite Howarth's counter-example, and *impact* is also identified as a collocate within the same span of *have*, albeit at a lower level of significance.) In the absence of any convincing evidence to the contrary, then, it is reasonable to continue to regard small spans as effecting the best available compromise between speed and efficiency of processing on the one hand, and comprehensive coverage of data on the other.

Before moving on to discuss the corpus data to be used in this research, we need to establish how the output of an N&C analysis is to be interpreted as a measure of collocational development. Thankfully, we may be reasonably confident that more *does* mean better, here. The assumption is that words form complex networks or webs of associations with other words both on the page and in the mind (Hoey, 2005), and that the greater the number of statistically significant linkages, the more advanced the level of collocational development. Although this assumption rests principally on the corpus linguistic work of Sinclair and his associates, it is also arguably compatible with recent trends in psycholinguistics, and in particular with connectionist models of SLA, in which language learning is seen not as a rule-governed process, but as the gradual accumulation of enormous numbers of probabilistic associations among and between simple information nodes (e.g. Ellis, 1998, 2003; Christiansen and Chater, 2001; Randall, 2007).

Description of the data

The obvious choice of data for analysis would be to use the same corpus that was used in Nesselhauf (2005), that is, the German Corpus of Learner English (GeCLE), a precursor of the German component of the International Corpus of Learner English (Granger, 2003). However, at only 154,191 word tokens, GeCLE is too small to be suitable for either lexical bundle or N&C analysis, particularly as it would have to be partitioned into even smaller subcorpora representing groups of students who have spent different lengths of time in a native English-speaking environment. Accordingly, I decided instead to make use of the Uppsala Student English Corpus (USE), a corpus of undergraduate student essays written by Swedish university students compiled by Margareta Westergren Axelsson and Ylva Berglund of the Department of English, Uppsala University, Sweden, between 1999 and 2001. At 1,221,265 words, USE is substantially larger than GeCLE and thus much more amenable to statistical analysis, even when subdivided into smaller subcorpora for the purposes of this study. The USE corpus was also ideal for my research because it comes with an extensive set of metadata which, among many other things, records the number of months each student has 'spent in an English-speaking environment, broadly defined as "where English is used every day, abroad or in Sweden"' (Axelsson, 2003: 9).

I used these metadata to create two new corpora representing two groups of students. The first, called USE 0, consists of texts written by students who have spent less than one month in an English L1 environment; the second, called USE 12+, consists of texts written by students who reported having spent at least one calendar year living in a native English-speaking environment. The final composition of the two corpora is summarized in Table 2.1 below.

As can be seen, the two corpora are very well balanced overall and may thus be regarded as highly comparable for present purposes. (It is interesting to note, however, that USE 12+ boasts 6.84 per cent more word types than does USE 0 even though it has six fewer texts.)

Lexical bundle analysis

Two-word, 3-word, 4-word and 5-word lexical bundles were extracted from both USE 0 and USE 12+ using *AntConc* (Anthony, 2006). The cut-off point for both analyses was set at a relatively high level of 10 occurrences per 250,000 words (i.e. 40 per million). This is because there is a particular danger when studying small, specialized corpora such as USE 0 and USE 12+ that the data may be skewed by idiolectal preferences, or by the relatively homogeneous nature of the topics covered by the texts in the corpus. As an additional safeguard in this respect, any given bundle had to occur in at least five texts in order to be included in the analysis (cf. Cortes, 2004).

Table 2.2 presents the results of this analysis. The numbers of bundles obtained from USE 0 consistently surpass those obtained from USE 12+,

Table 2.1 Basic composition data for USE 0 and USE 12+

	USE 0	USE 12+
Word tokens	253,481	253,483
Word types	12,672	13,603
Texts	308	302

Table 2.2 Frequency of lexical bundles in USE 0 and USE 12+

		USE 0	USE 12+	Difference
2-word bundles	Types	3,142	3,111	1%
	Tokens	97,953	93,048	5%
3-word bundles	Types	956	821	16%
	Tokens	18,386	15,360	20%
4-word bundles	Types	163	116	41%
	Tokens	2,577	1,926	34%
5-word bundles	Types	23	12	92%
	Tokens	273	167	63%

and the type and token differences between the two corpora become more pronounced as the bundles increase in length.

These results may indicate that the USE 12+ learners are relying less on an overused set of known lexical bundles, or that they are using smaller quantities of a greater number of bundles, or that the formulaic sequences that they do use are inflected by a greater degree of constituency and positional variation than is the case with the students in the USE 0 group. Or it may be that the trends in Table 2.2 are a result of all or some of these factors in combination. Unfortunately, the only way to test these hypotheses from within the lexical bundle research paradigm itself would be to repeat the analysis at a significantly lower cut-off point (say, three or five repetitions per corpus).[1] This would be a highly unreliable exercise, as the data yielded may well be skewed by the idiolects of individual writers, or by the topic foci of individual texts. What is needed, therefore, is an alternative form of analysis that does not require collocations to recur very frequently in precisely the same structural sequences in order to be detected. It is to an account of precisely such an analysis that we now turn.

Node and collocates analysis

While the N&C approach is much broader and more flexible than the lexical bundle approach in most respects, it is more constrained in that it requires the researcher to pre-specify a list of node words for analysis. This is problematic as it may intentionally or unintentionally lead to selections that are biased towards a particular outcome. Usually, the easiest way to avoid this is to implement a random selection procedure. However, this was not viable in the current research because the corpora themselves are (in corpus linguistic terms) very small, and most of the words obtained in test selections simply did not occur frequently enough for a statistical collocation analysis to be performed on them.

Table 2.3 Rank and frequency data for the top 10 prepositions in USE 0 and USE 12+

USE 0			USE 12+		
Rank	**Word**	**Frequency**	**Rank**	**Word**	**Frequency**
4	*of*	6,589 (+1%)	3	*of*	6,533
7	*in*	5,161	6	*in*	5,363 (+4%)
12	*for*	2,228	11	*for*	2,301 (+3%)
16	*as*	2,018	12	*as*	2,220 (+10%)
19	*with*	1,561	19	*with*	1,594 (+2%)
23	*on*	1,377	20	*on*	1,508 (+10%)
33	*from*	1,012 (+6%)	35	*at*	952
35	*at*	931 (+5%)	41	*from*	888
40	*by*	892 (+6%)	44	*by*	836
50	*about*	767 (+3%)	52	*about*	748

I therefore decided to focus on the 10 most frequent prepositions in each corpus.[2] Quantitatively, prepositions are highly suitable for frequency-based analysis insofar as they occur very frequently in even the smallest corpora. Furthermore, in the case of USE 0 and USE 12+, these words also turned out to be highly comparable; as can be seen in Table 2.3, the same top 10 prepositions occur in both corpora, in almost exactly the same rank order, and with very similar frequencies. (Percentage differences between these two sets of raw frequency figures are shown in brackets.)

Qualitatively, prepositions were deemed a good choice for collocational analysis because of the significant role that they are known to play in a wide range of phraseological sequences (Francis, Manning and Hunston, 1996, 1998; Hunston, 2006), and because of the difficulties that these sequences are known to cause for even advanced-level learners. Consider, by way of illustration, the potential challenges posed by the semantically related sequences *interested in*, *keen on*, *crazy about*, and *fascinated by*.

I carried out t-score and MI analyses of all 10 prepositions in both corpora using *AntConc* (Anthony, 2006). For all analyses, the span width was set at ±4 words of the node term. A minimum collocate frequency level of 10 occurrences was applied, and the threshold score for statistical significance was set at 2.0 (Clear, 1993; Barnbrook, 1996).

The results of the t-score analysis are presented in Table 2.4. This analysis finds that there are more collocation types in USE 12+ than there are in USE 0 in six out of the 10 prepositions studied (*of, in, for, as, with* and *at*). Only three prepositions (*on, from* and *about*) reverse this trend, and in one case (*by*) the same number of types is found in both datasets. Similar findings are observed for t-score collocate tokens;

Table 2.4 Collocation types and tokens identified by t-score analysis

	USE 0		USE 12+	
	Types	Tokens	Types	Tokens
of	684	48,136 (+1%)	**701 (+2%)**	47,485
in	573	37,332	582 (+2%)	38,766 (+4%)
for	272	14,543	**282 (+4%)**	15,008 (+3%)
as	228	13,171	**253 (+11%)**	14,369 (+9%)
with	192	9,356	**204 (+6%)**	**9,607 (+3%)**
on	**180 (+3%)**	8,436	175	9,187 (+9%)
from	129 (+7%)	**5,571 (+17%)**	121	4,774
at	119	5,611	**122 (+3%)**	**5,677 (+1%)**
by	106	**4,589 (+8%)**	106	4,256
about	**114 (+6%)**	3,729	108	**4,235 (+14%)**

Table 2.5 Collocation types and tokens identified by MI analysis

	USE 0		USE 12+	
	Types	Tokens	Types	Tokens
of	663	**47,643 (+2%)**	**673 (+2%)**	46,882
in	558	37,034	570 (+2%)	38,520 (+4%)
for	267	14,443	**276 (+3%)**	14,864 (+3%)
as	218	12,880	**245 (+12%)**	14,102 (+9%)
with	186	7,681	**200 (+8%)**	**7,939 (+3%)**
on	**175 (+1%)**	8,374	174	9,143 (+9%)
from	125 (+5%)	**5,513 (+17%)**	119	4,713
at	117	5,587	**121 (+3%)**	**5,664 (+1%)**
by	104	**4,559 (+8%)**	**105 (+1%)**	4,232
about	**111 (+6%)**	3,672	105	**4,135 (+13%)**

for seven of the 10 node words studied here (*in, for, as, with, on, at* and *about*) the USE 12+ data exceed the USE 0 data. The results of the MI analysis are highly consistent with the above findings, as can be seen in Table 2.5.

In summary, then, in the N&C analysis above it seems that collocational usage and time spent abroad are more positively than negatively correlated. There are two possible objections to this claim, however. The first is that some of these figures may be attributable to, or at least affected by, the raw frequency differences between the two corpora noted in Table 2.3 earlier. Although is not possible to establish whether or not this is the case, it must be acknowledged as a possibility. Accordingly, I have used bold highlighting in Tables 2.4 and 2.5 to indicate where a proportional increase is at least 1 per cent greater than the raw frequency difference between each preposition across the two corpora, and where we may therefore be somewhat more confident that the result obtained is not just an effect of raw frequency differences. Even when we take this into account, the USE 12+ occurrences still substantially outweigh the USE 0 occurrences overall.

The other objection is that there has been no attempt to establish how many of these collocations are qualitatively correct and therefore valid as quantitative data. One rejoinder could be to argue that non-native 'lingua franca' varieties of English may have their own distinct collocational characteristics, and that it would be inappropriate to assess these according to British, American or other native-speaker norms (Jenkins and Seidlhofer, 2001; Seidlhofer and Jenkins, 2003; Seidlhofer, 2005, 2007). However, for the purposes of this research, it was assumed that the USE students do aspire to nativelike collocational usage patterns, and that it would therefore be interesting to submit the USE data to an additional qualitative analysis. As it would clearly be impossible to look at every single collocation identified by the N&C analysis above, this was done by means of a concordance sampling procedure. Specifically, five random 100-line concordance samples were obtained for each preposition and searched manually for possible collocation errors. I checked the validity of my judgements as to the acceptability or otherwise of a particular collocation by searching for the same combination in both the Bank of English and on the Internet using the Google™ search engine. Errors that were judged to be primarily syntactic or morphological rather than collocational (e.g. *I do it when I want to be* ***sured about*** *my guesses regarding the new words meaning*) were ignored. The total number of errors for each preposition was then divided by five in order to obtain an average score. These mean scores (rounded up or down to the nearest whole number and expressed as percentages of all instances of each preposition) are presented in Table 2.6.

Although both corpora are characterized by a very high degree of collocational accuracy, the USE 0 data consistently contain more collocational errors than do their USE 12+ equivalents. (Collocations featuring the preposition *on* seem to be particularly problematic for the USE 0 group, and it might be interesting for a future study to investigate whether L1 influence may be at work here.) Overall, the average error rate for USE 0 is almost twice that of USE 12+, at 2.3 and 1.2 respectively. A Wilcoxon Signed Ranks test[3] found this difference to be significant at $p<0.05$ ($z=-2.456$; $p=014$). In summary, while the above analysis is clearly in line with Nesselhauf's claim that 'the length of stays in English-speaking countries does correlate with a decrease in deviations' (Nesselhauf, 2005: 236), it is less clear whether it supports Nesselhauf's additional claim that 'this decrease is not dramatic'

Table 2.6 Percentage frequencies of collocation errors for 10 prepositions in USE 0 and USE 12+

	Example	USE 0	USE 12+
of	They no longer agree **of** how to lead their life	4%	2%
in	My knowledge **in** writing comes from reading a lot	2%	1%
for	I am positive **for** starting with english as early as possible.	3%	2%
as	[No errors identified]	0	0
with	Of course there is nothing amazing **with** that statement.	1%	1%
on	Some of the responsibility must lie **on** the producers of violent films	5%	1%
from	Questions aroused **from** tv should be discussed in school	3%	2%
at	To explain this i would like to point **at** the description of nature in the novel.	2%	1%
by	Swedish pop charts have been crowded **by** new, young swedish music.	1%	1%
about	I feel rather competent **about** my english at this point.	2%	1%

(Nesselhauf, 2005: 236). On the contrary, given that the prepositions studied here are among the most frequent words in the English language (Leech, Rayson and Wilson, 2001), it is possible to interpret the improvements in collocational accuracy observed above as very substantial indeed.

Conclusions

This chapter has used the tools and methods of corpus linguistics to investigate two claims: firstly, that there is a negative relationship between time spent in an L2 environment and the number of collocations produced by L2 learners; and secondly, that collocational accuracy is only slightly improved by an extended period of immersion in an L2 environment. My conclusion in respect of the first claim is that much depends not only on the way in which the concept of collocation itself is defined and operationalized, but also on how the results of a particular method of analysis are interpreted. If we define collocations as lexical bundles, we find that the number produced does seem to decrease with time spent abroad. However, I have argued that this apparent decrease may actually indicate an underlying positive trend, as learners acquire more phraseological sequences, and/or introduce more variation into the sequences that they already know, thereby rendering them invisible to the lexical bundle search procedure itself. Support for this latter argument comes from the node and collocates analysis of the 10 most frequent prepositions in each corpus, which finds a much clearer positive correlation between number of collocations produced and time spent in an L2 milieu.

As regards the second claim, I found not only that collocational accuracy does appear to be positively correlated with L2 immersion, but also that the difference between immersion- and non-immersion groups may be more substantial than Nesselhauf (2005) suggests. However, it should be borne in mind that these findings are based on the analysis of a small selection of words taken from just one word class, and must therefore be regarded as subject to confirmation or challenge by future research.

In the meantime, my overall conclusion is that doubts as to the pedagogic value of time spent in an L2 environment may not be warranted after all. Even so, it remains clear that the process of L2 collocational development is likely to be a slow and occasionally painful one quite irrespective of the linguistic environment in which the learner happens to be immersed. The challenge that remains for researchers, therefore, is to find out whether, how, and to what extent, explicit instruction can speed this process up.

Notes

1. A qualitative structural and functional analysis of the lexical bundle data was carried out in the hope that it might cast some light on these issues, but this proved quite unilluminating and will therefore not be discussed here.
2. The word *to* was excluded from this list on account of its frequent use as an infinitive marker.
3. The figures are from concordance samples, which by definition merge lots of individual students together. The Wilcoxon Signed Ranks measure is used here on the assumption that spread of prepositions provides a representative sample of each corpus. The measure treats each pair of prepositions as matched pairs and allows us to compare the two groups for these cases (albeit in a somewhat unorthodox fashion).

Acknowledgement

I would like to thank Ylva Berglund Prytz, Jeannette Littlemore, Oliver Mason, Carole Patilla, Brent Wolter and the two editors of this volume for providing assistance and support at various stages of the research reported in this chapter.

3
Sound Evidence: Phraseological Units in Spoken Corpora

Phoebe M. S. Lin and Svenja Adolphs

Introduction

With the advent of the rapid development of corpus over the past decade, we see an ever-increasing body of research on collocations. As Moon (1997: 41) puts it, 'it is difficult and arguably pointless to study such things [i.e. collocation] except through using large amounts of real data'. However, there are different views of collocations, and the one that we adopt is in line with that of Sinclair (1991) who regards collocations as recurrent, continuous or discontinuous, word combinations that may be retrieved from a corpus based on raw or adjusted frequency measures. This view of collocation essentially overlaps with what corpus linguists commonly call *phraseological units* or *phraseology* in the field. As Sinclair (1991) points out, these phraseological units play a central role in language production, and research (e.g. Biber, Conrad and Cortes, 2004; Biber et al., 1999a; Bolinger, 1976; Cowie, 1988; Wray, 2002) shows that they are essentially building blocks of discourse in spoken and written registers.

While corpus-derived phraseological units often place strong emphasis on their frequency of occurrence, the psycholinguistic nature of these phraseological units remains under-explored. If second language learners are to benefit from the reduced online processing load brought about by the use of phraseological units, we have to assume that they store and process phraseology as holistic units in the mental lexicon. However, the investigation of the psycholinguistic nature of phraseological units has proved difficult. The psycholinguistic methods that researchers have used include self-paced reading (Conklin and Schmitt, 2007; Schmitt and Underwood, 2004), eye-tracking (Underwood, Schmitt and Galpin, 2004) and the use of grammaticality judgement tasks (Jiang and Nekrasova, 2007). These methods, however, only focus on the perception of written phraseological units under experimental conditions. There is a need for new methods to be developed that allow us to explore the production of spoken phraseological units in naturalistic, non-experimental settings. Among other alternatives, Wray (2004) suggests the tracking of pauses and intonation, which, together with a number of other phonological features, are subsumed under the criterion of *phonological coherence* in Hickey (1993), Peters (1983) and Wray (2002). The underlying assumption is that if learners process phraseological units as holistic entities, phonological coherence should provide evidence to support this process.

In this chapter, we will test the idea of phonological coherence as a technique to explore the psycholinguistic nature of phraseological units.[1] We report the findings of our study, which attempts to profile the phraseological unit *I don't know why*, and examine whether this phraseological unit displays phonological coherence. The study is based on the assumption that if phraseological units are always phonologically coherent, phonological coherence might be established as an alternative to the psycholinguistic methods currently adopted to explore the reality of holistic storage and processing of phraseological units.

In the next sections, we will explore the definition of phonological coherence and how it has been used as evidence of chunking in psycholinguistic research. We will also discuss ways in which the notion of phonological coherence of phraseological units might be challenged. The second half of this chapter reports on the findings from our study of the phraseological unit *I don't know why* extracted from our 230,000-word Chinese learner subcorpus taken from the Nottingham International Corpus of Learner English (spoken) (abbreviated as NICLEs-CHN hereafter).

The notion of phonological coherence

Defining phonological coherence

The term *phonological coherence* was first used by Peters (1983) in her list of criteria for identifying formulaic sequences in child language. She suggests that a phonologically coherent sequence is always produced fluently as a unit with an unbroken intonation contour and that there is an absence of hesitations. She calls these two criteria, that is, the absence of hesitation and the presence of a single intonation contour, the dual criteria because the satisfaction of both is required for phonological coherence. Elsewhere in Wray (2004) and Moon (1997) similar points are made about phraseological units in adult language. Wray (2004) notes that a formulaic sequence ought to be relatively resistant to internal dysfluency and inaccuracy and predicts that there would be far fewer pauses and errors within formulaic strings than between them. Note that while Wray (2004) argues there are far fewer pauses and errors within formulaic strings, this does not mean there should be no pauses or errors at all. Moon (1997: 44), on the other hand, proposes the 'phonological criterion' as one of the criteria that should distinguish holistic multiword items from other kinds of strings. The criterion implies that holistic multiword items should form single tone units. In other words, the most ideal case will be when the intonation unit (IU) boundaries match exactly the phraseological unit boundaries as shown schematically below, where ■ represents the phraseological unit, — the surrounding single words and ⌒ the span of an intonation unit.[2]

The main argument supporting the idea that phraseological unit boundaries should match intonation unit boundaries is that these multiword units are believed to be building blocks of fluent speech. As Bolinger (1976: 1) suggests,

> our language does not expect us to build everything starting with lumber, nails, and blueprint, but provides us with an incredibly large number of prefabs, which have the magical property of persisting even when we knock some of them apart and put them together in unpredictable ways.

This comparison of phraseological units with prefabricated building blocks has highlighted not only the efficiency achieved through using phraseology, but also the fact that individual words in these units form chunks that are closely held together even though they are made up of semantically transparent single words.

While these phraseological units are processed as a prefabricated unit, some researchers, including Wray (2002, 2004), Schmitt and Underwood (2004) and Underwood, Schmitt and Galpin (2004), actually go further in suggesting that such units are stored and retrieved as holistic units in the mental lexicon. Regardless of the psycholinguistics behind phraseology, the idea here is that these units are holistic to a certain extent. This forms the basis of the prediction that the holistic nature of phraseological units will also be revealed phonologically even without any reference to their psycholinguistic reality.

Phonological coherence as evidence of chunking

The question, then, is why the holistic nature of phraseological units should be revealed phonologically. Here we will look at how the notion of phonological coherence in general is used in psycholinguistic research to reveal the underlying processes of language production. The aim is to establish why and how phonological coherence reflects that a sequence of words has been processed as a chunk.

The history of using phonological coherence as psycholinguistic evidence can be traced back to prosodic disambiguation studies in the 1970s when the ideas of deep structure and surface structure under generative grammar proliferated. Researchers were interested in how the surface structure ambiguity in sentences like *The old men and women stayed at home* and *Steve or Sam and Bob will come* (Lehiste, 1973) could be resolved. One of the solutions was to look at the prosodic features of these sentences (cf. Lehiste, 1973; Price et al., 1991; Schafer et al., 2000; Warren et al., 2000). If the underlying structure is *the old men and some women*, a prosodic break is expected between *men* and *and*. This is also true of syntactically ambiguous sentences involving unclear prepositional phrase attachment like *The cop killed the robber with a gun* where a prosodic break between *robber* and *with* will lead us to make the interpretation that the weapon belongs to the cop rather than the robber. The absence of a break, however, will lead us to infer that the weapon is actually the robber's. Through the placement of prosodic breaks, we can see how chunking happens. Thus, we should be able to find phraseological units, which are chunks, as being delineated by prosodic breaks.

Challenging the idea of phonological coherence

While the discussion so far has pointed to the plausibility of the suggestion that phraseological units are phonologically coherent, there are a few issues we have to consider as this idea and its application may not be as simple as it first appears. We mentioned earlier that the ideal case will be for us to find complete matching of phraseological unit and intonation unit boundaries in *all* phraseological units. If it were the case that these two types of boundaries always match, phonological coherence would be a fairly reliable indicator of the formulaicity when we identify phraseological units in a spoken text. However, the situation is actually more complicated because the extent to which the two types of boundaries may match may also depend on the type of phraseological units we are looking at. Phraseological units that are full clauses, such as *conversational routines* (Aijmer, 1996), may have a greater tendency to have boundaries that also match the intonation unit boundaries.

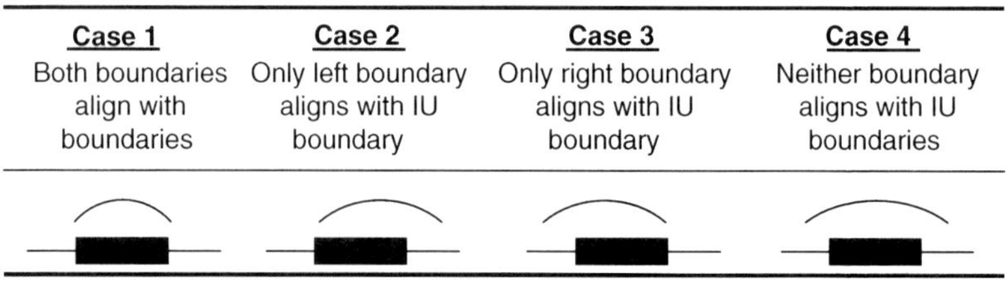

Figure 3.1 The four possibilities with phraseological unit boundary/intonation unit boundary matching

Units that are not full clauses, such as sentence builders and semantically transparent two-word collocations, on the other hand, may have a lower tendency to demonstrate matching of the two types of boundaries. The length of the phraseological unit is another factor that complicates this issue. In terms of processing load, longer phraseological units may have a greater tendency to form phonologically coherent sequences than shorter ones. While we are not predicting that short phraseological units cannot be phonologically coherent, it may not be straightforward to apply phonological coherence as a criterion to shorter units.

When we examine the nature of the phraseological unit/intonation unit boundary alignment, there seem to be four possible outcomes (i.e. Cases 1 to 4), presented schematically in Figure 3.1. While Case 1 means phonological coherence is achieved and Case 4 the opposite, it is not clear how Cases 2 and 3 should be handled.

All of the questions raised so far point to the need for the notion of phonological coherence to be refined further. One of the ways to do this is by scrutinizing this notion in the light of real spoken language data. In the next section, we will present the findings of our study, which sets out to test whether phraseological units are phonologically coherent, as Coulmas (1979), Hickey (1993), Peters (1983), Moon (1997) and Wray (2004) suggest. We have aimed to develop a phonological profile for the most frequent 5-word unit[3] *I don't know why* in our 230,000-word NICLEs-CHN subcorpus. From there we can evaluate the validity of phonological coherence to be listed as one of the criteria for identifying phraseological units.

Profiling the phonology of *I don't know why*

The NICLEs-CHN learner corpus

The 230,000-word NICLEs-CHN subcorpus is made up of interview data collected longitudinally from 17 Chinese EFL learners who were studying in a British university. The participants were interviewed by a native speaker of British English three to five times on a regular basis on topics such as their life, study and English language learning experience in the United Kingdom. To obtain a corpus that only includes learner language, the native speaker interviewer's turns were taken out. The longitudinal design of this corpus allows us to capture the development of learners' phraseological knowledge over time, as well as the idiosyncratic preferences of individual learners in their use of phraseological units.

The use of a learner corpus is well suited to the particular method we are exploring in this chapter. This is because the speech patterns of learners, which are generally slower and marked by more hesitations, make the presence of phraseological units as prefabricated building blocks more explicit. As a result, when learners do use phraseological units that are stored holistically, those parts of their utterance will be marked by fluency and specific phonological features. Dechert (1983), in his study of a German learner of English, finds that while the learner's spoken English was marked with hesitations, fillers and corrections, there were also smooth and fluent stretches in the output that he labelled 'islands of reliability' (Dechert, 1983: 184). These islands of reliability, in a sense, describe phraseological units. Wray (2004) also highlights the fact that a formulaic sequence ought to be relatively resistant to internal dysfluency and inaccuracy.

Patterns of use of *I don't know why* in the corpus

The phraseological unit *I don't know why* was identified by automatic extraction using WordSmith Tools 5.0 (Scott, 2008). The tool generated lists of 2-word to 7-word phraseological units. We regarded it important to select a target phraseological unit with a reasonable frequency of occurrence so that the scale of the phonological analysis would be manageable for us. Therefore, phraseological units of other lengths were not considered for they have either too many (e.g., there were 3,028 instances for the most frequent 2-word unit) or too few (e.g. there were only nine instances for the most frequent 7-word unit) instances. We finally got down to the most frequent 5-word unit *I don't know why*, which has a fairly substantial 56 occurrences in NICLEs-CHN and was widely used by the interviewees. Half of the eight participants used this phraseological unit, and each of them used it seven times on average.

We suggested earlier that the status of the target sequence as a full clause would also be a factor affecting the level of phonological coherence. In written language, we would expect *I don't know why* to function as a sentence stem to introduce a question to which the speaker does not know the answer. However, analysing the phraseological unit in our corpus, we found that only eight out of the total 56 instances functioned as a sentence stem while the majority (k=38) occurred as a full clause. These full clauses could be further broken down into *comment clauses* (k=6) and *disclaimers* (k=32) according to Altenberg's (1998) grammar-based categorization of spoken multiword units (see Figure 3.2 for examples).

The task of categorizing the 56 instances of *I don't know why* into these three functions was not as straightforward as it might appear. Without hearing the sound of the concordance lines, sometimes there was simply insufficient information in the concordance lines. In fact, it was possible to fit 18 per cent of all cases into either category. Example 1 below illustrates the ambiguity in categorizing such cases.

Example 1

S2: I had changed my address but I don't know why they also send the package to China.

Participant 009, Interview 3

This example could function as a sentence stem or a disclaimer. If we assume that the utterance was delivered at fast pace and contains no break in rhythm or intonation, Example 1 will tend to be classed as a sentence stem. However, if we assume that it was delivered in slow

sentence stem	**S2:** since the people around me are laughing but **I don't know why** [laughs] they laugh *Participant 004, Interview 5*
comment clause	**S2:** yeah sometimes we you know hang out to the pub or some party yeah **S1:** and do you go to the cinema or to **S2:** well actually I don't like you know go to the cinema but most of my friends **I don't know why** most of my friends they like you know go the cinema quite often and every weekend call me to go outside to watching them. *Participant 002, Interview 5*
disclaimer	**S2:** but it's really right decision. **S1:** mm mmm **S2:** yeah **I don't know why** but after that I think the world is more better than before here *Participant 003, Interview*

Figure 3.2 Examples of *I don't know why* as sentence stem, comment clause and disclaimer in NICLEs-CHN

pace, along the lines of *I had changed my address but ... I don't know why ... they also send the package to China*, it will tend to be classed as a disclaimer. In another empirical study of phraseological units, De Cock (1998) also notices this difficulty and develops the argument that it is important for researchers to get access to intonation information when investigating phraseological units in a spoken corpus.[4] However, we decided to keep the investigation of concordance lines separate from the investigation of the audio record so as to avoid circularity. The functional categorization in this investigation was thus based on textual data only.

To find out to what extent phraseological unit boundaries match intonation unit boundaries, we extracted from the audio records all 56 instances from their context. In other words, the clips contain approximately four seconds to the left and to the right of the target utterances. We then analysed these clips auditorily to mark the intonation unit boundaries. To complement our auditory analysis, we also used a sound synthesis and analysis program called Praat (Boersma, 2001) to draw an acoustic picture. We will discuss the acoustic analysis further below after presenting the quantitative findings from the auditory analysis.

Auditory analysis

The general picture

Earlier we pointed out that there could be four possible outcomes with the matching of the two types of boundaries (see Figure 3.1). Analysing all 56 instances, we found that 55 per cent of the instances of *I don't know why* matched the intonation unit boundaries on both sides (Case 1) and 4 per cent did not match at all (Case 4). In the middle were 14 per cent that matched only the left side of the phraseological unit and 16 per cent that matched only the right side. We also put 11 per cent of the instances in the miscellaneous group, which, as we listened to the audio data again, seemed to be *I don't know. Why ...* rather than our target sequence *I don't know why*, despite the fact that they were identical in form.

Another way of looking at these percentages is to see them as raw probabilities. In other words, when we encounter an instance of *I don't know why* in a spoken corpus, there is a 55 per cent chance that it is phonologically coherent in the sense that it will match the intonation unit boundaries on both sides, an 85 per cent chance (= 55%+14%+16%) that it will match at least one side and a 4 per cent chance that it is not phonologically coherent at all.

As the corpus is made up of interview data, natural turn-taking between the interlocutors also plays a role in the overall picture of intonation unit alignment. In other words, when *I don't know why* begins the speaker's turn, the intonation unit/boundary alignment that we find at the left boundary of the phraseological unit may not be as revealing as cases where we find the unit in the middle of a speaker's turn. The situation is similar when *I don't know why* occurs at the end of the turn. The turn-taking effect affected 41 per cent (23 out of 56) of the cases in this investigation, which was quite high.

Results by function categories

Table 3.1 shows the percentages and raw frequencies when we break down the numbers into Altenberg's (1998) categories. As we mentioned above, we predicted a higher tendency for full clauses (which functions as either comment clauses or disclaimers) to be phonologically coherent (Case 1). We submitted the raw frequencies in Table 3.1 to a chi-square test. The 5 x 4 chi-square analysis revealed that there was a significant relationship between type of intonation unit matching (i.e. Cases 1 to 4) and the function categories χ^2 (12, 56) = 35.1, p <.001. Despite this statistically significant finding, we are also aware that given our small sample size it may not be appropriate for us to draw conclusions out of this inferential statistical test that are too strong. As Oakes (1998)

Table 3.1 Results by function categories (raw frequencies in brackets)

	Sentence stem	**Comment clause**	**Disclaimer**	**Unclear**	**TOTAL**
Case 1 Both boundaries align with IU boundaries	—	5% (3)	41% (23)	9% (5)	55% (31)
Case 2 Only left boundary aligns with IU boundary	5% (3)	5% (3)	4% (2)	—	14% (8)
Case 3 Only right boundary aligns with IU boundary	2% (1)	—	5% (3)	9% (5)	16% (9)
Case 4 Neither boundary aligns with IU boundaries	2% (1)	—	2% (1)	—	4% (2)
Miscellaneous	5% (3)	—	5% (3)	—	10% (6)
TOTAL	14% (8)	10% (6)	57% (32)	18% (10)	99%* (56)

* The total does not add up to 100% owing to fractions being rounded up or down.

points out, to use the chi-square test, the number of items must be large enough to obtain an expected cell frequency of 5. Therefore, at this stage, we are inclined to discuss the results in terms of raw frequencies and percentages.

From the raw frequencies in Table 3.1, we worked out that if we know that an instance of *I don't know why* is a full clause, there is 74 per cent chance that this will be phonologically coherent.[4] But if we know that it is not a full clause (in which case it functions as a sentence stem), there is zero probability that it will be phonologically coherent.

While nearly three quarters (74 per cent) of the full clauses were phonologically coherent, we also wanted to find out why 25 per cent of the full clauses did not align with the intonation unit boundaries. Our analysis revealed that there were two main reasons for this non-alignment. The first reason was that the intonation unit also included conjunctions like *but* and *so* that occur right before or after these instances of *I don't know why*. Example 2 shows a case where we found that only the left boundary aligned with the intonation unit boundary (intonation unit is highlighted in bold).

Example 2

S2: but it's really right decision
S1: mm mmm
S2: yeah I don't know why but after that I think the world is more better than before here.

Participant 003, Interview 5

The second reason for a full clause to fail to align with intonation unit boundaries on both sides was the repetition at the beginning of the intonation unit. In Example 3 below, *I don't I don't know why* formed an intonation unit, thus leaving only the right boundary of the phraseological unit to align with the intonation unit boundary.

Example 3

S2: because I th= I don't like USA at all I don't I don't know why but I don't like it.

Participant 056, Interview 2

To deal with the non-alignment as a result of the conjunctions and repetitions as we see in Example 3, we have two options. The first option is to treat these cases of failure to align strictly with the intonation unit boundaries on both sides as *not* phonologically coherent. The second option is to refine the criterion of phonological coherence to make allowance for conjunctions and repetitions, which are arguably minimal and common speech phenomena. While both options are viable, the decision seems to depend on the purpose of the investigation into the phonological coherence of phraseological units.

When *I don't know why* functions as a sentence stem, it is not a full clause. So one would normally expect only the left boundary of the phraseological unit to align with the intonation unit boundary (i.e. Case 2). As seen in Table 3.1, we found the highest number of instances having only left boundary alignment. So it appears that the finding is as expected. However, given the infrequency of the phraseological unit as a sentence stem in this corpus, more data may be needed to draw conclusions on this point.

Acoustic findings

While quantitative analysis of the data offers an initial overview, a more detailed acoustic analysis adds an important dimension to the investigation of the matching of phraseological units and intonation unit boundaries. In this section we aim to show examples of how the intonation unit boundaries that we have identified auditorily can also be revealed in the waveform and pitch changes in graphs imported from Praat (Boersma, 2001).

In the literature, researchers find that intonation unit boundaries are associated with acoustic cues such as pauses, anacrusis (i.e. the speeding up of articulation at the beginning of an intonation unit), final syllable lengthening, a change in pitch level and/or pitch direction among unaccented syllables (Cruttenden, 1997), pitch reset and a final falling tone (Wichmann, 2000). So acoustically, we should be able to observe these phonetic cues at the boundaries of *I don't know why*. Figures 3.3 and 3.4 show the waveform and pitch changes of Examples 4 and 5 respectively. In Figure 3.3, what we can see is the 0.13 second and 0.94 second silent pauses at the left and right boundaries respectively of *I don't know why*. Also, right before the brief 0.13 second pause, we can also see the falling tone of the word *know*, which again points to the presence of an intonation unit boundary.

Example 4

S1: they are
S2: yeah I don't know I don't know why our tuition fees is the cheapest I think in our= in our university.

Participant 051, Interview 3

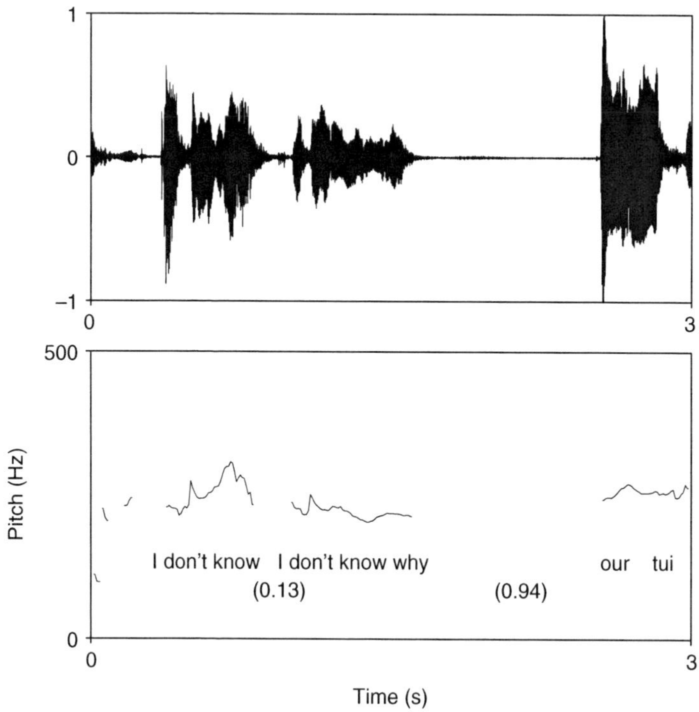

Figure 3.3 The waveform and pitch changes of *I don't know why* in Example 4

While the magnitude of the falling tone at the word *know* in Figure 3.3 may be small, the falling tone in Figure 3.4 at the word *why* is much more prominent. This prominent fall at *why* and the 0.42 second silent pause together explain why intonation unit boundaries are perceived on both sides of the phraseological unit.

Example 5

S2: but if every time I should write in this way I think it's rather boring I don't know why I should write in this [*laughs*] way and um when the first erm the first edition of my project.

Participant 004, Interview 3

Among all the phonetic cues that signal the presence of an intonation unit boundary, it seems that silent pauses and the falling tone are the most common and easiest to observe in graphs showing waveform and

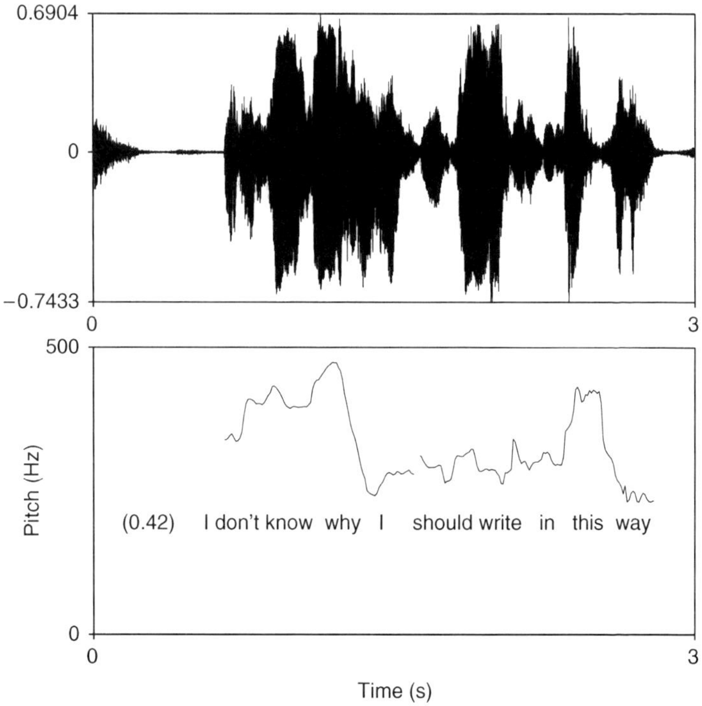

Figure 3.4 The waveform and pitch changes of *I don't know why* in Example 5

pitch changes. However, there does not appear to be a simple way to observe other phonetic cues such as anacrusis, final syllable lengthening, a change in pitch level and/or pitch direction among unaccented syllables, so the 'measurement' of these cues remains on the auditory level. Further research in this area should lead to an increase in objectivity with regard to the phonological analysis.

Concluding remarks and future directions

In this chapter, we have explored the idea of phonological coherence as a criterion for identifying phraseological units. While many researchers assume that formulaic sequences should display phonological coherence given their nature as holistic units, based on the 230,000-word NICLEs-CHN subcorpus, our investigation revealed that the phraseological unit *I don't know why*, as an example, demonstrates phonological coherence (defined as the alignment of the phraseological unit boundary and intonation unit boundary on both sides) only 55 per cent of the time. This implies that phonological coherence alone may not be as powerful an indicator of formulaicity as we assumed. We also found that natural turn-taking played a role in this figure. When we examined the cases that failed to demonstrate phonological coherence, we found that repetition and the insertion of conjunctions were the main factors. We therefore suggested that in future the idea of phonological coherence might be modified to make allowance for these minimal structures, which are frequent in speech. Finally, we also looked at how acoustic evidence might complement our auditory analysis of intonation unit boundaries.

While we looked at the level of phraseological unit/intonation unit boundary alignment, we did not deal with issues of internal dysfluency and hesitation phenomena, which are also part of the definition of phonological coherence. This will be an interesting topic to pursue in future research, but there does not seem to be an easy way to address this issue. Beyond giving the type of general, impressionistic remarks that learners appear to be more fluent and hesitate less within sequences of formulaic language, it seems difficult to determine quantitatively if there are significantly more dysfluency and hesitation phenomena in non-formulaic language than within phraseological units.

The value of investigating the notion of phonological coherence, as mentioned at the beginning of this chapter, is that it is one of the very few existing methods for exploring the production of spoken phraseological units in non-experimental settings. Our investigation implies, to some extent, that if phonological coherence (combined with automatic extraction) is used as a method to identify phraseological units, the success rate will be 55 per cent. However, this figure is far from conclusive considering the exploratory nature of the study and the limited focus on only one of many possible criteria for analysing holistic storage. An alternative approach might be not to begin with a pre-selected phraseological unit but to take a more exhaustive approach by identifying all phraseological units and all intonation units in the corpus. An analysis could then be carried out at the level of phraseological unit/intonation unit boundary matching. Such an approach would also allow us to determine quantitatively whether the phraseological unit is an accurate predictor of intonation unit boundaries.

Our study has offered an account of the phonology of collocations, with particular reference to the notion that they are processed as holistic units. This opens up a new perspective of describing and identifying collocations in learner language and has implications for a number of different areas of language research, both descriptive and applied. Advances in acoustic coding and corpus development should make it possible to refine the methods we have described here even further and allow us to generate a better understanding of the processing and use of collocations in learner and native speaker language.

Notes

1. Among the very few studies that have explored the technique, Dahlmann and Adolphs (2007) and Erman (2007) look at pauses as evidence of the psycholinguistic reality of phraseological units or formulaic sequences.
2. This schematic representation is inspired by Park (2002: 647).
3. Computationally, the abbreviated form *don't* is often counted as two words. In keeping with the conventions of our search tool, WordSmith Tools 5.0 (Scott, 2008), we count *I don't know why* as a 5-word unit.
4. This figure is calculated by dividing Case 1 full clauses (i.e. 3+23 = 26) by the sum of Cases 1–4 full clauses (i.e. 3+3+23+2+3+1 = 35) under the *comment clause* and *disclaimer* columns in Table 3.1.

4

Exploring L1 and L2 Writing Development through Collocations: A Corpus-based Look

Randi Reppen

Introduction

This chapter explores how English first and second language elementary students (ages 8 to 12) writing in English, use 3-word lexical bundles in various writing tasks (for example, expository, narrative, and taking a position). Lexical bundles are sequences of words that are empirically identified through the use of a computer program, rather than a researcher thinking up phrases or groups of words that are noticeable in discourse and then searching for those sequences. In other words, the bundles emerge from the corpus rather than from the researcher as a starting point, in contrast to most phraseological studies (Moon, 1998). Because the bundles are identified computationally and not by the human eye, these bundles are not always complete structural units, for example: *take a look at, can I have a* (Biber et al., 1999b). In this chapter, I use the lexical bundles found in student writing to explore writing development across three grade levels of elementary students and also the influence of first language on the use of lexical bundles.

Lexical bundles

There are a number of terms that are frequently used by researchers to refer to groups or sequences of words. Some of the terms used include extended collocations, clusters, fixed expressions (Moon, 1998), formulaic sequences (Schmitt, 2004), chunks (Lewis, 1993), and lexical bundles (Biber et al., 1999b). Each of these terms has slight definitional nuances and also sometimes methodological differences. I use the term lexical bundles to refer to the sequences of words that will be explored in this chapter. A lexical bundle is not a predetermined piece of language;

rather, it is a recurring sequence of words that is identified through the use of a computer program. The computer searches through the texts in the corpus and identifies the recurring word sequences of the length that the researcher has specified (e.g. 2, 3, 4 or 5 words). In this study I have used the computer program Collocate (Barlow, 2004), an accurate and very user-friendly tool, to identify the recurring word sequences in the corpus of student writing. There are also studies that have identified lexical bundles that are more typical of spoken or written discourse (Biber, 2004). Lexical bundles can also be categorized according to their functions (Biber et al., 1999b; Reppen and Vásquez, 2007). Because lexical bundles are sometimes seen as building blocks of language, this provides a useful starting point for exploring the writing development of elementary students writing in both their first and second language.

The corpus

The corpus used in this chapter is a subcorpus of a larger six-year project (Reppen, 2001) that involved students in Grades 3 through 6 in 26 classrooms from across the state of Arizona in the southwestern United States. The students in this study range in age from 8 to 12 years old and speak either English or Navajo as a first language. Each month, the students wrote in-class essays on topics designed to elicit different types of writing (for example, description, narrative, taking a position). The topics are similar to writing tasks that elementary students regularly encounter. Each month, all of the classes wrote on the same topic, therefore allowing accurate comparisons to be made across grades and language groups while controlling for the effect of topic. Table 4.1 provides a list of the topics and the pre-writing activity that was used by the classroom teacher to introduce the writing prompt. Providing a brainstorming, or pre-writing, activity with the monthly writing prompts ensured that there was a similar treatment of the task across all the classrooms that were participating in the study.

The type of writing being elicited was also cycled across the school year so that, for example, the narrative topics did not all occur at the beginning or end of the year. Students in each grade level wrote on the same topic, and the topics varied each month over the course of the academic year (September–June). In other words, each month the students were presented with a topic, participated in a brainstorming activity and then were asked to write on that topic in class. By having students writing on the same topic, comparisons can be made across grade levels and also across first languages.

Table 4.1 Writing prompts used for compiling the corpus

Month	Brainstorming directions for the teacher	Writing prompt
September	Talk about famous people (remember they can be historical, scientific, popular etc.). List some on the board if you desire. What would your life be like if you were ________?	You can be any famous person: Describe who you would be.
October	Discuss how much TV students watch. Talk about different types of shows (cartoons, talk shows, news, movies). What are some advantages and disadvantages of watching a lot of TV?	Should kids watch a lot of TV: Why or why not?
November	Discuss different Thanksgiving plans and different traditions.	What will you do for Thanksgiving?
December	List games or sports on the board. Discuss how to describe a game/sport that someone has not played.	Choose your favorite game or sport. Describe how to play your game or sport to someone who has not played it.
January	List what you like about your school. What would you include in your ideal school? What else would you put in your ideal school?	Explain what the ideal school would be like. How would this ideal school be similar or different to the school you are in?
February	Discuss what a time machine is. Where can you go in a time machine? List some places that students would like to go if they had a time machine. Relate to Social Studies and what it was like 200 years ago. Emphasize this is 200 years BACK: not "Back to the Future."	You have traveled **back** 200 years in a time machine. What did you see? Tell a story about what happened.
March	What is a good friend? How do you decide who is your friend? Discuss ways to describe friends (e.g. physical characteristics, inner qualities).	Describe your best friend.
April	No pre-activity.	What is your favorite subject and why? What is your least favorite subject and why? Be sure to say why you like or do not like the subjects.

(Continued)

Table 4.1 (Continued)

Month	Brainstorming directions for the teacher	Writing prompt
May	Discuss how to write so that people who do not see something can understand what happened. Relate it to a news report. If possible read a news article to the class. Discuss what the students understood? What did they "see?"	Picture series: Write about what is happening in the pictures. Write so that someone who has not seen the pictures will know what happened.

From reading the essays and conferring with the classroom teachers, we can confidently assume that the students' writing is typical and representative of the writing produced at these grade levels from the students at these schools. The L1 English students are from a school in a small city in the southwestern US. The Navajo L1 students are from a school located on the Navajo Nation, also in the southwestern US. In both cases, the students are in a context where their first language and culture are dominant.

Method

By using the carefully designed corpus of student writing (Reppen, 2001; 2007) described above, we can address the specific questions posed below.

1. How do 3-word lexical bundles vary by grade level?
2. What impact does the writer's first language have on the 3-word lexical bundles used?

The questions explored in this study – writing development across grade levels and the influence of first language on the use of lexical bundles – require the corpus to be analyzed in two ways to answer the research questions. First, the results are explored by grade level, and, second, by the influence of first language.

Table 4.2 provides an overview of the corpus with a breakdown by words and essays by grade level and first language. The total number of essays reported in Table 4.2 represents class totals, so in many cases there are nine essays written by the same student but on different topics. Most of the participating classes had between 15 and 25 students. Only students who had written on seven of the nine prompts that were given during the school year were included in this study.

Table 4.2 Total number of essays and words by grade and L1

L1	Essays	3rd Grade	5th Grade	6th Grade
English	Total texts	137	151	154
	Total words (tokens)	10,622	13,423	18,144
	Average essay length	77	89	118
Navajo	Total texts	125	122	147
	Total words (tokens)	5,828	22,239	23,089
	Average essay length	47	182	157

Table 4.2 provides some useful insights about the similarities and differences across grade levels and first languages. We see that regardless of first language the third-grade students write less than their older peers. This is not entirely a surprising finding since they are less experienced writers, having only been in school three or four years. It is interesting to note that by fifth grade, the L1 Navajo students write quite a bit more than their L1 English counterparts, almost twice as much as their native English-speaking peers. If we look at average length of essays, this is certainly the case. The reasons for the differences in the amount of writing produced between the L1 Navajo and English students is a question that cannot be answered through a corpus investigation; however, it is an issue that can be discovered through this type of empirical investigation and then followed up through interviews and classroom observations. Without taking a general quantitative look at the writing produced in these classes, the differences in the amount of writing produced would never have surfaced.

In order to explore the use of lexical bundles found in the student essays, I processed the various subcorpora using Collocate (Barlow, 2004). Each set of essays was run separately by grade level and first language to obtain the counts for the 3-word bundles in that set of essays. Because the total number of words varied for each grade level, it was necessary to convert the raw counts to normalized counts so that accurate comparisons can be made. For example, if one text has 100 words and another text has 200 words and each have a count of eight modals, it is not accurate to say these two texts have the same rate of use of modals. The text that was twice as long had a rate of half of the shorter text. The process of normalizing is a standard procedure to allow accurate comparisons across texts of unequal length (Biber, 1998). For this study the counts were normalized to per 10,000 words. The procedure was as follows: (raw count/ total number of words) × 10,000 = normalized count.

Results

In Tables 4.3 and 4.4 we see the counts for the top 20 most frequent 3-word bundles by first language and grade level normalized to 10,000 words. Table 4.3 has the results for the L1 Navajo students, and Table 4.4 has the L1 English students' top 20 3-word lexical bundles.

Variation by grade level

To answer the question of how 3-word lexical bundles vary by grade level, we will begin by looking across the three grade levels and not consider first language. The only identifiable pattern that we see across all three grade levels is the use of portions of the prompts appearing as lexical bundles. Bundles such as *my favorite sport, my favorite subject, least favorite subject, my best friend,* and *the ideal school* can each be directly traced to a prompt. It is interesting to see how the prompt exerts a similar influence across all grade levels, at least when looking at the top 20 lexical bundles. The students across all grade levels are able to use the prompts as a hook or introductory framing to the text that they are writing. A clear example of this is the use of "My favorite subject is ..." and "My least favorite subject is ... ." These are represented by several 3-word bundles: *my favorite subject, favorite subject is, my least favorite,* and *least favorite subject.* It is easy to see how these bundles serve as an introduction not only for an essay, but also for a paragraph. Students across all grade levels used this to create an effective introduction.

There are prompts that are not directly or clearly represented by lexical bundles, and this is also consistent across the grades. The two prompts that did not result in clear 3-word lexical bundles are the picture series task and writing about a famous person. At this point that seems to be all that can be reported about the patterns across the grade levels. Of course, this is a very preliminary pass through the data, and perhaps by looking at the less frequent bundles, greater insight could be gained. Less frequently occurring bundles might provide insights into the effect of topic on the essays, and this might vary across grade level, or across first language.

Variation by first language

Unlike the consistency found in the use of lexical bundles across grade levels, there appears to be some interesting patterns due to the influence

Table 4.3 Top 20 3-word bundles by L1 Navajo students by grade level

Grade 3		Grade 5		Grade 6	
46.33	my best friend	16.19	are going to	14.29	you have to
37.75	we are going	13.94	we are going	13.86	a lot of
37.75	i like to	11.69	a good friend	11.69	favorite subject is
36.03	are going to	10.79	a lot of	8.66	i would like
32.60	to be a	10.34	the time machine	7.80	i would be
29.17	it is fun	9.44	i would be	7.80	would like to
25.74	i want to	8.09	you have to	7.36	went to the
24.02	favorite sport is	8.09	know how to	6.93	go to the
24.02	want to be	7.64	we went to	6.93	my favorite subject
24.02	a lot of	7.64	i want to	6.93	least favorite subject
22.31	my favorite sport	6.74	the next day	6.93	the time machine
22.31	best friend is	6.74	i like to	6.93	my best friend
22.31	favorite subject is	6.30	go to the	6.50	i don't like
20.59	i am going	5.85	went to the	6.50	my least favorite
18.87	am going to	5.85	a friend that	6.06	to go to
18.87	is going to	5.85	favorite subject is	5.20	are going to
17.16	is fun to	5.85	learn how to	5.20	it would be
17.16	going to be	5.85	is going to	4.76	to have a
15.44	like to play	5.85	to go to	4.76	so we can
15.44	go to school	5.85	to play with	4.76	when they got

Table 4.4 Top 20 3-word bundles by L1 English students by grade level

Grade 3		Grade 5		Grade 6	
17.89	favorite subject is	21.65	a lot of	32.95	my best friend
14.12	a lot of	20.71	would have a	19.77	a lot of
13.18	we would have	20.71	favorite subject is	18.83	i would be
12.24	my least favorite	16.95	i would be	18.83	i would go
11.30	my time machine	16.00	i would have	16.00	i would like
10.36	i would like	15.06	my favorite subject	15.06	are going to
10.36	least favorite subject	15.06	school would be	15.06	best friend is
9.41	watch a lot	14.12	the ideal school	14.12	then i would
9.41	my best friend	14.12	my best friend	14.12	we are going
9.41	best friend is	14.12	ideal school would	14.12	there would be
9.41	lot of TV	11.30	if i could	14.12	favorite subject is
8.47	my favorite subject	11.30	because it is	12.24	my favorite subject
8.47	it is fun	11.30	my least favorite	11.30	my least favorite
7.53	we will have	11.30	would be a	11.30	to go to
7.53	like to be	10.36	would be like	10.36	my favorite sport
7.53	would like to	9.41	are going to	10.36	it would be
7.53	because it is	9.41	best friend is	9.41	one of the
7.53	for kids to	9.41	and i would	9.41	to be a
7.53	because she is	9.41	i like to	9.41	least favorite subject
7.53	of TV because	8.47	it would have	9.41	i would want

of the first language. First, there are six bundles that are used across all three grades in the L1 English group. Five of the 6 bundles are topic bundles – ones that are directly related to the prompt: *my best friend*; *best friend is*; *my favorite subject*; *favorite subject is*; *my least favorite*. The sixth bundle, which was used by L1 English students in all three grade levels, was *a lot of*. In the L1 Navajo group there were only three bundles that were used by all three grade levels, and only one of the three was topical: *favorite subject is*. As we can see from Table 4.3, there are other bundles that were directly related to the prompt, but there was enough variation in the way the bundle was realized that only one topic-related prompt was identical across all three grade levels of the Navajo students. The other two bundles that were used by Navajo students in all three grades were *are going to* and *a lot of*. The frequent use of the lexical bundle *a lot of* is a good example of a spoken language feature. In novice writing it is not uncommon to find oral features of language. As students increase their linguistic ability, they will use fewer features of spoken language in their academic essays (Grabe and Kaplan, 1996). In the writing of more advanced students, the bundle *a lot of* would probably be replaced by the single lexical items *many*, or *much*.

Another spoken feature that emerges across the language groups in the first 20 lexical bundles is the strong reliance on the use of *BE + going* by the first language Navajo students. Across the three grade levels, there are nine bundles with the *BE + going* pattern in the Navajo student writing and only three in the writing of the first language English students. The structure of *BE + going* is also strongly associated with spoken language (Biber et al., 1999b). The use of this characteristically spoken feature in writing is an interesting finding, and one that seems to point to the more spoken nature of the Navajo students' writing. This may be a result of these students writing in their second language and therefore initially relying more on spoken language features to express their ideas. This seems a plausible explanation since the use of *BE + going* decreases from third to sixth grade. In third grade writing, there are five different *BE + going* bundles and by the sixth grade only one.

Below are two essays from the same writing prompt both written by L1 Navajo students: one in third grade, the other in sixth grade. The essay prompt was "What will you do for Thanksgiving?" and involved students writing about their plans for the upcoming Thanksgiving vacation. The Navajo celebrate Thanksgiving as part of the blended culture that they live in; it is not part of their traditional culture. In the examples below, I have underlined the use of *BE + going* to highlight some of the differences between these two essays.

TEXT 1: Third grade Navajo essay

We are going to my Nali's* house. We are going to have Thanksgiving at my Nali's house. My Nali's is going to buy the turkey. Even my Nali is going to go to my house. She lives at Pxxx. She is going to invite my mom. We are going to have a dinner. We are going to eat at my Nali's house. We are going to invite my aunt. We are going to pick her up because it is her birthday. She is going to be 31 years old. She is going to be nice to me. She lives in Xxxx Xxxx. She is going to be nice to a lot of people at the party even her sister. She is going to be nice to people. <1883NFNX.093>
* Nali is a term used for grandmother.

TEXT 2: Sixth grade Navajo essay

On Thanksgiving my whole family from my mom's side goes to my grandma's house. We have a big dinner. But first we plan who brings what. Most of the time my family brings salad. The first thing we do is start off with a little prayer for the food. Then we let the older ones go first to serve themselves. The children go last. We eat till we're done. The kids play while the adults clean. We either play football, volleyball, or baseball. When the adults are done cleaning they relax for awhile. After that the families start going home with there full stomachs. Some Thanksgivings don't turn out like these ones. Sometimes we don't have our dinner till the next day after Thanksgiving. Or our parents have different plans. Or sometimes we just have our own 7 person dinner at our own home. But we mostly like to be with our family on Thanksgiving Day. <2196NFNX.123>

Text 1 written by the third grade student uses *BE* + *going* 13 times, while, in Text 2, the sixth grade student does not have one instance of *BE* + *going*. Instead, the sixth grade student frames the essay in such a way as to avoid the use of *BE* + *going*. The third grade text is framed in terms of reporting a future event, and uses *BE* + *going* instead of some of the modal options that could also be used. On the other hand, the sixth grade text approaches the text much like reporting an event using the historical present, thus avoiding the use of the progressive *BE* + *going* and also the use of future modals. These two texts typify the linguistic differences seen as students move from third to sixth grade.

Another trend that seems to be influenced by first language is the use of *I* or *my*. The Navajo students have 14 bundles with either *my* or *I*, while the English students have 22 bundles with *I* or *my*. It seems that this difference might be attributed to the cultural differences in the two groups. The native English speakers are Americans and typically there is a strong tradition of valuing individuality, while in the Navajo culture the group and the family often play a more central role than the individual.

Conclusion

The use of lexical bundles is a productive method for exploring elementary student writing development for both first and second language students writing in English. When looking across the grades we see that there are more similarities rather than differences. The students show a strong tendency to use certain prompts as frames for beginning their essays. This shows an awareness of the need to reference the prompt and help the reader to be aware of the topic being addressed. In analyzing the results for the second research question, regarding the influence of the first language on the use of lexical bundles, the first 20 lexical bundles revealed some interesting cross-linguistic differences and also warrant further exploration. The different use of *BE + going*, and also the different use of *I* and *my* that might reflect linguistic and cultural orientations, are insights that would perhaps be missed through other analytical approaches. These very preliminary results provide a method for further investigation that should prove to be productive for exploring writing development and possible cross-linguistic differences. Future analysis that examines all of the lexical bundles may reveal developmental patterns that are not apparent when only looking at the first 20 bundles at each grade level. Although the research findings presented in this chapter are preliminary, they point to some differences and similarities that are worth further investigation. As a methodology, lexical bundles provide a productive lens through which different questions to do with collocation can be examined across a range of language (and sociocultural) issues.

5
Commentary on Part I: Learner Corpora: A Window onto the L2 Phrasicon

Sylviane Granger

In his review of Lewis's (2000) book on teaching collocation, Barfield (2001: 415) highlights the exciting challenge offered by Lewis's lexical approach but laments the fact that 'the voices of typical language learners are largely omitted' in the volume. The three chapters in this section put learners centre stage and can therefore be seen as redressing the balance. All three studies contain thorough investigations of learner corpus data, but differ in terms of the research questions addressed, the type and size of corpus data used and the methodological approach chosen for the analysis. This multiplicity of perspectives opens the window wide onto the learner phrasicon.

Groom's research into the learner lexicon was prompted by a conclusion reached by Nesselhauf (2005) that increased exposure to the target language does not seem to lead to increased collocational use by learners. Startled by this counter-intuitive finding, Groom sets out to revisit the effects of exposure from a different theoretical perspective and with different types of data. The two types of multiword units (MWUs) he focuses on – contiguous recurrent word sequences (lexical bundles) and statistically significant word co-occurrences (nodes and collocates) – are very much in keeping with Sinclair's wide view of phraseology and contrast sharply with the types of units (idioms, phrasal verbs, proverbs, etc.) that were until recently considered as the most worthy of attention by both linguists and teachers. Groom identifies the MWUs fully automatically, an interesting methodological approach that provides an excellent illustration of a corpus-driven approach to phraseology (Tognini-Bonelli, 2001). As this method requires large corpora, Groom selects the one-million word Uppsala Student English Corpus (USE), which contains the rich metadata necessary to investigate the effects of exposure. Groom's two-pronged analysis reveals a positive correlation between L2 immersion and collocational accuracy, thereby contradicting Nesselhauf's conclusions. The phrasicon is multi-faceted, and Groom's study comes as a useful reminder that the results of a phraseological study can be very different according to the type of MWU investigated. The study also shows that what may at first sight appear to be a weakness in learner language, namely an underuse of lexical bundles, should in fact be interpreted positively, that is, as a sign that learners are using fixed phrases more creatively. This finding ties in with several recent corpus-based studies that have highlighted the variability of MWUs (Moon, 1998; Philip, 2008). More generally, Groom's study highlights the incremental nature of phraseological research. While there are occasional giant leaps forward – and Sinclair's theoretical and methodological framework certainly qualifies as one – most of the time research advances in small steps, with researchers questioning previous findings and building on or refining them to take the issue somewhat further.

Corpus-based phraseological research to date is extremely poor in studies of learner speech. De Cock (2000, 2004) is one of the very few researchers to have investigated the learner phrasicon on the basis of written and spoken corpora. In this largely unexplored field, Lin and Adolphs' study is particularly welcome, especially as the authors analyse actual speech, that is, the sound files, where other researchers have tended to disregard the sound files and restrict themselves to analysing transcribed speech. The starting point for the study is the observation that 'the psycholinguistic nature of [these] phraseological units remains underexplored' indeed, while it is generally assumed that learners will benefit from the reduced processing load provided by phraseological units, very few studies have actually gone about demonstrating this benefit. The few studies that have looked into learners' processing and storage of multiword units have come up with interesting – if mixed – results (Schmitt, 2004). However, most of these studies have used experimental data obtained via techniques such as eye-tracking or self-paced reading. Lin and Adolphs rightly highlight the need to supplement this kind of data with spoken data produced in naturalistic, non-experimental settings. Starting from the idea of 'phonological coherence' borrowed from Peters's (1983) investigation into child language, Lin and Adolphs explore the phonological coherence of 56 occurrences of the phraseological unit *I don't know why*. The study demonstrates the benefits of small-scale exploratory investigations aimed at testing out new methodologies. The analysis of as little as one chunk allows the authors to test available software (Praat) and to highlight both the advantages and disadvantages of the method and suggest ways of fine-tuning it for further analyses. For example, the relatively low rate of phonological coherence displayed by the chunk is found to result from repetitions and insertion of conjunctions. This finding opens the way to a more realistic operationalization of the concept of 'phonological coherence', that is, one that makes allowance for these minimal structures. More generally, this study highlights the need for SLA researchers to work hand in hand with psycholinguists in order to assess the psychological reality of multiword units. This is essential as holistic storage of MWUs and their ease of comprehension/production are presented as major arguments in favour of a phraseology-oriented approach to language teaching.

In the third chapter Reppen tackles another greatly under-researched field, that of the development of the learner phrasicon. Longitudinal corpus-based studies are still very few and far between because of the scarcity of longitudinal corpora. As pointed out by Belz and Vyatkina (2008):

> [T]he great majority of learner corpus research to date has employed a cross-sectional design wherein a synchronic slice of learner productions at a single moment in time is compared to a synchronic slice of NS productions (...). Although 'longitudinal' analyses have attracted more attention in recent publications (...), they are still under-represented in SLA research in general and in corpus linguistics in particular.
>
> (Belz and Vyatkina, 2008: 46–7)

The originality of Reppen's study is that it is both longitudinal and cross-sectional: she analyses the writing development of first and second language learners of English over a nine-month period. Unlike Groom and Lin and Adolphs, who have used corpora already collected and put together in other research projects, Reppen has compiled her own in a real classroom setting. While 'corpora for delayed pedagogical use' (Granger, 2009) like the USE are admittedly bigger and can therefore lay claim to greater generalizability, the 'localization' of smaller local learner corpora greatly increases their relevance for the teachers who collect them and the learners who benefit from the insights they provide. Reppen uses a highly rigorous methodology to compile the data, taking care to control for both text types and topics so as to ensure full comparability of the results. Three-word lexical bundles are extracted from the learner data and the top 20 are compared both longitudinally and cross-sectionally. The data confirm the speech-like nature of L2 learner writing already observed in other studies (for example, Granger and Rayson, 1998; Cobb, 2003) and concurs with Groom's finding that the overall number of lexical bundles tends to decrease as proficiency in the language increases. The chapter is of great interest to teachers as it shows that learner corpus compilation is not the exclusive domain of academics or publishers. As most of the writing now produced by learners is in electronic format, teachers can compile their own local corpora fairly quickly and using the lexical bundle approach, gain insights into the 'chunks' learners use and/or misuse.

The three chapters in this section raise a number of important issues that should be addressed in future research. The following three seem to me particularly worthy of comment: terminology of phraseological units, types of multiword units targeted, and types of learners investigated.

First, applied phraseological studies do not escape the terminological chaos that besets theoretical phraseological studies. Cowie's (1998b: 210) description of phraseology as a 'field bedevilled by the proliferation of terms and the conflicting uses of the same term' applies equally – if not more forcefully – to applied studies that either describe learners' use of MWUs or suggest ways of implementing a phraseology-oriented approach to teaching (cf. Granger, in press). This section is no exception. All three studies use the term collocation to mean something different. In addition, what Groom and Reppen refer to as a 'lexical bundle' is referred to as 'collocation' or 'phraseological unit' by Lin and Adolphs. This terminological fuzziness does not detract from the usefulness and value of each study taken independently, but, in a general way, it can prove detrimental to the field and can seriously hinder pedagogical implementation. As suggested in Granger and Paquot (2008), one way of solving this problem is to use different terminologies for linguistically defined units and quantitatively defined units. More particularly, we suggest keeping the term '*collocation*' in its traditional sense (usage-determined or preferred syntagmatic relation between two lexemes: an autonomous base and a collocate selected by and semantically dependent on the base) in view of its widespread use in that meaning in lexicology, lexicography and ELT resources in general, and using other terms such as *recurrent sequences* or *co-occurrents* for the quantitative units. Such overt reference to the quantitative basis of some units should serve as a reminder that the set of linguistic units extracted is a function of options taken by the researcher as regards frequency (how often a word sequence should appear to qualify as a lexical bundle), span (how many words to the left or right of the node are taken into account) and/or statistical measure (which test is used: MI, t-score, log-likelihood, etc.).

Let us now turn to the issue of which types of multiword unit should be investigated. There is currently a great deal of excitement about lexical bundles, which is perhaps understandable given that their pervasive role in both speech and writing has only recently been brought to light. Lexical bundles constitute the kind of virgin territory that researchers quite naturally want to explore in both L1 and L2 varieties. The tendency to focus on these units is reinforced by their ease of extraction, which is in sharp contrast to the difficulty of extraction of other types of MWUs that are neither fixed nor contiguous and therefore much less tractable. All three studies in this section demonstrate the value of focusing on lexical bundles, but it is important to bear in mind that these units are but one part of the phrasicon. Groom's study provides a clear example of how different the phraseological picture looks when examined through the lens of lexical bundles or collocations. As regards applications of lexical bundle research, it is important to bear in mind that lexical bundles should be viewed as raw material that needs to be refined to be pedagogically useful. In this connection, grouping is essential. Beside the structural and notional categories suggested in the literature (see, for example, Altenberg, 1998; Biber, 2004; Biber et al., 2003), our own research into English for Academic Purposes (EAP) vocabulary (Gilquin et al., 2007; Granger and Paquot, 2009) has shown the advantage of grouping slightly different versions of the same bundle. This makes it possible to uncover interesting differences between L1 and L2 users, such as the tendency for L2 learners to favour active structures with a verb like *argue* (*some people argue, many people argue, I argue*) where L1 writers seem to favour passive structures (*it can/could be argued, as argued by, as argued above*). This type of grouping can therefore be seen as a way of compensating for the rigidity of the lexical bundle approach, which treats recurrent sequences as different bundles, however slight the differences between them.

Finally, the three studies in this section highlight the need to abandon the notion of the generic L2 learner and distinguish between different types of L2 learners and L2 learning situations. Instead of referring to Learner English or L2 English, it would in fact be more appropriate to speak of Learner Englishes in the same way as indigenized L2 varieties are referred to as World Englishes (Gilquin and Granger, forthcoming). Researchers need to take into account the many variables that influence learner language when compiling learner corpora and interpreting the results. This concerns factors pertaining to the learner, such as the learner's mother tongue, degree of exposure (Groom, this volume) or the proficiency level (Reppen, this volume), as well as factors pertaining to the task such as the medium, genre or task, which have all tended to be neglected in learner corpus research (Nesselhauf 2006: 154). Investigating the influence of these variables in earnest – and carefully designed corpora are ideal resources with which to do so – will go some way towards bridging the gap that still exists between learner corpus research and SLA research to the mutual benefit of both fields.

Part II

L2 Collocation Lexicographic and Classroom Materials Research

6
Towards Collocational Webs for Presenting Collocations in Learners' Dictionaries

Susanne Handl

Introduction

Researching collocations in a foreign language requires both a detailed consideration of native speakers' habitual word combinations and an account of how those combinations can be made accessible to language learners. Whereas acquiring collocations in an L1 is a natural process based on constant exposure to language in context and co-text (see Handl and Graf, 2009) in the completely different situation of L2 acquisition, the teaching/learning environment and materials have to compensate for the lack of linguistic input. A major source of information for learners besides textbooks and teachers is the dictionary. Although a range of different dictionaries is available to help students cope with any linguistic task, it seems that on average they prefer a single book for everything. Thus, it would certainly be helpful, if as many collocations as possible could be integrated in such a dictionary.

In this chapter I propose a method that aims at improving the representation of collocations in advanced learners' dictionaries in a number of ways. Drawing on the findings of a large-scale analysis of collocations (Handl, in preparation) in the British National Corpus (BNC; Oxford University, 2005), the present study explores a new multi-dimensional classification for working out in detail the criteria by which collocations can be selected for advanced learners' dictionaries. Based on this, I present a method of display for collocation entries and also report on a pilot study evaluating this alternative.

Research basis

Theoretical background

Collocation has seen a wide range of classifications, from simple binary approaches (Firth, 1957c) and gradual classifications (Benson, Benson and Ilson, 1986a; Carter, 1998) to a prototypical account of the category of collocation (Schmid, 2003: 249). As collocation is a pervasive phenomenon that escapes clear-cut categorization, the prototype model and recent approaches instigated by corpus linguistics (Sinclair, 1996; Stubbs, 2002) seem most promising. They integrate statistical aspects of frequency to delimit – at least approximately – the scope of collocations. The fuzzy boundaries, however, are an obstacle to lexicographic description of collocations. That is the reason why, in the so-called significance-oriented approach, researchers like Hausmann (1984), Benson (1985) and Klotz (2000) promote clear-cut boundaries. They classify collocations typologically mainly on the basis of word classes and the semantic relation between base and collocator. To my mind, however, this approach misses out on incorporating psycholinguistic and cognitive factors that can be captured with the latest trends in corpus linguistics.

For a more detailed working definition, the basic notion of collocation as 'the occurrence of two or more words within a short space of each other in a text' (Sinclair, 1991: 170) needs to be enlarged with a set of further criteria. First, the frequency of such combinations and the respective co-occurrence measures can be used to rank significant collocations.[1] Another factor that points towards their classification on a continuum is the fact that collocations are more or less restricted in their choice of partners, and thus are characterized by a specific collocational range. In terms of idiomaticity, collocations are said to be semantically more transparent than idioms, yet more opaque than free lexical combinations. The most important criterion for identifying collocation is the famous notion of mutual expectancy[2] originally postulated by Firth (1957c). The constituents of a collocation mutually evoke each other, thus allowing a native speaker to predict the second partner when they encounter the first. So, two words that collocate are not governed by semantic compatibility but rather by lexical restriction, that is, by the norms of the language (see Coseriu, 1973). A consequence of this conventionalization is a certain associative bond that holds between the two partners of a collocation.[3] Sinclair (1991: 119 ff.) highlights this function in postulating the idiom principle of language where he claims that for a large part of text production we use semi-preconstructed phrases that we choose at one go when speaking or writing.

We can conclude that collocations are conventionalized recurring word combinations exhibiting more or less restrictedness, more or less semantic opacity and a certain degree of predictability for native speakers. Their main function – besides disambiguating the meaning of words – is to facilitate smooth communication by reducing the processing effort for speakers and hearers alike (Wray, 2002). This fluency and native-like communicative competence are of course also a major aim for non-native speakers.

The present state of dictionary collocation entries

British lexicographers have long specialized in monolingual dictionaries for advanced learners of English (Béjoint, 1994; Cowie, 1998c). The problem, however, is that learners' needs range from simple receptive tasks like understanding a text to translating it or producing an original text in the target language. For these diverse requirements completely different reference works like thesauri, idiom and collocation dictionaries or bilingual dictionaries would be useful. Most learners, however, seem to prefer the same book for all tasks. So, what is needed is an all-purpose dictionary, but still in compact form. A dictionary should not exceed a certain size, so that it remains affordable and manageable; within the entries, clarity of representation should be the guiding principle, that is, bold print, colours, underlining etc. should not be overused in order to avoid information overflow. Consequently, lexicographers have to find a way to reduce the amount of information given. This minimizing and specializing principle for print dictionaries can be contrasted with a maximizing and generalizing principle in electronic dictionaries, where compilers tend to include too much unfiltered information that is not oriented towards the target group of users.

Some brief examples from recent dictionaries can help illustrate the present situation. The *Macmillan English Dictionary for Advanced Learners* (MED; 2002) informs the user in its front matter that collocations are either shown in bold and illustrated with examples or, if a word has many collocations, the lexical entry ends with a box '*Words frequently used with*'. This is a user-friendly method, as the marking is clear enough and collocations are given special status. The *Longman Dictionary of Contemporary English*, 4th edn (LDOCE; 2005) follows a similar strategy, although it puts the collocation box at the beginning of the entry, sometimes also highlighting collocations only within example sentences. The *Oxford Advanced Learner's Dictionary*, 7th edn (OALD; 2005) integrates collocations into both examples and definitions or presents them as separate entries without keeping to a specific strategy. Table 6.1 shows how the entry for *attention* is organized in each of the three dictionaries. I have listed the collocations that are highlighted under the various senses, and indicated where they appear.

The comparison reveals that, although the three dictionary entries look quite similar, there are considerable differences.[4] In all three works the collocations are arranged under the respective lexical units. On the

Table 6.1 The collocations for *attention* in three dictionaries

MED	LDOCE	OALD
Five lexical units: 1 Interest/thought 2 Fact that you notice sth 3 Special care/treatment 4 Way of standing straight 5 Show of love/interest + **phrases**	**Five lexical units:** 1 Listen/look/think carefully 2 Interest 3 Notice 4 Repair/cleaning 5 Care + **idioms/phrases**	**Five lexical units:** 1 Listening/looking carefully 2/3 Interest 4 Treatment 5 Soldiers
1: Collocations in bold with examples: *turn your ~ to sth.- undivided/ full ~ - hold/keep your ~ - divert/distract ~ from - catch sb's ~*	**1: Collocation box + example sentences:** *sb's ~ is on sth - pay ~ - turn/ give your ~ to - sb's full/ complete/undivided ~ - keep sb's ~ - close/careful ~ - ~ to detail - sb's ~ wanders - may/could I have your ~?*	**1: Collocations in bold within examples:** *~ span - pay ~ - pay any ~ - attract the waiter's ~ - draw ~ to - caught my ~ - undivided ~ - has come to my ~ - called (their) ~*
2: Collocations in bold with examples: *sth comes to sb's ~ - draw sb's ~ to sth - bring sth to sb's ~*	**2: Collocations in bold as separate entries and within examples:** *~ he was giving her - attract/ receive/enjoy ~ - public/ media/press ~ - hold/keep sb's ~ - the centre of ~ - turned his ~s to*	**2: Collocations in bold within examples:** *attract great ~ - centre of ~*
3: No collocations	**3: Subsenses headed by idioms/phrases in blue:** *attract/catch/get sb's ~ - get ~ - draw/call ~ to sth - divert/distract/ draw ~ from sth - bring sth ot sb's ~ - come to sb's ~ - escape your ~*	**3: No collocations**
4: No collocations	**4: Collocation in bold within an example:** *need a bit of ~*	**4: Collocation in bold without example:** *for the ~ of*
5: No collocations	**5: Collocations in bold within examples:** *care and ~ - medical ~ - could do with a bit of ~*	**5: Collocation in bold without example:** *stand at/to ~*
Phrase section: *attract sb's ~ - for the ~ of sb - pay ~*	**Idioms & phrases in blue:** *stand to/at ~ - ~! - for the ~ of sb*	**No separate phrase section**

one hand, this enables users to master both meanings and usage of the lexeme; on the other, it may lead to double listings of collocations. This, for instance, is the case with *attract attention* in the LDOCE under Senses 2 and 3 and in the OALD under Senses 1 and 2. It remains questionable whether this collocation can really be used to illustrate different senses of the lexeme. The MED avoids this problem by listing *attract attention* separately in the phrase section. This practice then results in a different ordering of collocations. Whereas *pay attention* is listed at the beginning in LDOCE and OALD, a user of the MED has to go down the whole entry to find it in the phrase section. A further point is that the OALD treats the compound *attention span* as a collocation right at the beginning of Sense 1, but the MED presents it in a separate entry.

It seems there is no common denominator that guides the decision process for including or excluding certain collocations; space constraints do not allow a separate treatment of those habitual word combinations within the normal scope of a learners' dictionary either.[5] Thus, learners face the problem of deciding for themselves whether a word combination they encounter in the explanation or illustration part of a lexical entry is a collocation worth remembering. In the next section I will present an alternative corpus-based approach to classifying collocations that should enable lexicographers to guarantee a certain objectiveness and representativeness in terms of the selection and presentation of collocations.

Towards an alternative

Theoretical background

Based on the comparison of different classifications and definitions mentioned above, I have worked out an alternative conception of collocation as the intermediate stage between idioms and free combinations (see Handl, 2008). This alternative focuses on the prototypical kernel, thus facilitating an evaluation of significant collocations relevant to foreign learners of English. As some of the criteria for collocations like idiomaticity or restrictedness are gradable in themselves, the prototypical approach should be complemented by a multi-dimensional classification of collocations on three levels: the semantic, lexical, and statistical.

These three dimensions allow for collocations to be categorized by more detailed criteria. First, the semantic dimension determines the degree to which a collocation is opaque. Some collocations include lexemes in their literal sense, as for instance the adjective *vague* in *a vague idea*. Others often change their literal meaning[6] in specific combinations like *run a shop* or *run a risk*. If an expression only uses the non-literal meaning of lexemes (e.g. *kith and kin*), or if an individual meaning can no longer be extracted (e.g. *to hang fire*), we have left the area of collocation and reached the end-point of the semantic dimension, where idioms come into play.

The second criterion is collocational range, that is, the number of possible lexemes used as collocational partners. A central collocation will have neither a very wide range of collocates nor a very restricted one. The lexical dimension is where we can determine how active a lexeme is in building collocations. If it has a reasonable number of possible collocates, it is essential for a learner to memorize the lemma, as it may occur very often in such semi-preconstructed units. If it has a small collocational range, the other two dimensions (semantic and statistical) can be used to decide whether it is worth noticing. If a word occurs very rarely, but in almost every case with the same partner, then it has a tendency towards being used as fixed expression, one that in some dictionaries may as well be treated as separate entry or even go into an idiom dictionary.

For the criterion of statistical significance, I relate the constituents of a collocation to each other with the ratio between the combined frequency and the frequency of the individual lexemes in a corpus.[7] This collocational factor (CF) reveals the strength and direction of attraction between two collocational partners. Thus, there can be very strong collocations, where the link from one partner to the other is tight, as for example in *foreseeable* + *future*, with *foreseeable* being the dominant partner, because more than half of its occurrences are within that actual collocation. The lexeme *foreseeable* is thus determined by its collocating with *future*. In the case of *future*, however, there is a much larger variation of possible collocates and only two per cent of its occurrences are formed with *foreseeable*. This also seems to capture the psychological aspect of predictability, as it is much more probable that a native speaker will predict *future* on encountering *foreseeable* than vice versa.[8] Other collocations do not show such a clear direction from one partner towards the other, as they consist of lexemes with almost equal individual frequencies. They are then classified as collocations with a levelled attraction, where both partners play a similar role for the collocation, as would be the case in *wide* + *range*. The predictability in such collocations works in both directions.

Figure 6.1 illustrates the internal relationship between two lexemes of a collocation. The direction points from Lexeme A to B, which means that A attracts B because it is the collocationally dominant partner.

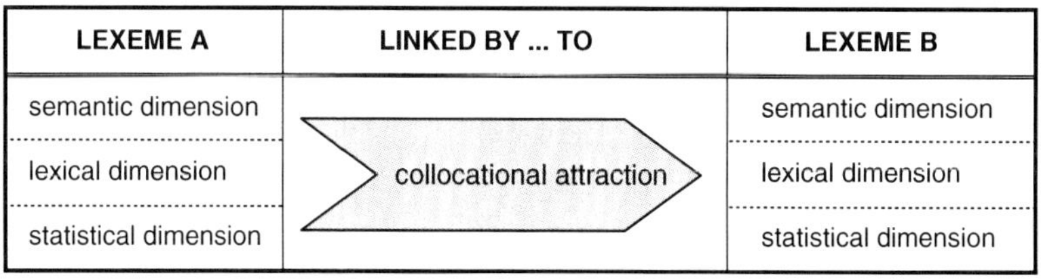

Figure 6.1 Two lexemes linked by collocational direction and attraction

The quality of the link, that is, the strength of attraction, is established on the basis of the statistical dimension. The collocational range can confirm the strength of attraction depending on the position of either partner on the lexical dimension. The semantic dimension is an additional means for establishing the stronger partner, that is, the one that needs the occurrence within the collocation to fully determine its meaning.

An interesting consequence of this statistical account of recurring word combinations is that collocations seem to behave differently depending on which of the partners we focus on. And this also holds for the other two criteria: they do not only apply to a collocation as a whole but to each partner separately. We can therefore reformulate the definition of collocation as follows:

> Collocation is a linguistic sign made up of at least two partners that have a certain internal relationship, determined by the collocational direction and attraction of one partner towards the other. This oriented relation is multi-dimensional for both collocation partners in three respects, leading to a positioning of each partner on the respective dimensions – semantic, lexical, and statistical.

This makes it easier to account for collocations in dictionaries, as now we do not have to categorize complete collocations and decide where to list them in the dictionary; rather, we can characterize the collocational behaviour of individual lexemes.

Alternative ways of presenting collocations in dictionaries

As already mentioned, the collocation display in dictionaries has to be a compromise between comprehensiveness and user-friendliness. With the multi-dimensional model rooted in large amounts of authentic language data, we can put the selection process on a broader basis and integrate aspects of the three criteria into the collocation entries. The collocational behaviour of each lexeme includes important information for learners such as the question whether it is the dominant partner or the dependent one that gets attracted by another lexeme or in how many relevant collocations the lemma takes part. The theoretical basis is found in collocational direction and the strength of the link on the statistical dimension, and the size of the collocational range on the lexical dimension. The question of how much of the individual, outside meaning of a lexeme is transferred to the collocation itself, and in how far the lexeme develops a different meaning inside the collocation is an additional aspect that helps to confirm the strength of the collocational link (see Figure 6.1).

These three aspects can be covered in a dictionary entry in different sections. Figure 6.2 illustrates such a refined entry as used in a small-scale pilot look-up study. According to the principle of collocational attraction, the entry begins with a list of all the partners the lemma attracts as the dominant partner (Section A). Collocations with a levelled attraction, being equally important for the lemma, are given as

trouble noun

COLLOCATION SECTION: ■ ■■ ■■

A: cause > much > lot > more > only > run > start > never > financial > real > keep > little > always > big > there > sort > begin > ask > heart > bit > police > might > mean > great > kind > bad > bring > far > money > source > ever > seem > expect > back > soon > stay > recent
B: serious > deep > save > avoid > enough > cause > deal > sign > less > before > hit > marriage > considerable > suffer > forget > arise > prevent > ahead > danger > pain

PROBLEM / WORRY
1 [U, C] trouble (with sb/sth) a problem, worry, difficulty, etc. or a situation causing this: *We have trouble getting staff. * He could make trouble for me if he wanted to. * The trouble with you is you don't really want to work. * Her trouble is she's in capable of making a decision.* The trouble is* (=

a trouble shared is a trouble 'halved
(saying) if you talk to sb about your problems and worries, instead of keeping them to yourself, they seem less serious

COLLOCATION CROSS-REFERENCES: ■ ■ ■ ■ ■ ■ ■

brewing > stir > strife > relegation > flare > spot > plague > brew > spell > dire > groin > beset > mar > hint > tummy > terrible > land > maker > shooting > marital > expense > crowd > testify > endless > erupt > bail > engine > deep > sense > northern > steer > immense > stem > outbreak > double > back > awful > boyfriend > root > diagnose > spot > head > stomach > desperate > store > spare > potential > provoke > guilt > rival > encounter > anticipate > smell > gender > lie > recover > major > constantly > fan > clear > lad > mate > emotional > experience > chest > indication > severe > load > domestic > crystal > dig > twin > victim > sort > warn > possibly

Figure 6.2 A refined dictionary entry as used in the look-up study

Section B. The next part contains usual information like definitions, example sentences, synonyms, antonyms, and usage labels. The entry ends with a cross-reference section to words, where the lemma is the weaker partner. An entry thus contains all collocations the lemma occurs in, and learners can access an unknown collocation from both sides. A lemma also gets a collocational indicator (represented by the square dots in Figure 6.2), which should give the user an idea of the collocational activity of the lemma as a dominant partner, that is, a collocation-builder, and also as collocation-supporter in the cross-reference section.

There are two obvious drawbacks to this method of presentation. The first is the strict separation between collocation boxes and denotational information in the entry. As collocation plays a crucial role for disambiguating the meanings of a lexeme, the semantic contribution of a collocational partner should be highlighted for the dominant partner by incorporating those collocations that lead to a meaning specification into the definition part. In order to integrate the directional information of such collocations, we would need specific typographic features that do not confuse and distract the user more than they help. A rough proposal, which was not tested in the pilot look-up study, is given in Figure 6.3. The symbols indicate the direction of the collocation, with the large black box marking the stronger, and the white box the weaker, partner. The number of boxes corresponds to the strength of the collocational link.

In this case, the entry begins with the cross-reference section, since the relevant collocational partners for the lemma are included in

pay verb

COLLOCATION CROSS-REFERENCE

tribute/attention/dividend/rent/fee/premium/tax/compensation/fine/sum/price/debt/salary/mortgage/fare/visit/wage/order/bill/liable/willing/royalty/subscription/shilling/low/cash/prepared/monthly/afford/quid/expense/levy/poll/deposit/contribution/cost/bonus/insurance/extra/pound/cheque/amount/penny/taxpayer/buyer/income/pension/gross/obliged [...]

1 pay (sb) (for sth) to give sb money for work, goods, services, etc.: *My* ***company***□··▪▪■***pays*** *well* (= pays high salaries). **Children must* ***pay***■▪··▪■ ***full*** *price. * He still hasn't* ***paid***■*me the* ■***money*** *he owes me.*

2 pay sth (to sb) to give sb money that you owe them: *Have you paid him the rent yet? *They only* ***pay***▪▪ *tax at a* ▪▪***rate*** *of 5%.*

3 [v] (of a business, etc.) to produce a profit: *It's hard to make farming pay. *an account that* ***pays***■▪▪·· □***higher***··▪▪■***interest***

4 to result in some advantage or profit for sb: [v] *Crime doesn't pay * It* ***would***□ *probably* ·▪■■***pay*** *you to hire an accountant.*

5[v]pay(forsth)to suffer or be punished for your beliefs or actions:

Figure 6.3 A dictionary entry with integrated collocation information

the explanation and illustration part. The list includes lexemes like *attention, fee, price* or *visit* as the partners that attract *pay*. The few lexemes where *pay* is the stronger partner (e.g. *would, interest, rate, high, company*) can then be included in the main sections with the respective markers for collocational attraction. This example shows that lexico-grammatical patterns like those given below are often also essential partners for a lemma:[9]

pronoun + *will/would* (*have to/not*) *pay*
it will (*not*) *pay*
noun + *will pay* + noun
if + pronoun + *pay* + pronoun + *will*
pronoun + *would be paid*
pronoun + *would be* + adjective (*liable/prepared*) + *to pay*.

This points us towards the second drawback of the method illustrated in Figure 6.2, namely that collocates are not given within their context. Thus, the wider collocational environment or patterns like *to run* + *into* + *trouble* or *the only* + *trouble* + BE are not made explicit. Integrated collocation information would solve this problem, but would in general also make the whole entry much more complex.

It seems that the above explained principles of collocation display can be better realized in electronic dictionaries, as the directionality and differing collocational strength of the partners can easily be visualized with the help of lines and arrows. Additionally, the interrelation between lexemes and their collocational behaviour can act as the basis for developing a collocational web. This is not dependent on the alphabetical order, so learners can define their own paths via hyperlinks between the single lexemes and their collocations. Ideally, they can gradually recreate such collocational webs in their minds. The electronic medium allows us to include a full range of sample sentences from a corpus and exact definitions wherever necessary, accessible via a simple click or even with a mouse-over device. Thus, the problem of semantic specification of lexemes within collocations is solved, turning the meaning into a constituent of collocations and not, as usual, vice versa. Figure 6.4 shows a rough sketch of such a collocational web for *pay* and *price*.

The large number of collocates to the right of the focus words *pay* and *price* corresponds to the cross-reference section in the print entries. These words are all dominant partners in collocations with *pay/price*. The words to the left of the focus are attracted by *pay/price* and words that are on

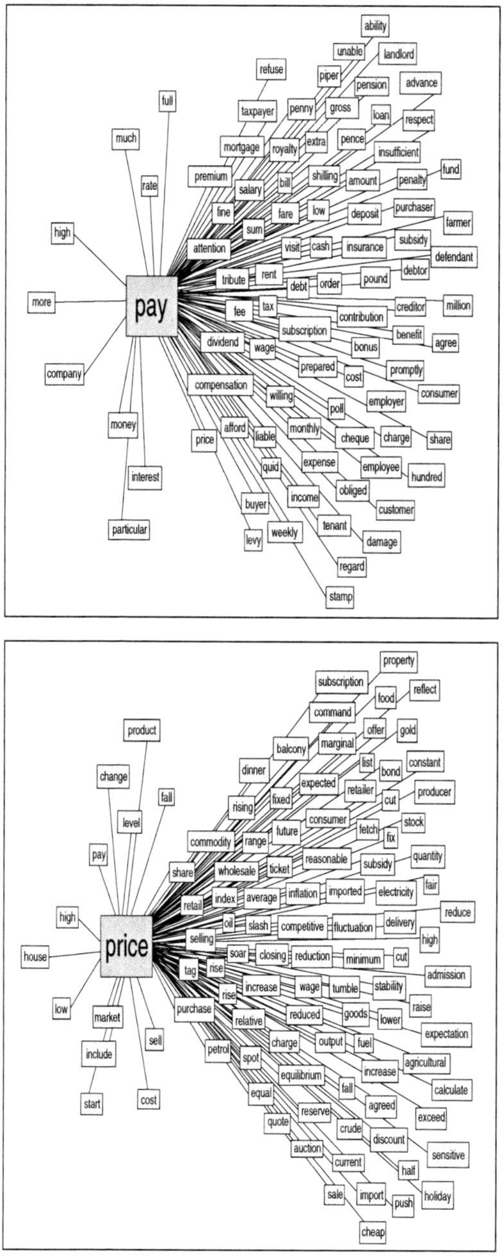

Figure 6.4 Example collocational webs

the same vertical level with the focus do not show a clear direction. The strength of attraction is visualized via the length of the lines, thus for instance *holiday* + *price* are not as strongly linked as *pay* + *attention* are.

Application

Designing the experiments

To test these ideas, I selected 15 target collocations from the large-scale corpus study mentioned above (Handl, in preparation), with some of them containing the same node word but different collocates, so that one dictionary entry could serve as source for different collocations. Table 6.2 lists the target collocations with identity numbers used in the questionnaire. Dominant partners are given in bold.

All 15 collocations were presented in the experiment within an authentic context taken from the British National Corpus (BNC; Oxford University, 2005), where both partners were deleted in turn to produce the gap-filling exercise. For the translation task the whole collocation was deleted and its meaning was given in brackets in German. The collocations were put in five separate questionnaires, each containing six gap-filling tasks and three translation tasks. These were given to a group of advanced learners of English together with an original extract of a learners' dictionary (OALD). Another group received the same questionnaires together with refined dictionary entries, containing collocation information as described above. Both groups had to solve the tasks with the help of the dictionary entries and to document their look-up processes. Examples from the questionnaire can be found in Figure 6.5.

Analysis

Fifty-two questionnaires were returned and used for the analysis; 28 of them used the original and 24 the refined dictionary entries. As the number of collocations tested is small, but the factors influencing the results are, however, multiple (direction of collocational attraction, original vs. refined dictionary entries, gap-filling vs. translation task), the study cannot be considered more than a pilot study. Although I made sure that the subjects' linguistic competence was similar, there are still less controllable aspects like the time spent for finding answers, learners' pre-knowledge about collocations or experience with monolingual dictionaries. Despite these limitations, we can use the results to make an initial comparison between conventional collocation dictionary entries and the alternative displays that I have proposed.

Table 6.2 Two types of target collocation

ID	Directional class	ID	Directional class	ID	levelled class	ID	levelled class
1	**fleeting** impression	7	held **responsible**	6	**close look**	15	**small business**
2	create **impression**	8	**legally** responsible				
3	pay particular **attention**	9	**dire** trouble				
4	**merit** attention	10	cause **trouble**				
5	close **proximity**	11	**generous** offer				
		12	not **entirely** clear				
		13	**major** change				
		14	prove **impossible**				

task	look-up protocol		solution
When she reached the bottom of the rather ornate staircase she hovered uncertainly for a moment, then with a defiant toss of her head she marched into the shabby splendour of the lounge before coming to a lame halt. Leo was crouched before the fire, and she had the odd **fleeting** _________ of power, a sort of unconscious arrogance that was only magnified when he turned his head. 1A1	I don't need a dictionary, I know the expression I look under the lemma found nothing - I look under I find a cross-reference to I'm not sure, so I look under I need more information, f. ex.		
A saint would break a diet under these circumstances. You need to consider those antecedent events that prompt you to break a diet, and then think about which of these things you can avoid or change in some way. The second part of your review of previous diet attempts involves a _______ **look** at your weight control behaviour. What diets have you tried? Which did you succeed most with and which did you fail badly with? 6A1	I don't need a dictionary, I know the expression I look under the lemma found nothing - I look under I find a cross-reference to I'm not sure, so I look under I need more information, f. ex.		
Also very useful in emergencies, you think of a - do you remember the ferry disaster? The one that was so bad, where a man used his back for other people to escape by? Now people there, those people would have been in _______ **trouble** if there hadn't been somebody who could do that. Now I always think of that as stamina cos I think that must have been a terrific stamina thing. He must have felt it and he must have suffered from it 9A2	I don't need a dictionary, I know the expression I look under the lemma found nothing - I look under I find a cross-reference to I'm not sure, so I look under I need more information, f. ex.		
This is a unique and fascinating book, which________ **attention** even though it is hardly hot from the presses. The author was born in Kronstadt, part of the ethnic German enclave in Transylvania, a region which was part of the Austro-Hungarian Empire at the beginning of the century but which had been handed over to Romania after World War I. 4A2	I don't need a dictionary, I know the expression I look under the lemma foundnothing - I look under I find a cross-reference to I'm not sure, so I look under I need more information, f. ex.		
In July 1773, following the three highly successful Italian visits, Mozart and his father again travelled to Vienna. The reasons for the visit are________ **(nicht ganz klar)** and Leopold's letters to his wife do not elaborate on his aims, their success or otherwise, since he was constantly concerned that the Salzburg censors were reading his mail. 12A3	I don't need a dictionary, I know the expression I look under the lemma found nothing - I look under I find a cross-reference to I'm not sure, so I look under I need more information, f. ex.		

Figure 6.5 Examples from the questionnaire

Table 6.3 Scoring the look-up process

Look-up step	Score
Lemma one	1
A cross-reference	2
Lemma two	3
Lemma three	4
Need more information	5
No or wrong solution	6

As the aim of the experiment was to account for the impact of the collocation display on the success of the look-up process, I filtered out all answers that students found without using a dictionary. The remaining answers were scored according to the number of look-ups and their results. Table 6.3 gives an overview of the scores attributed to the different look-up processes. Ideally, a correct solution would be found in the first look-up, leading to a score of 1. The higher the score, the longer it took the student to find the solution; wrong solutions or no solution at all were scored with 6. For each target collocation the scores were added and related to the total number of look-up processes.

For the gap-filling exercises the students' answers and their respective scores were divided into natural direction (the dominant partner was given) and unnatural direction (the weak collocational partner was given). The translation task involved finding both and was therefore treated separately. On the basis of these three types, I then compared the different results for the look-up processes using the original and the refined dictionary entries.

Results

The mean number of answers for each target collocation in the three types is 5.4 (SD 1.9) for the original and 4.6 (SD 1.0) for the refined dictionary; the mean number of look-up processes is 3.3 (SD 1.8) and 3.0 (SD 1.6) respectively. The look-up scores reveal a more detailed picture. The ideal score of 1 appears in all three groups, being twice as frequent for the natural and unnatural direction than for translation. This implies that finding a complete collocation for a mental concept requires more active knowledge of the language. The fact that the number of wrong or no solutions is also higher in this group suggests that the reception-oriented information in a learners' dictionary is not sufficient. In terms of the choice of look-up-lemmas, the translation task showed that learners tend to prefer nouns as in *create impression*, *generous offer* or *major change*. Still, there are some cases where either both partners are used as first look-up-lemmas or where the concept is accessed via other words, as with *deserve* for *merit attention* or *near* for *close proximity*.

Both for the unnatural and the natural direction the individual answers imply that filling in the gaps was easier. Thus, for the collocation *pay attention*, the weaker partner *pay* was found without look-up by all participants, for the other direction only one look-up was performed leading to a solution in the first step. For the levelled collocation *close look* it is vice versa. Difficult collocations, on the other hand, include *major change, fleeting impression* and *not entirely clear*. Surprisingly, the first is problematic in the natural direction with the lexeme *major* given, which predominantly leads to *problem* or *role* as answers, although *change* is explicitly mentioned in both dictionary extracts under the lemma *major*. The reason may be that non-native speakers are more familiar with the collocation *major problem/role* and that both fit approximately into the context given in the questionnaire. *Fleeting impression* is a problem, since the informants seem to be completely unfamiliar with the adjective, so they mostly choose a more frequent and familiar lexeme like *vague*. For *not entirely clear* the unnatural direction results in unidiomatic solutions, as the learners are not aware of the semantic prosody of *entirely* with a negative statement (see Partington, 1998: 60) and fill in the first intensifier they find.

Figure 6.6 gives a general overview of the results. It allows a comparison of the three groups both for the original and the refined dictionary entries. The numbers (shown with standard deviations in Table 6.4) represent the mean look-up scores for all 15 target collocations. It becomes evident that the degree of difficulty steadily increases from natural direction over unnatural direction to translation, although those learners who worked with the refined dictionary entries performed better in

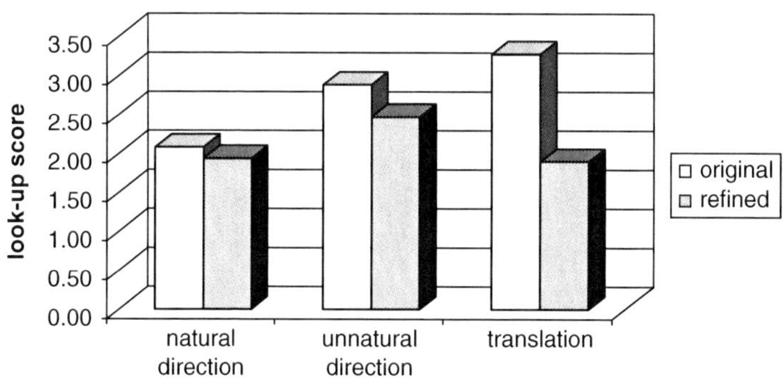

Figure 6.6 Look-up scores in relation to collocation display and task

Table 6.4 Mean look-up scores and SD

Task	Dictionary	Score	SD
Natural direction	Original	2.08	1.41
	Refined	1.94	0.98
Unnatural direction	Original	2.88	1.74
	Refined	2.47	1.58
Translation	Original	3.28	1.30
	Refined	1.90	0.76

the translation task than in the other experiment settings. The reason for this may be that the additional collocation sections provided them with more material to choose from.

A general comparison of the results for the original and the refined dictionary in all three groups suggests that learners make more effective use of the alternative collocation display than the traditional one.

Conclusion

The present chapter set out to explore a new method of collocation display in dictionaries based on an objective, corpus-based multi-dimensional classification of collocation as a directional relation between two lexical items. Such an alternative view has a number of advantages for a learner in determining the number and significance of the collocations, so that dictionary users encounter a limited range of more useful collocations. These can be presented in ways that let learners more easily identify words especially active in forming collocations, and the particular relevance of different collocations can be signalled so that learners can decide which combinations are worth attending to. While in print this method largely relies on typographic means and a cross-referencing of collocational partners, in electronic dictionaries it should ultimately be possible to arrange these partners in collocational webs that guide the learner through the vocabulary of English without the limitation of alphabetic order.

Besides preparing the theoretical ground for this alternative collocation display and illustrating the present practice in dictionaries with the help of examples, I also reported on a pilot study testing the new method in print dictionaries. A questionnaire using 15 target collocations in authentic context was given to two student groups, one of which worked with original dictionary entries, the other with refined ones. While filling in the collocation gaps and translating the German expressions into English collocations, both groups had to document their look-up processes. These provided the data for the comparison of traditional and alternative methods. Judging from the mean number of look-ups the users needed to arrive at an acceptable solution, the results point towards clear advantages in the new collocation display. For a comprehensive picture, however, a validation study with a much larger population would be needed to confirm these tentative findings. Also, in a larger-scale experiment, statistical tests would be needed to determine the significance of any differences in results. Furthermore, some problematic issues like the distinction of polysemous items, the inclusion of patterns and constructions into the representation and the preference of some collocations for specific wordforms would have to be tackled.

Future aspects for research in this area might include a psycholinguistic study that checks the predictability of directional collocations with native speakers, a clear typographic design for marking collocations within the single lexical units of a lemma and, eventually, the implementation of collocational webs in electronic dictionaries.

Notes

1. Statistical measures are calculated to exclude mere random co-occurrences in a corpus and thus determine a set of potential collocations.
2. For a contemporary illustration of the notion of mutual expectancy or predictability, see Jehle (2007: 54).
3. Aitchison (2003: 91) assigns a more fundamental function to collocations, when she says that word meaning 'is probably learned by noting the words which come alongside'.
4. See also the documentation of a dictionary look-up in Handl (2008: 45–6).
5. For an evaluation of electronic dictionaries in this respect, see Heuberger (2000) and Stein (2004).
6. The literal meaning is understood to be the meaning a word usually has when used in free combinations outside the collocation in question.
7. The calculations given here are based on an analysis of the examples in the BNC.
8. To prove the relation between collocational attraction and predictability association, experiments with native speakers will have to be conducted.
9. This phenomenon is at the core of recent theories like Pattern Grammar (Hunston and Francis, 2000) and Construction Grammar (Goldberg, 2006).

7
Japanese Learners' Collocation Dictionary Retrieval Performance

Yuri Komuro

Introduction

Recognition of the pedagogical significance of collocation dates back to the days of Palmer (Palmer, 1930, 1933b) or even before that. Palmer benefited greatly from the work done by Hidesaburo Saito, who noted in the preface[1] to his *Jukugo-Hon'i-Eiwa-Chu-Jiten* (*Saito's Idiomological English–Japanese Dictionary*, 1915), a monumental work in English pedagogical lexicography:

> Words are nothing in themselves, and everything in combination. In the case of words, combination comprises construction and association. A verb without its construction is no verb; and association is what makes the most significant words what they are. By association are meant the *idiomatic, proverbial*, and *conventional* expressions in which each word usually occurs.
>
> (Saito, 1915: 1)

Although Saito did not use the word *collocation*, what he meant by the *idiomatic, proverbial*, and *conventional* expressions certainly covered what is called collocation today. Several decades later, in the 1980s, when Pawley and Syder (1983) identified collocation as an underlying factor in the successful acquisition of 'nativelike fluency' and 'nativelike selection', the remarkable development of computer technology and the increasing availability of large corpora, including the British National Corpus (BNC; Oxford University, 2005), were enabling researchers to obtain fairly comprehensive data of words that co-occur frequently with each other. In the 1990s, teachers began to grant greater recognition to the pedagogical importance of collocation, too, and over the last decade, collocation dictionaries have also become more readily available. A primary example is the publication of the *Oxford Collocations Dictionary for Students of English* (OCDSE, 2002), the first collocation dictionary based on a large computer corpus, the BNC.

Critical reviews of collocation dictionaries, not only the OCDSE, but also the *BBI Combinatory Dictionary of English: A Guide to Word Combinations* (Benson, Benson and Ilson, 1986b), the *BBI Dictionary of English Word Combinations* (Benson, Benson and Ilson, 1997), are generally positive and usually focus on inclusion criteria by analysing what word combinations should or should not be included (Iannucci, 1987; Piotrowski, 1987; Herbst, 1988; Kaye and McDaniel, 1989; Paikeday, 1989; Howarth, 2000; Klotz, 2003; Marks, 2003; Komuro, 2004). However, so far little research effort has been expended on learners' actual use of collocation dictionaries (see Nuccorini, 2003: 385).

This chapter aims to look into dictionary look-up performance of Japanese learners of English by investigating how successful they are in retrieving appropriate collocates from a given entry. To this end, I will report on a small-scale study in which Japanese university students were asked to look for and single out appropriate collocates from (long) lists characteristic of collocation dictionary entries. I will consider the implications of this study for making collocation dictionary entries more user-friendly for such learners.

The entry structure of the OCDSE

First of all, let me give a brief explanation of how an entry in the OCDSE is designed to present collocation information. The wordlist of the OCDSE consists of nouns, adjectives and verbs, and each entry shows typical words that co-occur with a headword according to their parts of speech. A noun entry usually starts with giving adjective collocates marked with •ADJ., then shows verbs that take the noun headword as an object (•VERB + HEADWORD), verbs that take the noun headword as a subject (•HEADWORD + VERB), nouns that make compounds together with the noun headword (•HEADWORD + NOUN), prepositions that come before and after the noun headwords (•PREP.), and idiomatic phrases that contain the headword noun (•PHRASES).

Within each part-of-speech section, synonymous or semantically related collocates are grouped together and separated from each other by vertical bars. There is no semantic or other kind of information provided, no typographical signs used to mark (the beginning of) each slot, and collocates are presented without any definition. According to the preface, slots are arranged 'in an order that tries to be as intuitive as possible' (OCDSE, 2002: x). Example sentences are given for some collocates, and when they are given they are inserted at the end of each slot in italics. For example, in the entry for *meeting*, the adjective section goes:

> **frequent, regular** | **annual, biennial, half-yearly, monthly, quarterly, weekly, etc.** | **all-day, hour-long, two-hour, etc.** | ... **open, public** | **closed, private** | **secret** | **joint** *Management have called a joint meeting with staff and unions.*| ... | **endless, interminable, long** *We had endless meetings about the problem.* ◊ *The meeting seemed interminable.* | **angry, difficult, stormy** | ...
>
> (*s.v. meeting*, OCDSE)

Klotz (2003: 59) maintains that the overall entry structure is 'very clear', but is doubtful whether users can successfully make the most appropriate choices to express their ideas without having any information about how to distinguish the different synonymous collocates from each other (see Komuro, 2004 for further discussion). The part-of-speech categorization of collocates seems to be clear as each section is marked off with typographical signs; however, retrieving appropriate collocates from a long list of intuitively ordered slots, in which synonymous collocates are alphabetically ordered, does not seem to be an easy task, especially when there is no indication as to what each slot contains and in what context each collocate is preferably used.

Research questions

The present study aims to assess accessibility within an entry of the OCDSE. In the OCDSE, nouns, adjectives, and verbs make up the entries, and since nouns are 'much the most heavily represented' (Lea and Runcie, 2002: 825) I focus on noun entries and address the following questions:

1. Is the part-of-speech categorization clear to users as Klotz (2003) claims?
2. How successful are Japanese learners, in finding a place where target collocates are given without any semantic or any other kind of indicators provided within a part-of-speech section?
3. Do any differences arise in learners' performance according to the number of synonymous collocates presented together in one slot?

Method

The subjects were 26 first-year Japanese university students taking an English writing course at the Faculty of Law, Chuo University, Tokyo. The main objective of this Grammar and Translation course is to learn to compose English writing at the sentence level through Japanese–English translation exercises with a focus on accuracy and naturalness. Since collocation is regarded as a crucial factor in achieving naturalness, I teach students the concept of collocation, how to make use of general learners' dictionaries in order to retrieve collocational information, and how to use a collocation dictionary. Most of the students own electronic hand-held dictionaries, which contain several English dictionaries. Recent models sometimes contain the OCDSE, but it is often the case that students never use it. Out of the 26 students taking part in this study, just five knew of the OCDSE, and only one of them had actually used it before.

To explore the students' ability to retrieve collocations from the OCDSE, I prepared a translation exercise. In order to focus on the students' ability or skills to choose appropriate collocates, I wanted words that students were expected to know well, so I chose three entries, *progress*, *meeting*, and *law*. I made questions with three different types of collocations (Verb + Noun, Adjective + Noun, and Preposition + Noun) in order to see whether part-of-speech categorization worked well or not. I did not want students to spend longer time than they usually would in their dictionary-look-up process. I planned 30 minutes for the exercise, so that giving 30 questions (10 items per collocation type) meant one minute per item (see Table 7.1 for examples from the 30-item test).

The exercise asks students to complete English sentences containing different types of collocation in which the targeted collocate is left blank, according to the Japanese translation. In the following example:

その法律を施行するのは司法長官の仕事であって、ホワイトハウスの仕事ではない。
It is the Attorney-General's job to (...) the law, not the White House's.

Students are expected to understand the whole English sentence structure and see that an English verb corresponding to the Japanese verb 'shikou suru' (施行する) is missing here, then look for an appropriate verb collocate in the Verb + LAW section in the entry for *law*, and find *enforce* there. In some of the test items, the Japanese and English sentences are not structurally parallel. In the following case, the idea

Table 7.1 Example test items

Verb + Noun collocations
1. 50人以上の人がその大会に出席した。 Over a hundred and fifty people (...) the meeting.
2. なんとかして進歩を早めることはできないものか。 Can nothing be done to (...) progress?
3. その法律を施行するのは司法長官の仕事であって、ホワイトハウスの仕事ではない。 ... It is the Attorney-General's job to (...) the law, not the White House's.
Adjective + Noun collocations
1. 熱帯雨林破壊の止めがたい進行 The (...) progress of rain forest destruction
2. この条約はさらなる前進の足がかりを与えてくれる。 The treaty provides a bridgehead for (...) progress.
3. 代表団は総会のために午前10時に招集された。 The delegates were assembled at 10.00 am for a (...) meeting.
Preposition + Noun collocations
1. 国際空港建設計画が現在進行中です。 A construction project of an international airport has been (...) progress.
2. 妹の英語はとても進歩している。 My sister is making progress (...) her English.
3. 恐れ入りますが、彼女は今会議中ですので、後ほど折り返しお電話を入れるよう伝えます。 I'm afraid she's (...) a meeting – I'll ask her to call you back later.

expressed by a Verb + Adverb collocation in Japanese ('junchoni kaifuku suru' 順調に回復する) is translated by a Verb + Adjective + Noun collocation in English (*make good progress*) with the result that the adjectival collocate is targeted in the English sentence.

彼は手術後、順調に回復している。
He is making (...) progress after his operation.

This is an important, but not universal, structural difference in collocation patterning between English and Japanese, so the results from the test can help us understand in what ways this dissimilarity presents retrieval or encoding problems for Japanese learners.

When I administered the test in class, I first asked the students to do a warm-up exercise to learn what collocation is and get to know how entries are structured or how information is presented in the OCDSE. Here, I used 'Ideas into Words' taken from the study pages in the OCDSE (S2) together with a copy of the entry for *idea*. The exercise asks learners to look at the main three sections (ADJ., VERB + IDEA, and IDEA + VERB) and find (an) appropriate collocate(s) to express certain ideas. For example, one task involves finding adjective collocates to express 'an idea that is helpful, rather than being negative or impractical' from the adjective section, where one can find *constructive* and *positive* as possible answers. By doing these warm-up exercises, the students learned that collocates were presented according to their parts of speech, and that they had several choices available to them to express a particular idea.

The students were then instructed to do the 30-item collocation translation test. They were asked to choose the most appropriate word to fill in the blank from a relevant entry according to the given Japanese translation, by referring to copies of the three noun entries taken from the OCDSE. They were allowed to use English–Japanese dictionaries when they did not know the meaning of collocate words given in the entry. To score their responses, I counted all responses with appropriate collocates as correct even when they were given in the wrong form (as the research focus was on students' collocation retrieval performance). For example, in Question 7 for Verb + Noun collocations, the verb should be in its past participle form; however, if students responded with *convene* instead of *convened*, this was counted as correct.

In order to gather some individual feedback from the students, I asked the students to answer the following questions freely in Japanese: 'What did you find difficult when trying to make appropriate choices of collocates?' and 'Do you think the OCDSE is easy for you to use?' The responses to these questions would help me assess students' perceptions of the internal access structure of the OCDSE more properly.

Results and analysis

The results are separately tabulated below for Verb + Noun collocations, then Adjective + Noun collocations, and finally Preposition + Noun collocations. In each table, the number and percentage of correct answers students gave are shown, together with the number of acceptable answers in brackets when there were more than one acceptable response. The number of collocates grouped together means how many synonymous collocates are put together in the same slot as the correct answer(s). 'No answer' indicates the number of blank responses.

Verb + Noun collocations

The average for correct answers for Verb + Noun collocations was 61.2 percent, but as Table 7.2 shows, students did fairly well with some questions and not so successfully with others.

Table 7.2 Results for Verb + Noun collocations

Collocation	**Collocations grouped together**	**Correct answers**		**No answer**
1 attend/participate in the meeting	1	18 (11|7)	69.2%	2
2 accelerate/facilitate progress	2	15 (15|0)	57.7%	5
3 enforce the law	2	22	84.6%	1
4 adopt/enact/pass a law	3	20 (5|8|7)	76.9%	3
5 chair/conduct/preside over a meeting	3	14 (13|0|1)	53.8%	3
6 break/violate law	3	21 (11|10)	80.8%	0
7 call/convene/summon a meeting	6	16 (8|5|3)	61.5%	0
8 arrange/organize a meeting	6	12 (10|2)	46.2%	3
9 block/hinder/obstruct/ hamper/impede/slow (down) the progress	6	21 (8|7|4|1|1|0)	80.8%	3
10 assess/evaluate progress	10	16 (2|14)	61.5%	2
Average		15.9	61.2%	2.4

There seem to be three causes for the lower success rates for certain questions:

- structural differences between English and Japanese
- L1 interference
- the questionable semantic grouping of collocates.

First, Question 2 (*accelerate/facilitate progress*) has a low success rate and the most blank responses. Judging from various, incorrect answers given by the students, it was probably more difficult for students to see how the English and Japanese sentences corresponded to each other than to find an appropriate collocate from an entry extract.

Second, Question 5 (*chair/conduct/preside over a meeting*) can be considered to have a low rate of correct answers because of L1 interference. Next to the 13 correct answers (*chair*) ranks *host* (6 responses). Since the Japanese translation equivalent (*shikai wo suru*) for *host* – in the sense of acting as host for a television or radio programme – is close to that of *chair* (*gicho wo tsutomeru*), those students might have relied on Japanese more than meaning itself when they made their choice.

Third, Question 7 (*call/convene/summon a meeting*), Question 8 (*arrange/organize a meeting*), and Question 10 (*assess/evaluate progress*) have a relatively low rate of correct answers, and in these three cases the semantic grouping of collocates seems quite questionable. In the entry for *meeting*, *call*, *convene* and *summon* are grouped together with *organize* and *arrange*, although the former set focuses on the action and the latter on the process. Also, *arrange* and *organize* are categorized together in the same group as *schedule*. Here, 61.5 per cent of the students answered Question 7 correctly, but two filled in the blank with *organize*, and one with *arrange* instead of *call*, *convene*, or *summon*. Other wrong choices of verbs were *held* (2) and *open* (1).

As for Question 8 (*arrange/organize a meeting*), only 46.2 per cent of the students made an appropriate choice, and five students gave *schedule* as an answer, which can be considered an appropriate choice here. Although it is defined in the *Oxford Advanced Learner's Dictionary*, 7th edn (2005), as 'to arrange for sth to happen at a particular time' and the focus is rather on time than on process, arrangement or preparation, there is no context provided and the Japanese translation (会合を段取る) can mean fixing the date of a meeting. If *schedule* is counted as a correct answer, then the rate of correct answers increases from 46.2 per cent to 65.4 per cent.

Similarly, in the entry for *progress*, *evaluate* and *assess* form the same slot together with eight other collocates. Three of them, *check*, *monitor* or *review*, were chosen by four students (*check* 2, *monitor* 1, *review* 1), which reduces the success rate to 61.5 per cent. Considering these rough semantic groupings of collocates, having *attend* and *participate in* separately in the entry for *meeting* raises the question of what criteria are used for the semantic grouping of collocates. The results in Table 7.2 suggest that the number of synonymous collocates put together is not a key factor influencing students' performance in making an appropriate choice. This may mean that it is the appropriate semantic clustering of synonymous collocates rather than their total number that has a deciding influence on whether or not students can retrieve the information successfully.

Adjective + Noun collocations

The students' success rate for Adjective + Noun collocations was higher than that for Verb + Noun collocations; however, there were still a couple of cases where the rate of correct answers was relatively low (Table 7.3).

The small number of correct answers to Question 5 (*satisfactory progress*) may be a result of various interpretations of the Japanese phrase *moshibun no nai hayasa de* (申し分のない早さで), as other adjectives given as an answer include: *rapid* (5), *considerable* (3), *swift* (2),

Table 7.3 Results for Adjective + Noun collocations

	Collocation	Collocations grouped together	Correct answers		No answer
1	inexorable progress	1	18	69.2 %	4
2	further progress	1	20	76.9%	5
3	general meeting	1	22	84.6%	0
4	steady progress	2	19	73.1%	2
5	satisfactory progress	2	9	34.6%	2
6	summit/top-level meeting	3	20 (15|5)	76.9%	1
7	regular meeting	2	24	92.3%	0
8	economic progress	8	19	73.1%	2
9	considerable/dramatic/ great/impressive/ remarkable/significant progress	12	19 (3|4|3|1|8|0)	73.1%	1
10	good progress	12	16 (6|steady 5| satisfactory 5)	61.5%	1
Average			18.6	71.5%	1.8

excellent (1), *dramatic* (1), *substantial* (1), and *smooth* (1). The low success rate for Question 10 (*good progress*) may be explained likewise. The misinterpretation of sentence structure mentioned earlier is also a factor here. In this specific case, students were unable to see how the English sentence structurally corresponded to the Japanese translation. Consequently, some filled in the blank with an adverb such as *steadily*, *well*, and *smoothly*, all of which are presented under the entry for *progress*, verb. It is interesting that, while a very large proportion of the students successfully identified an appropriate collocate when it is presented on its own or with just one collocate, more students also left a blank empty compared to Question 9 (*considerable/dramatic/great/impressive/remarkable/significant progress*) and Question 10 (*good progress*), where as many as 12 collocates are presented together in the respective entries. It may well be the density of information that prevents the students from retrieving an appropriate collocate in such cases. Moreover, where no synonymous collocates are given, the students have no additional information for guessing the meaning of single collocates. It may be also worth mentioning that concrete notions such as *general meeting* and *regular meeting* have a higher percentage of correct answers than more abstract notions such as *satisfactory progress* and *good progress*. The results as a whole seem to support the interpretation made in the previous section that the length of each slot does not affect retrieval performance success rates to a great extent.

Preposition + Noun collocations

The results for Preposition + Noun collocations (see Table 7.4) generally seem to point to specific limitations in current entry structures. Compared to the results for Verb + Noun, Adjective + Noun collocations, fewer correct answers and more blanks were observed on the whole.

It seems that when learners do not know or cannot guess from a Japanese sentence the target Preposition + Noun collocation, which (succinctly) expresses an idea to be translated into English, they are unlikely to retrieve an appropriate collocation from the dictionary entry. Only half of the students could get the answer right for Question 7 (*against the law*), and it appears that most of those who failed could not identify the correct English collocation structure. The number of correct answers for Question 1 (*in progress*) and Question 10 (*within the law*) is very small, six and seven respectively, in comparison with those to other questions, and as many as nine subjects left the spaces blank. It can be hard for Japanese learners to connect the Japanese *shinko chu* (進行中), which some students tried to express by the progressive aspect in English, with the Preposition + Noun collocation *in progress*. Similarly, the Japanese sentence for Question 10 is not parallel to the English, so that it may be difficult to infer that *gouhou* (合法) can be expressed by the preposition + noun collocation *within the law*. On the other hand, the Japanese sentence for Question 9 contains *hanni nai de* (範囲内で), which is a translation equivalent of the preposition *within*, so that the

Table 7.4 Results for Preposition + Noun collocations

Collocation	Collocates grouped together	Correct answers		No answer
1 in progress	1	6	23.1%	9
2 progress in/with	5	18 (15|3)	69.2%	4
3 in a meeting	1	19 (is having 5)	73.1%	4
4 a meeting about/over	5	20 (17|3)	76.9%	4
5 a meeting with	5	9	34.6%	7
6 by law	4	22	84.6%	2
7 against a law	4	13	50.0%	5
8 above the law	4	17	65.4%	3
9 within the law (1)	4	18	69.2%	6
10 within the law (2)	4	7	26.9%	9
Average		14.9	57.3%	5.3

number of correct answers rises to almost 70 percent. The results for Question 3 (*in a meeting*) may also be likewise explained. While 14 students filled the blank with *in*, five students did so with *having*, which is also completely acceptable in this context. In contrast, Question 6 (*by law*) produced 22 correct answers, probably because of the similarity between the Japanese expression and the English collocation. However, Question 8 (*above the law*) produced 17 correct answers though the Japanese sentence for Question 8 does not have a parallel structure to the English one. A possible explanation for this is that the example sentence given in the OCDSE ('No one is above the law.') is similar to Question 8, 'No official is (...) the law', and this may well have led the students to the correct answer.

Qualitative feedback

I will now continue by looking at feedback from students about the usability and accessibility of the OCDSE. In terms of difficulties, 15 students commented that it was difficult for them to choose one collocate from several synonymous ones. Quite a few mentioned their difficulty in understanding the nuances of different words. Some students said that dictionaries did not help them to make a decision with confidence. They were unsure about which English word to use among those with the same Japanese translation equivalent. One student reported that he had tried in vain to find the differences between synonymous collocates by using both a monolingual and a bilingual dictionary. Another student pointed out that she found words that have a similar meaning in separate groups in the OCDSE and was confused about which one to use in a given sentence.

As to user friendliness, four students reported that the OCDSE was easy to use. Many more felt that it was difficult to use but would be very useful, at the same time, for English composition once they had got used to using the dictionary. Five individuals said that they would appreciate or need Japanese for better accessibility, and two students wanted more example sentences to help them to understand synonymous collocates better. All in all, the students acknowledged the usefulness of the OCDSE, but most of them did not find the dictionary user-friendly enough. They seemed to be, to some degree, overwhelmed with the rich mine of information all given in English.

Discussion

The overall results suggest that the OCDSE's part-of-speech categorization works well with users, but that it is not as clear as Klotz (2003) claims. The results, in particular for Preposition + Noun collocations, indicate that the students' performance was better with collocations whose structure is the same in English and Japanese. Once students get to the right section in a particular entry to start with, then they are quite successful in retrieving appropriate collocates in many cases; however, as to accessibility within a part-of-speech section, it may be said that a single collocate or a short list of collocates is more likely to be missed than a long one without any icon or number to indicate the beginning of each slot. On the other hand, it does not seem that the number of collocates put together in one slot affects the success rate for retrieval to a great degree. However, most of the students found it difficult to make a (final) choice from a (long) list of synonymous collocates.

Although the present study involved only a small number of learners, the results above tend to show the following:

- Categorization of collocates by parts of speech may bar access to some types of collocations when their corresponding expressions are not structurally parallel in users' L1. The students sometimes failed to get to the right part-of-speech section when they did not know or could not correctly guess a collocation type that expresses an idea to be translated into English. The results for Preposition + Noun collocations may suggest that a good deal of the information could be left unnoticed or unused if there is no explanation to lead users from ideas to collocations to express them.
- Some students left blanks empty when correct answers were given on their own or in rather short slots. It may help to make an entry more accessible by marking each slot in such a way that short slots do not get overlooked by users in an entry into which a lot of information is condensed.
- The level of learners' performance did not go down with long slots, but it did with slots where the semantic grouping of collocates was found to be questionable. Also, many students reported that they had difficulty in making decisions about which collocate to choose since it was hard to find information about the difference in meaning among near-synonymous collocates.
- The students, in general, saw the usefulness of the OCDSE, but they seemed to be, to some degree, overwhelmed by a large number of collocates presented together. Some students commented that they would welcome more example sentences with typical contexts or semantic explanations for each collocate.

When students did not know a word given as a collocate, they were allowed to look it up in an English dictionary, and most students used their English–Japanese dictionaries for help. Even in such cases, they sometimes ended up making wrong choices or were unable to fill in the blanks. This may mean that simply giving Japanese equivalents (translations) for each collocate will not be the perfect solution for creating a more user-friendly collocation dictionary for university students in Japan.

Concluding remarks

In this study, I tried to explore Japanese university students' information retrieval skills with the OCDSE. Students were happy to learn about the collocation dictionary and how to use it, but they also found it difficult to use. One factor seems to be the current entry structure, which is mainly based on forms of collocation, rather than their meaning, and several implications for improvement arose from the present study. However, this study dealt with a very small number of students and entries. Also, because the survey took the form of a classroom translation exercise, linguistic differences between English and Japanese affected students' performance to a certain extent. Large-scale user studies will be needed to discover users' look-up processes and problems, and to explore how to design more user-friendly entry structures.

Note

1. Saito's preface quoted from a paper he had read at the Second English Teachers' Conference in Tokyo in 1914.

8

Designing Pedagogic Materials to Improve Awareness and Productive Use of L2 Collocations

Jingyi Jiang

Introduction

This chapter is situated in the context of English language teaching and learning in China. To be specific, I attempt to look at the connection of corpus studies with materials development in China. I use two corpora, the Chinese Learner English Corpus (CLEC; Gui and Yang, 2003) and the Freiburg–LOB Corpus of British English (FLOB; Mair, 1997; Hundt, Sand and Siemund, 1998), to summarize explicit similarities and differences in collocation usage between Chinese English learners (CELs) and native speakers. My goal is to understand better Chinese learners' collocation knowledge and development in their process of learning English as a foreign language.

For the past decade and more, researchers have recognized the importance of teaching collocations in language education, and some have drawn on the results of corpus studies for materials and textbook writing (Richards, 2006). In China, language education specialists have shown a growing interest in studies based on Chinese learner corpora, including CLEC. They have investigated, among other things, semantic prosodies (Wei, 2002a), the effect of chunking (Miao and Sun, 2005), interlanguage errors and crosslinguistic influence (Yang, 1999), the use of prepositions (Gui, 2005), recurrent word combinations (Guan and Zheng, 2005), and erroneous Verb + Noun collocations (Zhao, 2005). In spite of all the invaluable insights gained about learner language, materials developers in China, nevertheless, have been slow to exploit corpus studies to create appropriate collocation tasks and activities.

In this chapter, I start by summarizing a comparative corpus analysis of a small set of target words used by CELs and native speakers respectively, and then look into how the target words and words of a similar nature are actually introduced in particular textbooks that are extensively used in China. I use the insights to present some self-designed collocation-focused pedagogic tasks to guide learners to become aware of, and then make use of, nativelike collocations. Finally, I present and discuss some learner and teacher feedback on these collocation-focused tasks.

The target CLEC words

The learner language data that I use come from CLEC, which is a national project (9th five-year plan, 1996–2000) sponsored by the Chinese government. Comparable to the size of FLOB, it is a one-million word corpus collected from writings by CELs at five different proficiency levels (senior secondary school students; first- and second-year non-English major college students; third- and fourth-year non-English major college students; first- and second-year college English majors; third- and fourth-year college English majors). The corpus is error tagged according to an error-marking scheme of 61 types of error, including various lexical, grammatical, semantic, and sentence level errors. For my study, I used CLEC to profile six target words, namely, *achievement, concept, conclusion, factor, method,* and *principle*, all of which are among the 2354 *Active Words* in the *College English Curriculum Requirements* (CECR; Department of Higher Education, Ministry of Education of the People's Republic of China, 2004),[1] a nation-wide guideline for tertiary-level English teaching. Chinese college students are expected not only to understand the meaning of the *Active Words* in the process of listening to or reading in English, but also to be capable of using them in speaking and writing. The list of active words was compiled with reference to Nation's 2,000 most frequent words of English and Nation's Academic Vocabulary (Nation, 1990), the *Longman Language Activator* Key Words List (Longman, 1993), and the Longman Defining Vocabulary used in the *Longman Dictionary of Contemporary English*, 3rd edn (Longman, 1995). Thus, the active words cover high-frequency words and words that frequently appear in academic texts regardless of subject areas.

Understanding Chinese learners' collocation use

Learner output is a genuine reflection of how learners actually use the target language and, in the case of this study, of how they typically use the target words with other collocates. By focusing on a small set of words, we should, to some extent, be able to come to some understanding of CELs' collocation knowledge by searching CLEC and analyzing how CELs have actually used these words in production. Table 8.1 below gives

Table 8.1 Target word collocates from the CLEC and FLOB

Target word	Word class	Collocates	
		CLEC	FLOB
Achievement	V	make*, get*, made*, gain*	*not significant*
	Adj	great, good*	*not significant*
Concept	V	is, have*, changed**, change	*not significant*
	Adj	traditional*, practical*, new	new
Conclusion	V	draw**, make*	is
	Adj	*not significant*	*not significant*
Factor	V	is	is, was
	Adj	important	important, activated, major
Method	V	is, find*, use	is, was, used
	Adj	good*, best**, new**, learning**, teaching**, cooking*, lecture*	*not significant*
Principle	V	is, has**	is, was
	Adj	important**	logical, general

* Indicates that the collocate is either not found in FLOB or not up to a significant level. A further search in the COBUILD Bank of English online (HarperCollins, 2007) does not find the collocate in either of the conditions.
** Indicates that the collocate is either not found in FLOB or not at a significant level, but it is used and is significant in the COBUILD Bank of English online.

a comparison of the adjectival and verbal collocates for the six target words as used by CELs (CLEC collocates) and native speakers (FLOB collocates). Collocates found both to the left and to the right of the target word, with a span of 5 words are considered, and only those that have a t-score >1.96 have been included in the table. I set the cut-off point at above 1.96 (2.0 to be exact), following the practice of many corpus researchers, since a z-score of 2.0 separates most 'accidentally occurring collocates, with the remaining ones significant' (Wei, 2002b: 107).

Table 8.1 lets us come to the following tentative conclusions:

- *Chinese learners are target-like with regard to the use of most collocates*: Though some collocates that are used in the CLEC are not found in the FLOB, a further search in COBUILD helps us find the corresponding native-speaker collocates as shown in Table 8.1. It may be said that after years of learning English as a foreign language, CELs have built up some basic sense of collocation usage in English.

- *A great percentage of collocates in CLEC and FLOB (93.6 per cent and 80 per cent respectively) fall in the first 2000 words in Nation's vocabulary list*: This result may be somewhat surprising as CELs very often tend to focus on so-called 'big and difficult' words and, in so doing, they naturally feel their vocabulary knowledge is good. This result may be used as good evidence to convince CELs that collocations are often not difficult words, but very frequent ones. Accordingly, vocabulary learning per se should not be taken as remembering as many difficult words as possible, but rather learning how to combine the more frequent ones.
- *Chinese learners are likely to use collocates that may be scarcely used by native speakers:* For some collocates used in the CLEC, neither the FLOB nor COBUILD reveals the same collocates, or at least not to a significant level in some cases, acceptable though they may be in the target language. In such cases, L1 influence is manifested in most of the unusual collocates (Yang, 1999; Gui, 2005). This usually results from word-to-word translation from Chinese and a lack of awareness of collocation appropriacy in English.
- *Chinese learners may overuse some collocates, whether the collocates are target-like or not:* Part of the possible explanation behind this language behavior is that the data collected are from prompted writing, hence the frequent use or over-use of some collocates. Another plausible explanation is that CELs tend to rely on those collocates they are familiar with, and overlook other possible choices.

The comparison shows that even though CELs have obtained minimum target-like competence in collocation usage, there is still a pressing need to help raise their collocation awareness further. Next we look at how English textbooks in China typically address collocation learning.

How collocation is typically dealt with in textbooks in China

In China, students enrolled in the same year learn from the same textbooks and their teachers (especially high school teachers and college English teachers) do not have a lot of autonomy as far as teaching materials are concerned. A conventional practice is that a couple of head teachers in charge decide what textbooks to use, and then a group of teachers (often as many as 40 or more) use the same textbooks to teach up to 5000 students for two years at almost the same pace. Achievement tests are given to the students at the end of each semester (16 weeks in total). Owing to the heavy reliance on textbooks at most Chinese schools, the importance of, and need

Type of vocabulary task
• Finding words and phrases from reading passages (with clues given) to fill in blanks, write a sentence, or replace with other words, phrases and idiomatic expressions
• Using words and phrases given to make sentences
• Filling in blanks with words and phrases given, or with the first letter of the word given
• Developing word formation/word families with different parts of speech, antonyms, synonyms, polysemous words, prefixes, suffixes etc
• Correcting wrong use of parts of speech in sentences and cloze tests
• Matching words with the definitions given
• Using words and phrases given to translate sentences from Chinese to English or vice versa
• Doing crossword puzzles
• Distinguishing pairs of confusable words and filling in blanks with the right words
• Using words and structures from reading passages to create sentences using the same words and structures
• Paraphrasing parts of sentences from reading passages

Figure 8.1 Summary of textbook vocabulary tasks

for, well-written, suitable textbooks is self-evident. But what language input is out there for the learners? How is collocation introduced and handled in such extensively used textbooks? How often do the target words appear, and how are they presented when they do?

To seek answers to these questions, I examined three sets of textbooks that are used at national level. I found in each of the three sets of textbooks that vocabulary is an important part of all the tasks at the end of every reading passage. There are different kinds of vocabulary practice in each set (see Figure 8.1), but only one of the three sets mentions in the preface of the teacher's book that attention has been assigned to word clusters. All six target words appear in the reading passages in the textbooks, some up to 12 times in one set, but none is practiced with a special focus on collocation usage.

We can see that vocabulary is considered a crucial part of learning English from textbooks and is practiced in many different ways. However, collocation as a very important part of vocabulary acquisition has been either overlooked or treated unsystematically, just as Coady and Huckin (1997: 256) noted over a decade ago: 'a key element of most language courses, other highly frequent word patterns – which is precisely what collocations are – have usually been ignored or at best been seen as marginal to courses'. As language learning involves 'learning sequences of words (frequent collocations, phrases, and idioms) as well as sequences within words' (Ellis, 1997: 130), I designed and piloted different collocation tasks to help learners raise their awareness of the appropriate use of multiword combinations. The example tasks are a tentative try in this direction. It should be noted, nonetheless, that no matter what materials or textbooks are used, they should meet the criteria of being entirely practical for class instruction and pedagogically possible in the context of English teaching in China. This is for two interrelated reasons: there is no time assigned exclusively to vocabulary teaching owing to limited instruction time, and, because of this, students should be encouraged inside class to work towards independent learning outside of class.

Example pedagogic materials

After I finished designing the pedagogic tasks and writing the instructions for how the materials should be used in class, I invited two teachers from two respective Chinese universities to use them with their students (75 altogether) for a duration of 12 weeks as a complement to their normal integrated English course. The materials are a combination of speed reading and collocation tasks, partly for in-class use but mostly for out-of-class self-study. In class students were given a reading passage of between 400 and 800 words. The time allowed to finish reading each passage, ranging from three to seven minutes, was decided based on the length and the difficulty level of the reading passage, that is, the number of possible new words and complexity of syntactic structures. Reading comprehension questions were discussed and checked in class at once after the allotted time was up. Afterwards, students were given other collocation-awareness-use tasks to finish on their own after class.

Let's take one specific reading passage as an example. This passage is a very short story about a girl's frightening experience. It is taken from *Breakthroughs in Critical Reading* edited by Benner (1997). In the story, the night before a girl called Nan boarded a flight to Florida, she had a horrible dream where she saw a man and a big, black limo that people usually used at funerals to carry coffins. The man said something weird to her: 'C'mon. There's room for you!' The next day when the girl was standing in line waiting to get her boarding pass, she saw the ticket agent, whom she recognized instantly as the same man in her dream, and this man said the same weird thing to her: 'C'mon. There's room for you!' She ran away in horror and didn't board her flight. Minutes later, the plane she was supposed to be on board crashed on the runway.

The following is a detailed introduction and explanation of the collocation tasks around this short story, where the tasks are composed of four major sections.

> ***Section One: Note down the good expressions***
>
> *Instructions: Write down in the space provided the good expressions in this story that you have noticed and want to learn.*

This section asks students to note down expressions in the reading passage that they have noticed and want to learn. Some of the examples students are expected to have noticed and written down are: *dialed the phone, woke up to this funny light, a weird dream, staggered over to a seat.* The purpose of designing this task is to guide students to go beyond comprehension, to push them to notice words and phrases in the reading passage and how they are used. It is hoped that by deliberately directing learners' attention to words and their collocates (see Schmidt, 1990), learners may get used to learning vocabulary in clusters.

In the second section, there is a common vocabulary task. The purpose of including this task is to emphasize the good expressions and the possible collocates as a reinforcement of what may have been noticed.

> ***Section Two: Use the right expression***
>
> *Instructions: Fill in the incomplete sentences with one of the expressions provided in the box and change the form where necessary.*
>
> *shook up ... wake up to ... stand in line*
>
> *1) Stop dreaming! _______ reality.*
> *2) The students were _______ to get into the lecture hall.*

The specific expressions are selected and put in a sentence in the hope that learners are able to use (or at least practice the controlled use of) the word cluster in different contexts.

> ***Section Three: Enhance your collocation awareness***

The third section concentrates on specific active words in order to enhance students' awareness of the collocates that often go with these active words. The activities are in different formats to ensure variety. Here are some examples:

A. Instructions: Complete each of the following sentences with a word or phrase in the box. More than one word or phrase may be possible for a blank. Make sure each sentence is grammatically correct as well.

shake ... seek ... tremble ... find
shoot out ... reach for ... grope for ... reach out

(1) Grandma's hand ________ as she lifted the glass to her lips.
(2) Her hand ________ the door handle as she can't see clearly.

B. Instructions: Nan's hand shook because she was frightened. So we can say 'Her hands shook with fright.' What else can we put after 'shake with'? Give at least four possible collocates as you can think of that can go with 'shake with'. Refer to a collocation dictionary if necessary.

shake with ________ / ________ / ________ / ________

C. Instructions: Nan's voice quavered when she was calling Tom. Listed below are other words that are similar to 'quaver', to describe someone's voice except one. Find out that word and cross it out.

a voice	*a. cracks ... d. falters* *b. quivers ... e. quakes* *c. shakes ... f. trembles*

D. Instructions: What words do you use to describe a dream? Add as many collocates as you can think of in each group. Give at least 4 collocates for each group. Refer to a collocation dictionary if necessary.

a(n)	*(1) bad* *(2) _____*	*dream*
	(1) pleasant *(2) _____*	

E. Instructions: We say 'A telephone rings.' What else do we say about a telephone? Give as many collocates as possible. Refer to a collocation dictionary if necessary.

... A telephone rings/ _______ / _______ / _______ / ________ / _______.

F. Instructions: Translate each of the following sentences into English using the words and phrases given in brackets.

> 她把脸转过去以免被人看见自己脸红。*(face away)*
> *(She faced away to hide her blushes.)*

All the activities in Section Three are closely connected to specific CECR requirements, so active words are emphasized in particular. Students are pushed to focus on the active words so that they may become aware of what collocates can go with a specific target word, which, in other situations, they might overlook. They are also encouraged to refer to a collocation dictionary when the need arises as most CELs are not familiar with collocation dictionaries.

> ***Section Four: Retell***
>
> *Instructions: Retell the reading passage in as much detail as you can remember by using words and expressions from the reading passage.*

The purpose of the retelling task in Section Four is to emphasize the connection between input and output. Swain (1995) pinpoints the role of output in interlanguage development, especially in grammatical competence. Though the focus in this activity is not grammatical, being pushed to produce by retelling the passage in as much detail as they can and using words and phrases from the reading passage, learners are directed to word clusters they may otherwise have overlooked.

To sum up, the collocation tasks consist of two main types: awareness tasks and production tasks. The criteria for including the above-mentioned tasks are dependent on the principles of noticing, retrieval/noting, and production. Awareness is a preliminary step towards acquisition, and the actual use of language helps promote acquisition.

Student feedback on the collocation-oriented tasks

At the end of 12 weeks when the students completed six units of fast reading passages and collocation-awareness-use tasks, I distributed a questionnaire to collect their feedback. The questionnaire was composed of two parts. The 10 Likert scale items in Part One asked for students' view on the role of collocation and the collocation-awareness-use tasks. The second part of the questionnaire consisted of open-ended questions for students to freely air their views. Table 8.2 summarizes the results obtained from the questionnaire, with raw totals given in the top line, and rounded percentages in the second line, for each statement.

Table 8.2 Feedback from the questionnaire (*N*=75)

Statement	Strongly agree	Agree	Not sure	Disagree	Strongly disagree
1. Memorizing word clusters helps me towards target-like use.	28 38.4%	39 53.4%	6 8.2%		
	92%				
2. There is a great difference between memorizing single words and word clusters.	3 4.1%	52 71.2%	10 13.7%	8 11.0%	
	75%				
3. Now I jot down a word and the company it keeps because I have recognized it is very important to remember word clusters.	25 34.3%	41 56.2%	7 9.6%		
	90%				
4. Collocations are often very easy words, but often I am not sure which words can go with which words.	17 23.3%	46 63.0%	8 11.0%	2 2.7%	
	86%				
5. Simply remembering many individual words does not really mean one is good in English.	48 65.8%	22 30.1%	2 2.7%		1 1.4%
	96%				

Table 8.2 Feedback from the questionnaire (N=75)

Statement	Strongly agree	Agree	Not sure	Disagree	Strongly disagree
6. If I was not asked to jot down the good expressions, I may have overlooked some collocations.	13 17.8% 82%	47 64.4%	9 12.3%	4 5.5%	
7. My first language Chinese influences my collocation use in English to some extent.	18 24.7% 84%	43 58.9%	3 4.1%	9 12.3%	
8. It helps to constantly remind myself to avoid possible Chinese-like collocations when I use English.	27 37.0% 92%	40 54.8%	5 6.9%	1 1.4%	
9. I am sure I will be more competent in collocation if I keep on jotting down good expressions.	28 38.4% 84%	33 45.2%	11 15.1%	1 1.4%	
10. The inclusion of collocation tasks in teaching materials is a very effective way to help me to become a better language user.	16 21.9% 88%	48 65.8%	7 9.6%	2 2.7%	

Responses to Statements 1, 3 and 5 show that most of the students recognized the importance of collocations in English learning. A great majority of the students also responded positively to the collocation awareness tasks as shown in Statements 6, 8, 9, and 10. However, when we look at the responses to Statement 2, which asks for students' views on memorizing single words and word clusters, the results are more mixed. Though 75 per cent of the students did think there is a great difference between memorizing single words and word clusters, 11 per cent of them, however, responded negatively, and 14 per cent were not sure (25 per cent in total). This underlines the fact that quite a number of CELs rely on memorizing individual words rather than word clusters to expand their vocabulary, a phenomenon that Moon describes as 'dangerously isolationist' (Moon, 1997: 40). Only a very low percentage of students (4 per cent) think that there is a great difference between memorizing single words and word clusters – this is much lower than the answers given to other statements. Finally, a small minority of students (12 per cent) replied that they didn't think that their mother tongue Chinese would influence their collocation use (Statement 7). Results obtained from the second part of the questionnaire shed more light on this.

The second part of the questionnaire consisted of six open-ended questions for students to air their views, unconstrained by the 5-level Likert scales used in the first part.

Question 1: *Did you pay much attention to collocation in the process of learning English before? Why or why not? How are you memorizing English words now? How would you like to develop further what you do to learn English?*

More than half of the students responded that they hadn't paid much attention to collocation before with reasons such as: *'didn't think it is important'*, *'being lazy'*, *'unaware of the importance'*, and *'didn't have enough time'*. Those who did give positive answers mentioned that they were not very serious towards collocation even though they paid some attention. Some of them did so only when writing in English. On the other hand, after taking part in this study, everybody reported that they recognized the importance of collocation and that they liked to jot down words and memorize them with the company they keep. Many of them also mentioned that they were now learning words in contexts and doing more reading. However, some also said that they tried to remember the spelling and meaning of single words, recite well-known sentences in literature works, or memorize English words with the help of Chinese. In other words, some students still focused more on memorization.

Question 2: *Were you told the importance of collocation in the process of learning English before the present collocation awareness tasks? If yes, who did it, when was that, and in what context?*

The responses here were rather surprising, though not unexpected. Two thirds of the students said that they had not been told about the importance of collocation in the process of learning English. Of the rest, some said that a couple of their high school English teachers mentioned collocation in doing exercises such as sentence-making and some mentioned that the tests they took emphasized collocation usage. Interestingly, a few of students specifically mentioned *New Concept English* (Alexander, 1967; Alexander and He, 1997), a series of textbooks by L.G. Alexander that are very popular textbooks in China that have been widely used for over 20 years. The passages in *New Concept English* normally are rather short, but, after each passage, there are different kinds of exercises focusing on comprehension, grammatical structures, and vocabulary use, and this may be the reason why these learners mentioned this book in relation to their initial collocation awareness.

Question 3: *Did you know that collocation dictionaries are useful tools in learning English? If yes, in your view what is the most useful effect of using a collocation dictionary for you? Are you going to get yourself a dictionary? Why or why not?*

Student responses here were indeed surprising. Almost 90 per cent of the students said that they didn't know there were collocation dictionaries. However, much to my satisfaction, about 85 per cent of the students said that now that they have realized the importance of collocation usage, they will get a collocation dictionary of their own, even though it may be expensive or heavy to carry around. They mentioned that they would look up the dictionary for word clusters when not sure of a right collocate. They also commented that a collocation dictionary would be good for writing, helping them towards target-like use and that it is fun to do so. However, some students (about 15 per cent) responded negatively. These students said that even if they had a collocation dictionary, they might still be too lazy to refer to it frequently. Some said they thought it would be better to expand their vocabulary via reading.

Question 4: *Of all the collocation tasks after the reading passages (jot down good expressions, use the right expression, enhance your collocation awareness, and retell), which type of collocation tasks do you like best and why? Please give two specific reasons why you like that particular task.*

Student preferences were evenly distributed across each of the four sections of collocation awareness tasks. The reasons students gave for their preferences are summarized in Table 8.3.

Students also gave some suggestions and comments about how to improve the collocation tasks used in the present study, such as doing

Table 8.3 Student feedback on the collocation tasks

Task section	Student feedback
Note down the good expressions	• without this, I may overlook some good expressions • they are easy to memorize • they help me learn a lot • they make a deeper impression
Use the right expression	• combine words and the whole sentence • interesting (can know more words and phrases) • collocations plus modeling and practice
Enhance your collocation awareness	• very focused • more important and useful than recitation • helps train my collocation awareness • provides intensive practice
Retell	• helps me learn how to summarize • helps me connect reading English with using English

intensive training, using more interesting materials, jotting down less frequently used collocations and using them in sentences, checking the dictionary often, making sentences with collocations, and reading more and reading faster. Some students even suggested that they have presentations on collocations in class, read more difficult materials, have systematic introduction of collocations, and prepare a special notebook for collocation use.

Teacher feedback on the collocation-oriented tasks

The interview with the two teachers was quite informal. We mainly focused on three points:

- the necessity and importance of emphasizing collocation usage in teaching;
- the effect of the materials on collocation learning;
- the possibility of integrating reading/collocation-awareness-use materials in the general intensive English course.

The discussion turned out to be fruitful and inspirational. Both teachers mentioned that it was important to give collocation teaching/learning a place in the syllabus. They often noticed in learner output inappropriate collocation usage and thereby felt it was necessary to have a systematic introduction to collocation. This would help learners become aware of – or *'alert to'* (as one teacher put it) – target-like collocations, especially those that may be quite different from those in their mother tongue.

As regards the pedagogic materials, the feedback was also positive. They expressed their appreciation and mentioned that, to the best of their knowledge, these were the first English reading materials focusing on comprehension and collocation usage in China. They strongly believed their students would benefit from the pedagogic tasks in terms of developing their English collocation ability. They expected more materials of this kind to assist them in their teaching.

They also felt that it would not be a problem at all to integrate the reading/collocation-awareness-use materials in their general intensive English course as the pedagogic tasks would be a welcome complement. They gave two main reasons for this. First of all, doing the fast reading didn't require much time (10 minutes at the most); it was thereby pedagogically feasible for the teacher to start the fast reading at any time. Besides, they found their students were very interested in the six fast reading passages. Secondly, the collocation-awareness-use tasks would be a great support in directing students towards becoming better autonomous learners. One teacher said: 'Often times learner autonomy is emphasized, but, without specific guidance, everything would turn out to be a beautiful dream, hard to be realized.' All in all, the feedback from the teachers confirmed the necessity and feasibility of including a collocation focus in the general English course.

Conclusion

It is necessary and important to raise learners' collocation awareness in the process of learning English as a foreign language. To do so, suitable materials are a must. Better connections must be established between materials writing and the invaluable insights provided by corpus research. It should be noted that the results of learner corpus studies in particular should be considered as such studies normally reveal the development of learner language, and, in the case of collocation usage, provide the baseline for innovations in materials development.

Note

1. The Department of Higher Education in the Ministry of Education invited a group of experts in education and language to draft the CECR. The reference here is for the 2004 trial version.

9
Commentary on Part II: Exploring Materials for the Study of L2 Collocations

Hilary Nesi

Introduction

These three chapters are all concerned with the design of materials to help learners recognize and reproduce appropriate collocations. All identify problems with existing materials, all tentatively suggest improvements, and, in support of their conclusions, all report on findings from a variety of sources, such as corpus analysis, materials analysis, test scores, and learner feedback. The chapters are multi-faceted, and bring to bear both knowledge of collocational theory and a practical understanding of learners' wants and needs.

Of particular interest is the attention paid to current constraints on publishers and classroom teachers, which make it difficult to provide students with the full range of collocational information that corpus evidence reveals. In the case of dictionaries, the greatest limitation seems to be that of space. Print dictionaries have to be small enough to carry around, but restricted entry length can lead to the loss of useful information, or the condensing of information to such an extent that it is difficult for the user to interpret. In the classroom lack of time is the biggest problem; teachers have to focus on the syllabus and prepare students for achievement tests, and tertiary English course materials such as those Jiang describes provide little opportunity to examine vocabulary in context. This commentary chapter will reflect on the three researchers' responses to these constraints, as revealed through their choices of corpora, their presentation of corpus data, and their suggestions for materials design.

Preliminary analyses

Corpus investigations of collocational behaviour are a starting point for all three chapters. The studies by Handl and Komuro feature the

100-million word British National Corpus (BNC; Oxford University, 2005), which provided Handl with the information to create her multi-dimensional classification of collocations, and was also used to compile the *Oxford Collocations Dictionary for Students of English* (OCDSE; 2002), discussed by Komuro. Jiang's teaching materials, on the other hand, arise from a comparison of collocation usage in the Chinese Learner English Corpus (CLEC; Gui and Yang, 2003) and the Freiburg–LOB Corpus of British English (FLOB; Mair, 1997; Hundt, Sand and Siemund, 1998). Jiang also refers to the Bank of English online (HarperCollins, 2007) as a larger source of collocational data, and finds significant occurrences of some collocates that were used by Chinese learners, but were not significant in FLOB. This suggests that a one-million word corpus is too small for comparative studies of this kind; without additional recourse to the Bank of English, Jiang would not have been able to demonstrate a distinction between plausible CLEC collocates such as *draw* and *conclusion*, and non-nativelike collocates such as *make* and *achievement*.

The shortcomings of existing materials also motivate further research in all three studies. Handl draws attention to differences in the treatment of collocational information in the *Macmillan English Dictionary for Advanced Learners* (MED; 2002), the *Longman Dictionary of Contemporary English*, 4th edn (LDOCE; 2005) and the *Oxford Advanced Learner's Dictionary*, 7th edn (OALD; 2005). She concludes that the selection and arrangement of this information is very varied, and probably does not help learners to decide which word combinations are worth remembering and which are not. Similarly, Komuro examines the entry structure of the OCDSE, where synonymous or semantically related collocates belonging to the same word class are ordered intuitively, without definitions or much contextual information, leading her to suspect that OCDSE users will find appropriate collocates difficult to retrieve and use. Having conducted corpus searches to assess the extent of Chinese college students' collocational knowledge, Jiang examines the treatment of the same target words in English language textbooks widely used in China. She finds that although the words appear in the reading passages, the textbooks pay little or no attention to collocation usage.

Pilot materials

All three researchers were interested in recording learner responses to learning activities, and in two of the three chapters this part of the research entailed the development and trialling of pilot materials. Handl created gap-filling and translation tasks based on specially designed collocation-rich dictionary entries, while Jiang created self-access collocation-awareness-raising tasks.

Handl's rationale for the design of her new type of learner's dictionary entry is at the heart of Chapter 6. This is a major contribution to collocation studies, involving the classification of collocations across three dimensions: semantic, lexical, and syntactic. From a semantic perspective, collocations can be mapped on a cline from 'transparent' (where the meaning is clear, and matches the literal meaning of the component words) to 'opaque' (where the meaning is highly idiomatic, and cannot be worked out by looking at the component words). From a lexical perspective, they can be classified in terms of the number of words each component collocates with. Some collocations include words that also form part of many other collocations, but others include a rare word that almost never collocates with other partners, and these might be considered fixed expressions, falling at the idiom end of the collocational spectrum. Finally, the statistical dimension of Handl's classificatory system takes into account the ratio between the combined frequency of the word partners and the frequency of individual words. This ratio reveals the strength of the collocation and the direction of the attraction (whether the first partner combines with a wider or a narrower range of collocates than the second).

Handl's multidimensional approach is a powerful way of describing multiple aspects of collocational behaviour, and she develops and explores its potential as a means of selecting and presenting collocational information. Although she discusses several alternative means of presentation, for her experimental study she used a three-part dictionary entry format (referred to as a 'refined' dictionary entry), where the usual dictionary definitions, example sentences, and usage information are sandwiched between a list of collocates that the headword predicts (as the dominant partner with a narrower range of collocates), and a list of collocates that predict the headword (as the weaker partner with a wider range of collocates). This has the practical advantage of condensing a great deal of collocational information into a confined space without too much typographic clutter, but, as Handl herself points out, it results in isolated lists of collocates, divorced from any information about their meaning and usage. In this respect, Handl's collocation cross-reference boxes suffer from the same defect as the OCDSE lists of semantically related collocates, described by Komuro. OCDSE entries indicate the word class of collocates, whereas Handl's refined entries indicate the direction of collocational attraction and the headword's collocational activity level, but neither type of entry indicates the strength of collocational links (another aspect of Handl's statistical dimension), or reveals how collocation affects the meaning and wider environment of the headword. Handl's alternative, and untested, proposal for an integrated dictionary entry seems to have greater potential as a guide towards appropriate production, but would however require more interpretative skill on the part of the user. The extensive use of symbols would also represent a reversal of the recent trend in learner dictionary design towards more transparent, less heavily coded dictionary entries.

Like Handl's refined dictionary entries, Jiang's experimental materials were also designed with practical constraints in mind. Jiang's speed reading passages only took up a few minutes of class time, and placed few demands on teachers. After a quick in-class comprehension check, the remaining activities could be conducted out of class. Teachers reported that they liked the way the tasks encouraged autonomous learning, and although they did not comment on the fact that the tasks fulfilled the *College English Curriculum Requirements* (CECR; Department of Higher Education, Ministry of Education of the People's Republic of China, 2004), this might also have been regarded as a point in their favour.

Jiang's tasks encourage students to notice collocations, in accordance with the precepts of second language acquisition theorists such as Schmidt (1990) who regard conscious noticing of L2 input as crucial for the conversion of input to intake. Subsequent activity stages in the materials involve selection and editing tasks that gradually increase the level of production, to the point when the student is required to retell the original story 'to emphasize the connection between input and output'. This approach too is in accord with the principles of L2 acquisition theory; for example, it aligns well with Gass's (1997) six-stage model, progressing from input to output. Thus, although Jiang focuses on her learners' attitudes rather than any measurable progress in second language acquisition, her chapter provides a useful model for the future development of materials to help learners acquire productive collocational knowledge.

Experimental method

The experimental work reported in the chapters did not involve large amounts of data: Handl used a series of five 9-item questionnaires, Komuro administered a 30-minute test of 30 items, and Jiang elicited feedback after trialling her materials with her students. For this reason it should be considered exploratory research, paving the way for future larger-scale studies, and the novel research methodologies employed should be regarded as contributing as much to the field as the research findings, if not more.

Handl's questionnaires contained gap-filling and translation tasks and a look-up protocol so that respondents could record their dictionary consultation process alongside their answers. The questionnaires were administered to two groups of subjects, a control group with access to an original extract from a learners' dictionary (OALD), and an experimental group with access to the refined entries. If subjects selected the first answer on the look-up protocol ('I don't need a dictionary, I know the expression'), their answers for that question were discarded, thus removing the risk that results might be influenced by prior knowledge, rather than the information provided in the dictionary extracts. The other answers in the look-up protocol monitored the number of times each subject had to return to the dictionary entry in order to arrive at a solution to the task – ideally the correct solution to the task would be apparent from the first look-up; longer searches and wrong answers were taken to indicate problems with the performance of the dictionary.

Although Handl writes in terms of longer and shorter searches, there is no record of how long it actually took the subjects to complete the tasks, because they filled out the questionnaire at a time and place of their own choosing. The look-up protocol facilitated response by offering multiple choice options, and only providing limited space to record additional information. Under tighter experimental conditions Handl might have had the opportunity to observe and time her subjects' look-up behaviour, and if she had set a think-aloud task or conducted face-to-face interviews, she might have been able to record more subtle responses to the tasks. The short questionnaires, on the other hand, made it easier for her to quantify her results, and presumably also improved the response rate of the learners involved.

Unlike the research by Handl and Jiang, Komuro's research focused on published rather than specially devised materials. Komuro's self-designed test to evaluate OCDSE entries combined gap filling and translation by requiring subjects to identify appropriate collocations with reference to Japanese versions of the test sentences. The task seems to have been quite demanding despite the Japanese translation support, because English and Japanese sentence structures differ so greatly. Structural differences in collocational patterning in the two languages were taken into account when analysing the test results, as one of the aims of the experiment was to identify the particular problems and needs of Japanese learners in relation to collocation dictionary use.

Komuro and Jiang both elicited feedback from their subjects to discover their attitudes to the tasks they had been set. The responses Jiang collected from students and teachers constitute her sole source of data regarding the success of her materials, and she did not attempt to measure any improvement in her students' language skills resulting from the introduction of the collocation tasks. This was probably a wise research design decision, as it is notoriously difficult to measure the language acquisition benefits of action research in normal teaching contexts, where other variables may also influence student progress.

The significance of the findings

Results from the experimental components of the research reported in all three investigations have a number of implications for materials design. In Handl's study the refined dictionary entries proved to be an improvement on the original OALD entries. The experimental group achieved higher overall scores and performed best when translating, whereas the control group had most difficulty with the translation task. Handl puts this down to the greater quantity of collocations available to the experimental group, and her findings imply that collocation lists are helpful to dictionary users even if they are isolated from the main entry information. Jiang also reports a successful outcome: her subjects indicated increased awareness of collocational issues, although there were still some traces of their earlier 'isolationist' approach to vocabulary learning, involving the memorization of decontextualized words. Komuro's results, on the other hand, confirmed her doubts about the difficulty of selecting appropriate collocations from OCDSE entries. The OCDSE method of categorizing collocations according to their word class was found to be problematic when learners translated from structurally dissimilar sentences in Japanese, and the undifferentiated lists of near-synonymous collocates in some OCDSE entries sometimes caused confusion.

The student feedback in Komuro's study that the OCDSE was 'difficult to use but would be very useful' recalls Laufer and Kimmel's (1997: 362) distinction between 'dictionary usefulness' (or 'the extent to which a dictionary is helpful in providing the necessary information to its user'), and 'dictionary usability' (or 'the willingness on the part of the consumer to use the dictionary in question, and his/her satisfaction from it'). There is a tension between usefulness and usability, and an improvement in one may sometimes lead to a decrease in the other, as Handl seems to be aware when she discusses the pros and cons of her refined and integrated dictionary entries. The integrated entry seems to be more useful, but also possibly less usable than the refined entry. Thus, Handl eventually reaches the conclusion that a visual display on a computer screen would be the most effective means of conveying collocational information.

Handl's proposed online collocational webs neatly visualize both the strength of collocational attraction and its direction, without the need for user-unfriendly codes and symbols, and with the option to reveal or hide definitions and example sentences. In fact, electronic reference tools such as *Visuwords*™ (Princeton University, undated) and *The Visual Thesaurus*™ (Thinkmap, Inc., undated) have already made it possible to create similar webs illustrating the semantic (rather than collocational) connections between words. An alternative approach to collocational mapping has been developed by Heyer et al. (2001) at Leipzig University. Heyer et al. created software to interlink entire collocational sets, illustrating collocational strength by length of line, as Handl does, but using the space surrounding the headword to illustrate collocational interconnectedness rather than collocational direction. Thus, in their graph for the polysemous headword *space,* there are three clusters of interconnected words, one cluster collocating with *space* in the context of 'real estate', one with *space* in the context of 'computer hardware', and one with *space* in the context of 'astronautics'. Webs of this sort distinguish very clearly between the specialist and non-specialist senses of 'cryptotechnical' words (common words that also have a specialized meaning, as described by Fraser, 2001). A visual representation of both interconnectedness and direction would probably be too difficult to interpret, so it would be interesting to investigate which of the two sorts of web would be most useful (and usable) for language learners.

Of course, the learner's willingness to use a dictionary is very much affected by its format, and it could be that full-screen graphic displays, though useful, will not be very usable for learners who do not have ready access to a computer. Personal experience in the classroom, and studies such as those of Deng (2005), Midlane (2005) and Boonmoh and Nesi (2007), suggest that pocket electronic dictionaries (PEDs) are becoming increasingly popular with learners. The small size of the PED screen might discourage learners from scanning whole dictionary entries, and might also preclude the display of semantic and collocational webs, but the portability, ease of use, and relative affordability of PEDs mean that they score highly for usability even if they are often perceived to be less useful than the established print and CD-ROM publications. Left to their own devices, learners are likely to rely on the bilingual components of PEDs, but in fact many also include a monolingual learners' dictionary such as the OALD, and some even include the OCDSE, as Komuro points out. This suggests that PED use might prove a good solution for Jiang's respondents, 85 per cent of whom intended to acquire a collocations dictionary, even though it might be 'heavy to carry around'.

Conclusion

Taken together, the findings from these three studies suggest the need for a variety of pedagogical and lexicographical resources, and continued research into their effects. Handl's refined dictionary entries seem to provide more useful collocational information than standard learners' dictionary entries, but Komuro's Japanese learners might have found the isolated lists of collocates hard to digest, and might have fared better with Handl's proposed graphic display, where words could be linked with definitions and examples. Jiang's practice materials seemed to promote new collocational awareness, but her students also expressed a desire for collocational dictionaries; they perhaps might have benefited from more information about the range of lexicographical materials on offer, including the print and PED versions of the OCDSE, and the print and CD-ROM versions of general learners' dictionaries.

It is revealing to compare small, separate and geographically distant studies, as this chapter has done, to discover further insights unavailable to the original authors. Given the fast pace of technology, and the constant emergence of new lexicographical products, there remains plenty of scope for further work relating to L2 collocation research and teaching. The studies contribute to this in three ways: at the level of analysis, through detailed description of various kinds of collocational relations; at the level of methodology, by proposing new ways of measuring the success of L2 collocation resources; and at the level of resource development, by critiquing existing practices, and suggesting innovative ways of improving teaching and reference materials.

Part III

L2 Collocation Knowledge Assessment Research

10
Evaluating a New Test of *Whole* English Collocations

Robert Lee Revier

Introduction

Much of the L2 experimental research on the assessment of collocation knowledge (e.g. Marton, 1977; Channell, 1981; Fayez-Hussein, 1990; Bahns and Eldaw, 1993; Farghal and Obiedat, 1995; Herbst, 1996; Schmitt, 1998; Gitsaki, 1999; Bonk, 2000) has relied heavily on a single elicitation method that involves presenting test takers with a node-word prompt (e.g. *attention*), and asking them to select or supply one or more collocates (e.g. *call, draw, pay*) of that node word. Although responses elicited by test items of this kind may well give an impression of the depth of test takers' knowledge of the node word, they offer little or no direct insight into the nature of test takers' knowledge of the *whole* collocation (e.g. *pay attention*). This shortcoming is a logical consequence of the common practice of adopting what can be referred to as the word-property view of collocation. Collocation as a word property (Nation, 2001) is said to interact with several other word properties (Richards, 1976), such as orthography, grammatical behavior, meaning, association, frequency, and style. Together, these properties are said to characterize the form, meaning, and use of a word. The word-property approach to collocations has led researchers and teachers alike to view collocation knowledge as a subcomponent of word knowledge rather than as independent knowledge. The word-property approach has also resulted in a focus on the individual words (e.g. *strike* and *claim*) that combine to form a collocation, rather than on the whole collocation itself (e.g. *strike a claim*).

The research reported in this chapter explores an alternative approach to the study of L2 collocation knowledge. This approach is characterized by four underlying assumptions. First, collocation knowledge can be viewed as an independent construct. Second, collocations constitute lexical items in their own right and, as such, feature formal, semantic, and usage properties similar to those borne by single words. Third, the semantic properties of the constituent words that combine to form collocations are likely to play a role in EFL learners' ability to 'produce' English collocations. Fourth, testing of L2 collocation knowledge needs to focus on the recognition and production of *whole* collocations. It is this set of assumptions that the new collocation test presented in this chapter is designed to probe. More specifically, the test is designed to assess L2 learners' productive knowledge of *whole* collocations of the verb object–noun syntactic type (e.g. *make a complaint*). It is also designed to explore whether test takers' ability to generate targeted English word combinations is influenced by the semantic properties of such items.

The chapter consists of two parts. In the first part, I address a number of theoretical and practical issues informing the experimental study. Once I have described how collocations are defined and classified, I go on to explain how collocation knowledge is conceptualized and operationalized in the present research and how the collocation test was designed and developed. In the second half of the chapter, I present a description of the study before I report and interpret the results in terms of reliability and validity.

Theoretical and practical issues

Defining and classifying collocations

In an early phase of this research, in which word combinations were extracted from a national corpus, I broadly defined collocations as a recurring combination of words (e.g. *commit suicide*) forming a particular syntactic unit (e.g. verb–object noun). This definition was subsequently refined in a later phase, when the computer-extracted collocations were manually classified according to their semantic properties. Adapting a three-way classification system employed by Howarth (1998b: 164) and Nesselhauf (2003: 226), I resolved to use a single criterion to establish category membership, namely the semantic property of both the verb and the noun constituent. Thus, if both the verb and the noun constituent are used in their literal or core sense, as in *make tea*, then the combination as a whole is classified as transparent. If the verb constituent is used in a non-literal or extended sense and the noun constituent in a literal sense, as in *make a complaint*, then the combination is classified as semi-transparent. If neither the verb nor the noun is used in its literal sense, as in *run the show*, or the two constituents form a unitary meaning that cannot be derived from their literal senses, as in *make the grade*, then the combination is classified as non-transparent. I relied primarily on the *Oxford Advanced Learner's Dictionary*, 7th edn (OALD; 2005) to establish the semantic property of the individual constituents. The senses of a given lexical entry in the OALD are generally organized such that the literal come before the extended. Thus, if the meaning of a constituent word (e.g. *make* and *tea* in *make tea, complaint* in *make a complaint*) matched one of the sense meanings listed at the beginning of the entry for that word in the OALD, then I assumed the constituent is used in the literal or core sense of that word. If, on the other hand, the meaning of the constituent word (e.g. *make* and *grade* in *make the grade*) matched none of the senses or if the meaning (e.g. *make* in *make a complaint*) matched one of the senses toward the end of the entry for that word, then I assumed the constituent is used in an extended sense of that word. However, since there is no clear division in the OALD between literal and extended meaning, I occasionally found myself falling back on native-speaker intuition. Furthermore, whenever I was in doubt about the semantic status of a given constituent, I simply dropped the word combination from consideration.

Conceptualizing the construct

The knowledge construct that the collocation test was specifically designed to probe is an adaptation of one first proposed by Revier and Henriksen (2006). In line with their original proposal, collocation knowledge is conceptualized here as an independent construct comprising knowledge of whole collocations that bear formal, semantic, and usage properties similar to those of single words. Going beyond their proposal, the present construct embraces three knowledge subcomponents – knowledge of transparent collocations (e.g. *take the money*), knowledge of semi-transparent collocations (e.g. *take a course*), and knowledge of non-transparent collocations (e.g. *take sides*). This dimension of the construct rests on the assumption that the semantic categories of verb–object noun collocations outlined above are psychologically real, not just for native speakers of English but also for learners of English as a foreign language. Additionally, following the original proposal, productive use of whole collocations is assumed here to require both *knowledge* and *ability*. Possessing productive *knowledge of* a verb–object noun collocation involves not just knowing its core lexical constituents and their combined meaning. It also involves having knowledge of its grammatical elements (e.g. noun determination and number). This second assumption bears implications for the way in which the different semantic categories of collocation are likely to be learned and processed. Since the lexical constituents and grammatical elements contained by collocations of the non-transparent and semi-transparent category are often subject to restrictions beyond those imposed by compositional semantics and general grammar, it follows that the *ability to use* collocations of this kind (accurately) in production may depend largely on storing and accessing them in the mental lexicon as *holistic units*, rather than piecing them together on the basis of general semantic and grammatical knowledge. The *ability to use* transparent collocations by contrast is more likely to be dependent on general lexical knowledge and grammatical knowledge. Holistic processing is no doubt most applicable to non-transparent collocations and, to a lesser degree, semi-transparent collocations. Although neither transparency nor syntactic regularity necessarily precludes a word combination from being processed holistically (Warren, 2005), the constituents of transparent collocations are much more likely to be learned and processed compositionally (i.e. as separate items) by both foreign language learners and native speakers.

Operationalizing the construct

With the aim of identifying an item format suitable for operationalizing the knowledge construct described above, I reviewed previous L2 experimental studies looking for a format that would meet three main conditions. The format would (a) test productive knowledge of whole Verb + Noun collocations, (b) allow the elicitation of relatively decontextualized collocations (i.e. ones independent of a coherent text longer than a sentence), and (c) be suitable for learners of different L2 proficiency levels.

Only three item formats emerged from the review as possible candidates. The first is translation, which was employed in a number of studies, including those by Marton (1977), Biskup (1992), Bahns and Eldaw (1993), Herbst (1996), and Gitsaki (1999). The second is the sentence-generation task proposed by Schmitt (1998). The third is the sentence cloze, which was employed to elicit verb collocate responses in studies by Bahns and Eldaw (1993), Herbst (1996), Gitsaki (1999), and Bonk (2000). Although none of these formats was found fully adequate in their traditional forms, I hoped that the latter could be modified to suit the needs of the present research.

I therefore considered making three modifications to the sentence-cloze format. I first considered leaving out the whole collocation. I dismissed this modification because I felt that it would invite multiple responses, not just in the form of verb–object noun sequences but also in the form of single-word verbs. Next, I considered restricting responses to the cloze gap by providing the first one or two letters of the two missing lexical constituents together with a choice of articles. This format was trialed together with a verbal protocol on first-year Danish university students of English. The protocol revealed that the test takers became so preoccupied with identifying any words that at all could match the letters that they lost sight of the propositional meaning projected by the sentence prompt. I was therefore forced to abandon this modification as well.

The third and final modification I considered resulted in the format called CONTRIX, which restricts responses to the cloze gap by offering a selection of choices. As in the following example, the CONTRIX consists of a sentence prompt containing a gap that corresponds to a whole collocation (i.e. Verb + (Det) + Noun):

The quickest way to win a friend's trust is to show that you are able to [ ].	tell	a/an	joke
	take	the	secret
	keep	—	truth

Alongside the prompt is a constituent matrix (hence the name CONTRIX) consisting of three columns, each of which represents one of the three constituents and features three word choices. Test takers are asked to select (circle) the combination of verb, article, and noun that best completes the sentence. Since the CONTRIX involves selection it is likely to be perceived as a receptive measure. Convention aside, however, it could also be said to tap productive knowledge for test takers must not only create (i.e. produce) meaning by combining lexical constituents, but they must also grammatically encode the noun constituent for determination. An informal pretrial run on first-year Danish university students of English showed this format to be potentially suitable for the purposes of this research.

Test design and development

Using the CONTRIX as the sole elicitation method, I developed a pilot test to measure Danish EFL learners' knowledge of whole collocations. The main considerations shaping the design of the CONTRIX test were target-item selection, sentence-prompt writing, distractor selection, and native-speaker norming.

In terms of items, I wanted to select a set of word combinations that would be representative both of the above-mentioned three semantic categories and of the 100-million-word British National Corpus (BNC; Oxford University, 2005). The selection process was carried out in two phases. The first phase involved the automated extraction of verb–object noun combinations from the BNC using the Phrases in English (PIE) extraction interface (Fletcher, 2003). The PIE extraction was guided by the following criteria:

- the constituents had to occur immediately adjacent to one another;
- the combination had to contain one of 15 highly polysemous verbs (i.e. *break, carry, catch, change, cut, draw, get, give, hold, make, pay, play, raise, run,* and *take*) in its infinitive form;
- the combination had to have a frequency ranging from .04 to .47 occurrences per million in the BNC.

The second phase involved a manual selection of a subset of collocations from those extracted in the first phase. I used these criteria to guide me:

- the noun constituents had to belong to the first 3,000 most frequent word families as determined by the *Web VocabProfile / BNC-20* (Cobb, 2006);
- the combination had to match one of the three semantic categories delineated above.

The resultant subset, consisting of 45 items, was balanced for (a) semantic category (15 items per category), (b) verb constituency (3 items per verb), (c) item frequency, and (d) noun-constituent frequency. An overview of the frequency properties is provided in Table 10.1.

In the next stage of designing the test, I aimed to come up with short, stand-alone contexts that would adequately pitch the meaning borne by the missing collocations. To ensure contextual authenticity, I looked

Table 10.1 Properties of the target item subset

Semantic category	Number	Item frequency*		Noun constituent frequency	
		Mean	SD	Mean	SD
Transparent	15	.20	.14	2.5k	2.1k
Semi-transparent	15	.21	.11	1.7k	1.2k
Non-transparent	15	.19	.12	2.3k	2.2k

*Per million words in the BNC.

at PIE and/or GOOGLE™ concordances containing the target item to get a general impression of how the target item is typically used by native English speakers. I then selected or fabricated a representative sentence, making sure that the depicted situation was as explicit as possible without unnecessary detail. Finally, to enhance sentence comprehension (and distractor recognition), I tried to restrict the lexis used in the sentence prompts (and matrices) to high-frequency words. A frequency analysis of the pilot test computed using the *Web VocabProfile* showed that 96 per cent of the words used in the sentence prompts and matrices fell within the range of the first 3,000 most frequent word families.

In selecting distractors, I wanted to have a matrix that could generate multiple word combinations, some of which would be perceived as acceptable English word combinations, but only one of which would accurately complete the sentence (i.e. bear the meaning projected by the sentence). I tried to ensure that most of the combinations formed by the distractors in a single matrix would reflect the target item in terms of their semantic properties. Thus, for a transparent target item (e.g. *hold the baby*), I sought verb and noun (e.g. *carry, bear; toddler, kid*) distractors that would in their core sense combine compositionally to form transparent word combinations (e.g. *carry the baby, bear the toddler*). For semi-transparent target items (e.g. *run tests*), I had to keep in mind that verb distractors (e.g. *make, take*) should ideally bear extended meaning and the noun distractors (e.g. *samples, probes*) core meaning. Non-transparent target items (e.g. *carry the day*) by contrast required verb (e.g. *bear, make*) and noun (e.g. *weight, battle*) distractors that would combine to form unitary meaning (e.g. *bear the battle, carry the weight*).

A 45-item pilot version of the CONTRIX was normed by a panel of three adult native British English (BrE) speakers. They were unanimous in their selection of 42 of the 45 target word combinations. With respect to the other three items (13, 35, and 38 in Table 10.4), where disagreement involved article choice, the targeted response in each case was given by two of the three BrE speakers, which was taken as sufficient norm evidence to retain these items for an initial test administration.

The study

This study constitutes a trial administration of the CONTRIX. My main purpose in conducting the trial was to obtain quantitative data from a cross-section of Danish EFL learners in order to evaluate the reliability and validity of the collocation test.

Three intact English classes (N=56) were volunteered by their teachers[1] to participate in the study. These classes represent three different education levels:

- 1st-year gymnasium (10th grade, n=20),
- 2nd-year gymnasium (11th grade, n=17), and
- 1st-year university (n=19).

All participants were assumed to have begun their formal study of English in fourth grade, which meant that they had had between seven and ten years of formal English instruction.

The test battery was administered in the participants' regularly scheduled classrooms and instruction times. In addition to the CONTRIX, the test battery included a background questionnaire and a vocabulary test. The questionnaire, which was administered to account for the participants' formal and informal (English) language learning experience, has at this stage of the research only been used to screen out exchange students. The results of the vocabulary test are not reported here.[2] The CONTRIX was administered first. Test takers were given oral and written instructions. They were also led through two sample items to ensure familiarity with the new format. The time required to complete the CONTRIX varied slightly according to education level. The 10th graders took 35 minutes, the 11th graders 30 minutes, and the university students 25 minutes.

The test takers' responses to the CONTRIX were scored as either correct (1) or incorrect (0). In order to be judged correct, responses had to match the whole target item (i.e. verb, article, and noun). Test-item scores, test-section scores, and a total-test score were recorded for each test taker.

Results and discussion

Test reliability

For aggregate participants (N=56), the test as a whole (k=45) had a moderately high internal consistency (Cronbach's α = .89). The reliability for each of the test sections (k=15) was somewhat lower (transparent = .68, semi-transparent = .76, and non-transparent = .74) than for the test as a whole. This is to be expected since, as Bachman (1990: 220) points out, reliability is affected by test length (i.e. the number of test items), in addition to the homogeneity of the items and the heterogeneity of the test takers.

Descriptive statistics for the CONTRIX

The descriptive statistics for section scores and total-test scores are shown in Table 10.2. One of the main objectives of the data analysis was to determine whether the test was able to distinguish among learners of different general proficiency. The mean total-test scores presented in the last row of Table 10.2 not only appear to differ across the three education levels, but they also indicate an increase from one level to the next. For example, the total score grows from 17.2 for the 10th graders, to 21.8 for the 11th graders, and to 28.8 for university students. This increase is also seen in the mean section scores across the three education levels. The following analysis looks into whether these observed differences are statistically significant.

Test validity

Two methods were used to obtain evidence for test validity. The first method, advocated by Henning (1987: 98), involved determining whether the CONTRIX could distinguish among learners of different proficiency levels. I compared mean total scores using a one-way between-groups ANOVA. An alpha level of .05 was used for this and all subsequent statistical tests. The results were statistically significant $F\ (2, 53) = 18.4$, $p = .000$ with a very large effect size ($\eta^2 = .41$). Scheffe post-hoc tests were conducted to determine which groups differed from one another. Both the 10th graders (M = 17.2, SD = 6.4) and the 11th graders (M = 21.8, SD = 6.4 were found to be significantly different ($p = .000$ and $p = .004$, respectively) from the university students (M = 28.8, SD = 5.1). However, the 10th graders were found not to

Table 10.2 Mean scores (M) and standard deviations (SD) for three proficiency levels

Collocation type	10th grade (*n*=20)		11th grade (*n*=17)		1st-year U (*n*=19)		Aggregate (*N*=56)	
	M	SD	M	SD	M	SD	M	SD
Transparent (TT) (*k*=15)	7.4	2.8	8.8	2.5	10.3	1.9	8.8	2.7
Semi-transparent (ST) (*k*=15)	5.0	2.2	7.0	2.4	9.8	2.1	7.2	3.0
Non-transparent (NT) (*k*=15)	4.8	2.4	6.0	2.1	8.7	2.1	6.5	2.7
Total (*k*=45)	17.2	6.4	21.8	6.4	28.8	5.1	22.5	7.7

differ significantly from the 11th graders. In other words, the CONTRIX results show a significant difference between Danish learners separated by two years of English instruction (i.e. the 11th graders and the first-year university students), but not between learners with a gap of only a single year (i.e. the 10th graders and the 11th graders).

The second method involved establishing evidence for the validity of the internal construct of the CONTRIX. The CONTRIX consists of three test sections, each representing a collocation knowledge subcomponent. Thus, to obtain evidence for internal construct validity, I conducted a set of one-way within-subjects ANOVAs comparing the three mean test-section scores for the participants as an aggregate. The results were statistically significant (Wilks' Lambda = .45, F (2, 54) = 32.7, p = .000, η^2 = .55). To reveal which test sections differed from one another, I performed pairwise comparisons using Bonferroni t tests, which automatically adjusted the observed significance level for multiple comparisons. As can be seen in the last column of Table 10.3, all paired differences were found significant. These results give preliminary evidence for the validity of the internal construct underlying the CONTRIX.

From a developmental perspective, the CONTRIX would offer greater insight if the knowledge subcomponents (i.e. semantic categories) could also be shown to be psychologically real at different proficiency levels. For this reason, I carried out a second set of one-way within-subjects ANOVAs comparing the three mean test-section scores within each of the three education levels. The results, as computed by Wilks' Lambda (= .38, .30 and .60 respectively), were significant at each education level: 10th graders F (2, 18) = 14.5, p = .000, η^2 = .62; 11th

Table 10.3 Test-section comparisons for three proficiency levels and aggregate-mean differences (MD) and confidence levels (p)

Pair	10th grade (n=20)		11th grade (n=17)		1st-year U (n=19)		Aggregate (N=56)	
	MD	p	MD	p	MD	p	MD	p
Transparent (TT)-Semi-transparent (ST)	2.4*	.000	1.8*	.002	0.5	.806	1.6*	.000
Transparent (TT)-Non-transparent (NT)	2.6*	.000	2.7*	.000	1.6*	.009	2.3*	.000
Semi-transparent (ST)-Non-transparent (NT)	0.3	1.000	0.9	.124	1.1	.109	0.8*	.013

*Mean difference is significant at the .05 level.

graders F (2, 15) = 17.8, p = .000, η^2 = .70; and university students F (2, 17) = 5.59, p = .014, η^2 = .40. To reveal which test-section scores differed from one another, I carried out Bonferroni t tests on each of the three groups. The results are presented in Table 10.3. With respect to internal construct, a slightly different picture emerges when the participants are grouped according to education level rather than as an aggregate. Four comparisons did not show significance: (1) the ST–NT pair for the 10th graders, (2) the ST–NT pair for the 11th graders, (3) the TT–ST pair and (4) the ST–NT pair for the university students.

These insignificant differences do not, in my opinion, necessarily represent evidence against the psychological reality of these knowledge subcomponents. On the contrary, if viewed together with the significant differences, they appear to give an impression of how the three subcomponents are likely to develop over time. In an early stage of development, represented here by the 10th graders, knowledge of transparent collocations clearly exceeds that of semi-transparent and non-transparent collocations. Not only is knowledge of semi-transparent and non-transparent collocations underdeveloped, but it is also not well differentiated, as is indicated by the lack of significance. Although the next stage, represented here by the 11th graders, features only a small but significant growth in overall collocation knowledge, from 17.2 to 21.8, this growth marks the onset of a qualitative shift in collocation knowledge whereby knowledge of semi-transparent collocations begins to catch up with that of transparent collocations. The third stage of development, represented here by the 1st-year university students, not only displays a large overall growth (from 21.8 to 28.8) but also reveals that knowledge of semi-transparent collocations has reached a level that is nearly comparable to that of transparent collocations – hence the lack of significance between transparent and semi-transparent collocations at this stage.

Item analysis

Adopting the classical approach to item analysis (Bachman, 2004: 120–8), I calculated facility values and discrimination indices for each of the items making up the three test sections. The results shown in Table 10.4 are based on the aggregate (N=56). For norm-referenced tests such as this one, the following guidelines are recommended. Item facility (IF), the difficulty level of a test item for a given sample of test takers, should range from .20 to .80, with an average of .50 being ideal (Bachman 1990: 138). Item discrimination, measured here as item-total correlation (ITC), refers to how well the item discriminates between individual test takers who score high on the test as a whole and those

Table 10.4 Item facility (IF) and item-total correlation (ITC) for each test item

Transparent			Semi-transparent			Non-transparent		
Item	**IF**	**ITC**	**Item**	**IF**	**ITC**	**Item**	**IF**	**ITC**
01 get a message	.73	.38	**07** draw the curtains	.77	.47	**02** hold the fort	.29	.29
06 catch the culprits	.25	.42	**08** raise the matter	.30	.29	**03** break the ice	.79	.35
11 break a leg	.84	.15	**10** cut jobs	.45	.58	**04** raise a finger	.71	.32
13 pay a ransom	.04	.04	**14** hold elections	.30	.43	**05** give a hand	.89	.23
19 draw a map	.88	.55	**18** run tests	.38	.51	**09** make history	.71	.50
20 take the money	.84	.21	**23** get a taxi	.98	.01	**12** run the gauntlet	.07	.31
22 cut a hole	.52	.50	**24** play tricks	.68	.62	**15** draw breath	.05	.20
25 hold the baby	.77	.27	**26** break the silence	.88	.53	**16** catch a cold	.68	.45
29 change direction	.63	.54	**27** change trains	.70	.01	**17** take sides	.79	.33
30 give money	.64	.26	**34** take a course	.57	.52	**21** cut corners	.32	.51
32 carry a gun	.73	.44	**35** carry the risk	.12	.30	**28** carry the day	.02	.28
38 make tea	.55	.23	**37** give consent	.12	.44	**31** change hands	.57	.52
39 run a race	.52	.08	**40** make trouble	.07	.15	**33** get the sack	.25	.35
41 play chess	.77	.61	**42** pay a visit	.71	.48	**36** play the field	.29	.51
45 raise prices	.09	.23	**44** catch fire	.23	.44	**43** pay dividends	.05	.43
M	.59	.33	M	.48	.39	M	.43	.37

who score low. Discrimination indices, following Henning (1987: 53), should ideally be .25 or higher, though ones as low as .19 may be acceptable. Although the section means observed for both IF and ITC meet the guidelines outlined above, a number of items distributed across the three sections nonetheless exhibit poor performance. If a subsequent analysis of item prompts and distractors fails to reveal the source of the problem, these target items may well have to be replaced. For now, however, I would like to make use of IF values to assess the effect of noun-constituent frequency. Seven target items (i.e. items 2, 6, 12,

13, 37, 41, and 43) containing low-frequency noun constituents were incorporated in the CONTRIX to explore the extent to which noun-constituent frequency plays a role in test takers' ability to combine verb and object constituents. As it turns out, four of these items (i.e. 12, 13, 37, and 43) are among the nine most difficult items (i.e. those exhibiting an IF value below .20). This clearly suggests that noun-constituent frequency played a key part in the test takers' ability to generate English collocations. This in turn implies that the low-frequency items will have to be replaced if frequency is to be adequately controlled in the design of the CONTRIX.

Concluding remarks

Despite being in an early stage of development, the CONTRIX performed surprisingly well, both in terms of reliability and validity. Although the scores obtained in the trial indicated that the internal consistency of the CONTRIX was moderately high, the performance of a number of individual items was nonetheless poor, suggesting that with improvement the test has the potential to generate even more reliable scores. Some evidence was also presented for the validity of the CONTRIX as a measure of Danish EFL learners' productive knowledge of whole English collocations. The observed total-test scores representing the test takers' overall collocation knowledge demonstrated that the CONTRIX has the capacity to distinguish among learners of different L2 proficiency levels, as the university students scored significantly higher than the 11th graders and the 11th graders in turn performed moderately (albeit not significantly) better than the 10th graders. Likewise, the observed section scores showed that the CONTRIX also has the potential to discriminate at the subcomponent level, highlighting strengths and weaknesses in test takers' knowledge of transparent, semi-transparent, and non-transparent collocations. In short, the results of the study suggest that the CONTRIX has the potential necessary to probe collocation knowledge as an independent construct comprised of three knowledge subcomponents. Yet, notwithstanding such promising potential, a number of issues related to the validity of the CONTRIX require further consideration. To be sure, further validation of the CONTRIX will need to involve sample sizes larger than the present. Representativeness of the knowledge subcomponents could be improved by increasing the number of items per section, though a lengthier test might, on the other hand, lead to lower reliability owing to loss of concentration, particularly among test takers of low proficiency.

Notes

1. I would like to thank the following high school teachers for having both volunteered their students and sacrificed valuable classroom time in support of this research: Kirsten Hegelund Ive, Tine Kilian Albæk, and Corinne Bilancio.
2. The vocabulary test was meant to serve as an independent measure of language proficiency. This could have been employed as an alternative means by which to group the participants if the analysis of collocation knowledge across education levels had failed to yield interpretable results.

11

Toward an Assessment of Learners' Receptive and Productive Syntagmatic Knowledge

June Eyckmans

Introduction

From the start of corpus linguistics, co-occurrence phenomena, especially collocations, have been considered an important area of research (Sinclair, 1991; Ellis, 2002; Colson, 2003). With the 'phrase' seen as the basic level of language representation, psycholinguists hold that most language utterances are determined by collocational restrictions and semantic prosodies (Ellis, 2008). However, different empirical studies on language learners' command of the target language reveal that learners tend to produce non-idiomatic word combinations because they neglect the idiom principle (Sinclair, 1991) in natural language and overuse 'creative' word combinations. Learners' lack of awareness of the existence of collocational patterns often results in excessive reliance on L1 to L2 transfer. Consequently, many sentences generated by language learners sound unnatural or foreign even though they are perfectly 'grammatical' (Pawley and Syder, 1983; Farghal and Obiedat, 1995). Not only in foreign language acquisition do collocations – and phrases in general – prove to be a stumbling block. Research in translation studies has also demonstrated the prominence of mistakes owing to a lack of phrasal command in the source or target language (Colson, 2003; Tirkkonen-Condit, 2002; Poirier, 2003; Colson, 2008).

When it comes to measurement of phrasal knowledge, standardized tests tapping into the syntagmatic competence of learners are not available yet. This can be explained by the fact that phrases make up a category that is difficult to define. They are very diverse in lexical composition as well as function, and they comprise the whole stock of collocational patterns of the language. It is no wonder that attempts to measure the 'phraseomaticity' of learners' interlanguage are scarce.

Over the years, my colleagues and I have carried out several research projects in which language learning is directed at enhancing bottom-up processing skills. In the first of these projects, we have tried to validate Lewis's Lexical Approach (1993, 1997) by measuring the effect of input-driven learning with noticing of multiword expressions on learners' oral proficiency (Boers et al., 2006). The results confirmed the hypothesis that spontaneous fluent speech is facilitated by exemplar-based knowledge. Blind judges who were asked to listen to learners' oral production tended to award higher oral proficiency scores to those learners who had used more phrases in their language production. However, in this project and the subsequent ones (Eyckmans, Stengers and Boers, 2007b; Eyckmans, 2007; Stengers, 2007), we have had to rely on volunteers to engage in the time-consuming activity of counting all the phrases in the participants' language production in order to have a measurement of our learners' phrase knowledge and use. It would benefit our research immensely if we were to find a user-friendly test that could serve as a reliable indicator of learners' phrasal knowledge. Such a test could function as an indirect reflection of the amount of language exposure and language intake that has taken place. So far we have mapped out learners' phrasal knowledge in different ways depending on the particular research project. We have used phrasal recognition in context (Eyckmans, Boers and Stengers, 2007) and a format called Deleted Essentials Test (Eyckmans, Boers and Demecheleer, 2004) as receptive measures, and phrase counts (Boers et al., 2006; Eyckmans, 2007; Stengers, 2007) and rational cloze tests targeting phrases as productive measures. Still, we felt there was a need for a more reliable – and preferably corpus-based – measure to track our learners' development of phrasal knowledge. That is why the Discriminating Collocations Test (DISCO) was designed.

Reasons for developing measures of phrasal knowledge – and specifically collocation knowledge – are manifold, as the following selection of arguments illustrates:

1. It has been suggested in the literature that learners' knowledge of word meanings does not change radically over time whereas knowledge of syntagmatic relationships does (Schmitt, 1998). If this is true, then tests of phrasal knowledge could be much more suited for measuring learners' progress (especially at an advanced level) than the vocabulary measures we tend to employ today (Eyckmans, Stengers and Boers, 2007a).
2. Since empirical studies into foreign language acquisition have shown collocations to be notoriously challenging for L2 learners

(Granger, 1998b; Schmitt, 1999; Nesselhauf, 2005; Barfield, 2006), it seems only logical that language testers should attempt to develop measures directed at filling this void. Because collocations are often comprehensible in the input, they may not be recognized as problematic by language learners. The errors mostly appear in language production. By evaluating language learners' (lack of) collocation knowledge a positive backwash effect may be created toward raising learners' awareness of the idiomatic nature of the target language.

3. Conventionalized language use also relates to other kinds of linguistic development in learners. Yorio reports correlations between grammatical proficiency and the successful use of conventionalized language and claims that 'although fluency is possible without grammatical accuracy, idiomaticity is not' (Yorio, 1989: 68).

In this chapter I will report the results of a study in which learners' receptive knowledge of collocations – more specifically, their ability to distinguish idiomatic Verb + Noun combinations from non-idiomatic word pairs – is seen in relation to their productive use of phrasal language and their language proficiency at large. Previous test use was centered on verifying the test's reliability in cross-sectional data collections (Eyckmans, Boers and Stengers, 2006). In this chapter I have taken the complementary angle of developing a longitudinal study in which the development of receptive collocation knowledge of a group of advanced English language learners is traced. The study serves to validate the DISCO by means of a design in which the test will be used as a pre- and post-measure in a 60-hour instructional setting. Comparison of test scores with scores on global proficiency (oral proficiency scores on interviews) as well as scores on phrasal productive competence (phrase counts in interviews, rational cloze tests) will shed light on the test's ability to capture learners' progress. But first I will address the issue of content validity when designing corpus-based measures of phrasal knowledge.

Content validity: The issue of representative coverage

From a measurement perspective, good sampling is a prerequisite for obtaining a test score on which to base generalizations. In order to select a representative sample of collocations for the DISCO, the concept of collocation needs to be delineated within the wide realm of frequently co-occurring word pairs. Unfortunately, collocation as a principle of lexical organization is ill-defined. It has been investigated from different angles and different researchers have approached the concept within the confines of their particular field of study (Nesselhauf, 2004). The dominating traditions in the twentieth century are referred to as the frequency-based tradition and the phraseological tradition (for a comprehensive account, see Gyllstad, 2007: 7–17). In the electronic mega corpora that are available nowadays, the concept of collocation is defined quantitatively: statistical significance computation scores indicate the probability of co-occurrence of words within a certain span. However, these 'lexicometrics' need to be interpreted with caution as they are purely mathematical analyzes of all items occurring in a set span. Given the prevalence of homonymy and polysemy, it is very hard to obtain unambiguous data and manual checking of the extracted collocations is indispensable (Eyckmans, Boers and Stengers, 2006; Stengers, 2007; Moreno Jaén, 2007).

In the operational definition of collocation that I put forward, however, defining characteristics of the frequency-based approach are combined with elements from the phraseological approach. This is because collocations need to be delineated from other frequent word combinations. Thus, Nesselhauf's (2003) criterion of 'arbitrary restriction on substitutability' was used to delimit collocations from free Verb + Noun combinations. She argues that the restriction that makes word combinations part of the idiomatic inventory of a language is non-semantic. In the word combination *tell the truth*, the verb *tell* cannot be substituted by its semantic cognate *say*. However, in my use of the principle of restricted substitutability, I have modified Nesselhauf's criterion by omitting the assumption that the restriction is arbitrary. Cognitive linguists have shown that the fact that certain synonyms are used in particular word combinations and others are not is linguistically motivated (Walker, 2008). In this study collocations are defined as frequently co-occurring Verb + Noun combinations that are different from free Verb + Noun combinations in that there is a restriction on the substitutability of their parts.

To my knowledge, five research projects to date have used computer corpora for the selection of test content when developing a test of collocation knowledge (Mochizuki, 2002; Barfield, 2006; Gyllstad, 2007; Eyckmans, Boers and Stengers, 2006; Eyckmans, Stengers and Boers, 2007a; Moreno Jaén, 2007). Of these, Eyckmans, Boers and Stengers (2006), Eyckmans, Stengers and Boers (2007a) and Moreno Jaén (2007) put a corpus-based approach into operation, whereas the other authors' sample selection could be called corpus-verified, that is, they used the corpora for checking the lexicometrics of the pre-selected collocations rather than sampling a set of collocations through corpus extraction.

In order to meet the criterion of content validity of the test, the following systematic procedure for collocation selection was used for the DISCO:

1. A total of 40 base verbs was selected from the General Service List (West, 1953), a set of 2000 words selected to be of the greatest 'general service' to learners of English.
2. With these verbs as search nodes, collocates were extracted from the British National Corpus on the basis of frequent co-occurrence for which z-scores were used. The co-occurrences of collocates with these verbs were selected within a default 3:3 span. This resulted in a list of the most frequent collocates of each verb for which the likelihood of co-occurrence was calculated. Only those Verb + Noun combinations whose z-score was higher than a threshold level of 3.0 were retained.
3. The outcome of this procedure was a set of Verb + Noun combinations that were not necessarily all idiomatic. In order to distinguish the true collocations from free word combinations, the criterion of restriction on substitutability was used (Nesselhauf, 2003).
4. A second corpus, the Collins COBUILD Bank of English (HarperCollins, 2007), served to enhance the content validity of the collocation selection (see also Moreno Jaén, 2007). Because corpora are best equipped for the retrieval of (semi)-fixed word strings, I used a query syntax to re-establish the joined frequency of the selected Verb + Noun combinations, for example, break@+1rule@, where the '@'-sign allows retrieval of all inflected forms of the lemmas 'break' and 'rule'. These joined frequency indications told me exactly how many times the particular form of a collocation (namely, the form in which it would be presented to the learners in the test) occurred in the Collins COBUILD Bank of English. Concordance lines were checked to ascertain the idiomatic use of the combinations. On the basis of their joined frequency, the set of collocations was divided into three frequency bands.
5. Native speakers were asked to run through the test in order to check the selected collocations and free word combinations.

A marked difference between the sampling procedure employed here and many others is that, although the collocations were originally extracted from the corpus using a word-centered approach, a true phraseological approach was used in the second phase where the absolute frequency of the phrase was used to assign it to one of three frequency bands regardless of the frequency of their constituent words. Since we are dealing with mental representations of chunks as wholes, I felt there was no point in selecting the collocations according to the frequency of the individual constituent words. Knowledge of the collocation is not per se a function of knowledge of the component parts. I find support for this logic in Nesselhauf's (2003) claim that Verb + Noun collocations can prove to be quite difficult for advanced learners, particularly when common delexical verbs such as 'take' and 'make' are concerned, that is, verbs that most learners are very familiar with.

Research questions

The main goal of this empirical study centers on the validation of the Discriminating Collocations Test. To this end, the development of receptive collocation knowledge of a group of advanced English language learners is traced in a longitudinal design in which the test will be used as a pre- and post-measure in a 60-hour instructional setting. The principal research questions are:

1. Is the Discriminating Collocations Test sufficiently sensitive to reflect the learners' progress? In other words: does the learners' ability to discriminate between idiomatic and non-idiomatic Verb + Noun combinations relate to their global language proficiency? Pre- and post-test scores will be compared to the learners' oral proficiency scores before and after the 60 hours of instruction.
2. Does the Discriminating Collocations Test have predictive validity with reference to the productive syntagmatic knowledge of the learners? In other words: does the ability to distinguish between idiomatic and non-idiomatic Verb + Noun collocations relate to learners' production of phrasal knowledge at large and can it therefore be used as a reliable replacement of the time-consuming phrase counts we used in previous experimental designs? Test scores will be compared to pre- and post-instruction phrase counts and learners' performance on rational cloze tests targeting syntagmatic knowledge.

Method

Participants

Participants were 25 students of modern languages, majoring in English, at the Erasmus University College in Brussels, Belgium. They were in the second year of their four-year translation and interpreting training, and their ages ranged between 19 and 22. Their proficiency in English was estimated to be of upper-intermediate level.

Procedure

The study involves a longitudinal design in which measures of English proficiency and of phrasal knowledge are used as pre- and post-tests in a 60-hour instructional setting. The data for this study were gathered in a general proficiency course covering the themes of popular psychology and socio-economic topics. The proficiency course was spread over an eight-month period. Besides working on the four skills, the teacher aimed at a maximum amount of authentic language exposure. This means that the course comprised a lot of reading and listening activities (estimated at about 60 per cent, compared to 40 per cent of speaking and writing tasks). The text types were written in educated journalistic style and the listening materials consisted of authentic radio and TV recordings. In order to enhance the students' bottom-up language learning processes, most of the classroom time was devoted to exposure to, and exploration of, authentic discourse. Learners' awareness of syntagmatic patterns in language was enhanced through noticing activities such as underlining multiword combinations in texts and filling in the keywords of phrases.

Materials

The participants' English proficiency was estimated before and after the 60 hours of instruction by means of a L1 to L2 re-tell task (henceforth called pre- and post-oral proficiency task). Participants were presented with a one-page Dutch text on the life of single men and women in society. After reading the text, they handed it back in, and received a list of English key words (not phrases) as a memory aid for reconstructing the content of the text in English.

The oral proficiency tasks were recorded, and these recordings (pre and post) were sent to three independent blind judges who were asked to listen to them and score them on the parameters of fluency, accuracy, and range of expression. These blind judges were experienced EFL teachers. They were given a descriptive scale of assessment based on the Common European Framework of Reference (Council of Europe, 2001) with scores that ranged from one to 15 for each parameter.

The participants' phrasal knowledge was assessed before and after the 60 hours of English proficiency instruction with the following tools:

Discriminating collocations test

The test format is based on a test of receptive vocabulary size – the Recognition Based Vocabulary Test (Eyckmans, 2004) – in which words and so-called pseudo-words are paired and learners are asked to discriminate between them. Using the same format with collocations seemed a logical next step. However, initial try-outs with the format revealed that the 50 per cent probability of getting the right answer (inherent in a paired format) resulted in ceiling effects, which seriously decreased the reliability of the test administrations. I therefore decided to turn the test into a multiple answer format. The test consists of 50 items that are each made up of two Verb + Noun combinations that are idiomatic in the target language (e.g. *seek advice, pay attention*) and a third Verb + Noun combination that is not idiomatic (e.g. **express charges*). Both idiomatic combinations of the item have to be ticked by the learners in order for them to obtain full marks for the item. The construct of receptive collocation knowledge as measured in this test is the ability to distinguish collocations from free word combinations in the English language. The test is computerized and does not allow the learner to tick only one out of three stimuli.[1]

Pilot test administrations with English language learners at intermediate level showed the test to be reliable (with Cronbach's alphas between .88 and .92, with the exception of some rather low alphas of .70 when homogeneous groups were involved). Item-total correlations were satisfactory (mean of .30) and indicative of the test's discriminatory power (Eyckmans, Boers and Stengers, 2006).

A 50-item computerized test consisting of idiomatic and non-idiomatic Verb + Noun combinations was administered. Items consisted of two Verb + Noun collocations of the same frequency band and one distractor.[2] The test contained 15 high frequency items, 15 medium frequency items and 20 low frequency items. The instruction was in Dutch (the participants' mother tongue) and read: *This test contains 50 items. Each item is made up of two idiomatic and one non-idiomatic Verb + Noun combinations in English. Tick both idiomatic Verb + Noun combinations to obtain full marks for each item* (author's translation).

Phrase counts

The recorded oral tasks (pre and post) were sent to three blind judges (different from the ones who scored the oral tasks for oral proficiency) who were asked to listen to the recordings and count the number of multiword combinations they considered to be 'phrases' in English. This is a procedure we had used in previous empirical studies (Boers et al., 2006; Eyckmans, 2007). The judges were EFL teachers who were familiar with the SLA literature on phraseology. They were also provided with guidelines concerning the identification of phrases in natural discourse (involving institutionalization, frequency of occurrence, fixedness, and non-compositionality).

Rational cloze

A 30-item Rational Cloze targeting multiword combinations was administered after the 60 hours of English proficiency instruction. The subject of the text corresponded to one of the general themes of the course (popular psychology).

Results

Oral proficiency (pre and post)

Because the measurement of oral proficiency is an intricate matter, a level of 'inter-subjectivity' was aimed for by weighing the scores awarded to the same students by different assessors. This inter-rater reliability was calculated for both the pre- and the post-Oral Proficiency Task by means of a Spearman Rank Coefficient for the parameters fluency, accuracy, and range of expression. Values ranged between .53 and .70 (p <.01). These values were considered fairly reassuring indications of the raters' agreement on their ranking of the participants' oral performances.

The assessors had been handed assessment sheets in order to warrant an acceptable level of intra-rater reliability as well. Their consistency in scoring was verified through Spearman Rank Correlations *between* the different parameters they had to score (fluency, range, and accuracy). These coefficients were significant (with p values <.01) and ranged between .81 and .88 for all raters. Since the inter- and intra-rater reliability had been verified, I decided that the most reliable indication of the participants' oral production would consist of the mean score of the three raters for each of the parameters. For simplicity's sake, I decided to compute one global oral proficiency score on the basis of the three parameters (fluency, accuracy, and range of expression).

A comparison of scores in the pre and post oral proficiency task was carried out using a mixed model repeated measures ANOVA with time as a 'within subject' factor. Including main effects only, the analysis revealed a significant effect of time on the participants' oral proficiency scores, F (1, 24) = 4.60, p <.05. With a mean of 8.7 in the pre-test (SD 2.4) and a mean of 9.9 (SD 2.0) after the 60 hours of instruction, the participants' oral production showed clear signs of progress.

Phrase production

It is self-evident that the number of multiword units produced by language users is highly dependent on the length of their speech production. A closer look at the digital recording showed that the length of the speeches varied strongly (from approximately 2 to 4.5 minutes). Instead of working with the raw phrase counts of the blind judges, I therefore decided to calculate the number of phrases per minute. The degree of inter-rater reliability between the three judges is reflected by Spearman Rank Correlation Coefficients from .51 to .85 (p <.01) in the pre-test and from .49 (p <.05) to .71 (p <.01) in the post-test. A mean of their counts was used for further analysis.

A repeated measures ANOVA revealed a significant difference in the mean number of phrases produced in the pre- and the post-tests, F (1,24) = 13.18, p <.001). With a mean of 8.35 phrases per minute (SD 2.81), the participants used significantly more multiword combinations after the 60 hours of instruction than before (mean of 6.43 phrases per minute, SD 2.24).

Spearman Rank Correlation Coefficients between the number of phrases produced per minute and the oral proficiency scores suggest that the use of multiword combinations can indeed play a part in students' coming across as more proficient speakers (r_s pre-test: .65, p <.01; r_s post-test: .69, p <.01).

Discriminating Collocations Test

Cronbach's Alpha reliability index for the pre-test came to .90, which is reassuring. However, when the participants took the test again at the end of the instructional treatment (eight months later), the alpha dropped to a mere .64. This difference in reliability estimates is most probably a reflection of the learners' progress in terms of collocation knowledge. Table 11.1 shows the obtained results on the Discriminating Collocations Test.

In order to fathom the effect of the frequency bands in the Discriminating Collocations Test, an analysis of variance was carried out with 'frequency band' as a 'between subject' factor. This analysis revealed a significant effect of this factor on the score distributions, F (2, 47) = 3.60, p <.05. A more detailed analysis of the contrast table shows the significance to be strongest between low-frequency and

Table 11.1 Results on the Discriminating Collocations Test (N=25)

	Pre-test	Post-test
M	29.80	36.08
SD	9.99	4.43
Range	36	22
Minimum score	6	26
Maximum score	42	48

high-frequency collocations, which is not surprising. This is indirect evidence of the content validity of the test and the way the collocation sampling was performed when developing the test. This has important implications when it comes to constructing test batteries for use with learners of different proficiency levels.

With a mean score of 36.08 (SD 4.43), the participants obtained higher scores after the instructional treatment than before (mean score of 29.8, SD 9.9). A repeated measures ANOVA shows this difference in scores to be significant, $F\,(1, 24) = 11.11, p = .003$). The small standard deviation in the post-test confirms the assumption that the participants formed a much more homogeneous group after the instruction, as a result of which the test does no longer discriminate sufficiently between the test takers. This is confirmed by the item-total correlations.

Rational cloze

The 30-item Rational Cloze obtained a Cronbach's Alpha reliability index of .75. With a mean of 12.33 (SD 4.42), the scores on the test were low, ranging from 6 to 22. In order to investigate the relation between the receptive collocation knowledge measured in the Discriminating Collocations Test and the productive phrasal knowledge targeted in the Rational Cloze, the Spearman Rank Correlation Coefficient between the scores was calculated. This rendered a moderate value of .45 (p <.05). This means that only 20% (r^2 = 19.98) of the variance between both measures was shared. The predictive value of the test results of one measure for the outcome of the other, in other words, is limited.

Discussion

On the basis of the results of this study, some preliminary answers to the research questions can be distilled. The scores obtained on the pre- and post-oral tasks indicate that the 60 hours of input-driven instruction benefited the learners' oral proficiency and their phrasal knowledge. Not only did the learners receive significantly higher oral proficiency scores after the treatment, they also produced significantly more phrases in the post-test than in the pre-test. The correlation coefficient between the oral proficiency scores and the phrase counts gives reason to assume that the learners' increased production of phrases led to a more idiomatic and fluent language output, which was rewarded by the judges who assessed the oral proficiency.

The design was set up to establish validation evidence for the Discriminating Collocations Test. One of the main research questions concerned the relationship between the learners' oral proficiency scores, on the one hand, and their ability to distinguish idiomatic from non-idiomatic Verb + Noun combinations, on the other. The test performed well in this respect. The test scores of the participants in the post-test are significantly higher than the scores they had obtained eight months earlier. It seems that more phrases (including collocations) are welded into learners' memories as a result of an increase in exposure. The test thus seems sufficiently sensitive to reflect the learners' phrasal progress. This can be interpreted as evidence for the claim that tests of collocation knowledge are powerful measures for evaluating progress in advanced students.

The Discriminating Collocations Test also seems to have predictive validity with reference to the productive syntagmatic knowledge of the learners, although the picture is slightly more muddled here. The learners' increased production of phrases after the 60 hours of instruction coincided with significantly higher scores on the Discriminating Collocations Test. This seems to suggest that the cognitive processes involved in taking the test – distinguishing salient Verb + Noun combinations from non-salient ones – relate to the learner's set of stored mental representations that are ready for productive use. However, this would need to be confirmed by a quantitative analysis of the phrases that were produced during the oral task. At this point no results can be presented as to the exact development of the learners' phrasal repertoires. Also, the correlation coefficient that was calculated between the test scores and the scores on a Rational Cloze Test targeting syntagmatic knowledge was unconvincing. However, I should also mention that, although correlational studies are the most commonly used design for investigating concurrent validation, the group of test takers in this longitudinal study is too small to be able to provide sufficient evidence. Correlations obtained with much larger populations should be gathered in order to shed light on the relation between the receptive and productive knowledge of phrases and/or collocations.

Conclusion

In this chapter I have set out to validate a receptive test for measuring learners' knowledge of Verb + Noun collocations. In discussing the development of the test, I argued the case for a corpus-based item selection because it holds more promise in terms of validity than a corpus-verified one. It is, however, much more difficult to put into operation because of the sometimes unwarranted optimism about the benefits and possibilities of corpus use for certain types of phrasal research (such as comparative research and test sampling). Checking all the concordance lines of generated collocation lists is such a time-consuming activity that one could begin to question the highly sung advantages of mega-corpora. Hopefully, natural language processing tools will undergo further development in the years to come so that future corpora will contain comprehensive linguistic annotation (semantic as well as syntactic) and word sense disambiguation. I have also argued against a solely word-centered approach in the extraction of collocates from corpora. Although psycholinguistic research (Schmitt, 2004; Wray, 2002) claims that L2 learners differ from native speakers in how they organize new vocabulary (first learning individual words and later blending them into phrases), test representative sampling requires the selection of those collocations that are used by native speakers in natural language settings.

The main goal of this empirical study centered on the validation of the Discriminating Collocations Test. To this end the development of receptive collocation knowledge of a group of advanced English language learners was traced in a longitudinal design in which the test was used as a pre- and post-measure in a 60-hour instructional setting. The test appeared sufficiently sensitive to capture the learners' progress. With a mean test taker time of under eight minutes, the test can be considered a user-friendly format for assessing language learners' receptive collocation knowledge.

Future research will be directed at a larger-scale validation with different test formats (among which the Rational Cloze and the Deleted Essentials Test: Eyckmans, Boers and Demecheleer, 2004) in which the patterns of correlation among different sets of scores will be analyzed through exploratory factor analysis. Hopefully, this will offer more insights into the extent to which knowledge of collocation may be indicative of phrasal competence in general and language proficiency at large. A second avenue concerns the investigation of learners' reaction times when taking the Discriminating Collocations Test. These reaction times could shed light on whether learners actually store chunks (and thus collocations) holistically in their mental lexicon, that is, as native speakers are believed to. Finally, a parallel test for Spanish as a foreign language has meanwhile been designed and piloted. One of the aims of that study is to investigate whether the corpora available allow for reliable collocation identification across languages.

This and other research in the field of collocation testing also contributes to language acquisition research in that it reveals the importance of enhancing learners' awareness of the idiomatic dimension of language. Efficient classroom instruction should involve a lot of exposure to authentic discourse and include the explicit targeting of phrases from low-frequency bands. This calls for new pathways for insightful teaching and learning of multiword lexis. Fortunately, these are now slowly becoming available (e.g. Boers and Lindstromberg, 2008; Lindstromberg and Boers, 2008).

Notes

1. We also piloted another format, in which collocations and pseudo-collocations were presented to learners in a list (resembling the well-known checklist format). Learners were asked to tick those word combinations they considered to be idiomatic in English. As was demonstrated for the Yes/No Vocabulary Test (Eyckmans, 2004), the results obtained with this format were skewed by a response bias. The test performance was influenced by test takers' inclination to over- or under-estimate their collocation knowledge, that is, attributes that are external to the construct we wished to measure.
2. The word combinations that serve as distractors in the test are not only non-idiomatic, but an investigation of their z-scores also showed them to have no significant co-occurrence in the corpus (e.g. **observe a limit*, z-score < 3). This means that the distractors are pseudo-collocations (or non-collocations) from a frequency-based perspective as well as from a phraseological perspective.

12

Designing and Evaluating Tests of Receptive Collocation Knowledge: *COLLEX* and *COLLMATCH*

Henrik Gyllstad

Introduction

Despite the fact that collocation knowledge has received increasing attention over the last decades as an important aspect of L2 proficiency (see, for example, Biskup, 1992; Bahns and Eldaw, 1993; Farghal and Obiedat, 1995; Howarth, 1996; Granger, 1998b; Schmitt, 1998; Gitsaki, 1999; Bonk, 2001; Mochizuki, 2002; Nesselhauf, 2005; Barfield, 2006; Revier and Henriksen, 2006; Keshavarz and Salimi, 2007), there is a conspicuous lack of properly validated tests capable of measuring this knowledge. It is unfortunately not uncommon for researchers to draw far-reaching conclusions without presenting any evidence of the validity or reliability of the test instruments used in their studies. In this chapter, I will report on the development and validation process of two test formats called COLLEX and COLLMATCH, both aimed at measuring receptive knowledge of English collocations.[1] First, I explain primary considerations and the rationale behind the tests. Secondly, I present a study in which over 300 learners sat the two tests in a large-scale administration. Finally, I briefly discuss the results of the study and address points for further research.

The test development process

Primary considerations

In the process of constructing any language test, there are a number of important steps to be taken along the way. McNamara (2000) compares the process of developing a test with that of a car manufacturer getting a new car on the road. The process of getting both products ready involves a design stage, a construction stage, and a try-out stage before the product is fully operational. However, a cyclic rather than a linear process characterizes the development of a test, in the sense that the use of the test produces evidence of its qualities.

Our first point of business when constructing a test is to define the 'construct' we intend to measure; the psychological term 'construct' is used to denote the mental ability that a test is intended to measure (see, for example, Chapelle, 1998; Alderson, Clapham and Wall, 1995; Bachman and Palmer, 1996). Bachman (1990) recognizes the need for a three-stage analysis in terms of linking a construct to an observed performance:

- the construct needs to be defined theoretically;
- the construct needs to be defined operationally;
- procedures must be established for the quantification of observations.

The theoretical definition is a specification of the relevant characteristics of the ability we intend to measure, and its distinction from other similar constructs. If there are several subcomponents to a construct, then the interrelations between these must be specified. The operational definition of the construct involves attempts to make the construct observable. To a great extent, the theoretical definition will govern what options will make themselves available. With respect to the third stage, our measurement should be quantified on a scale (nominal, ordinal, interval, or ratio; see Bachman, 2004). In the next section, I continue by discussing how I applied Bachman's three-step procedure to evaluating L2 collocation knowledge.

Collocation as a linguistic concept: The theoretical definition of the construct

It is not an exaggeration to say that 'collocation' has been defined with a high degree of heterogeneity in the research literature (see Fontenelle, 1998: 191; Stubbs, 2004: 107). However, it should be acknowledged that despite its definitional heterogeneity, 'collocation' was traditionally approached from two different angles in the literature of the second half of the twentieth century (see Chapter 1 of this volume). My own view of collocation essentially straddles the frequency-based and the phraseological traditions, in the sense that I broadly see collocations as frequently occurring word combinations realized in various syntactic patterns (see Gyllstad, 2007 for a detailed account). More specifically, in my own research, I have employed the working definition shown below as Figure 12.1. Thus, I see collocations as associative connections between word abstractions in the mental lexicons of language users, which in their textual instantiations are conventionalized word combinations consisting of:

two syntagmatically related and frequently co-occurring orthographic words, either adjacent or separated by a specified distance, where one of the words is used in a figurative, delexical, or technical sense, and where the meaning evoked by the combination as a whole, sometimes requiring additional lexical elements for grammatical wel-formedness and usage convention, is either compositional or non-compositional, and varies in its degree of opaqueness.

Figure 12.1 A working definition of 'collocation'

The notion of figurative, delexical, or technical senses follows Howarth (1996). As an example, consider the word sequence *say a prayer*. This sequence consists of two main elements. These elements are two syntagmatically related orthographic words: a Verb + an Object Noun. In addition, an indefinite article is present for sake of grammatical well-formedness. The verb *say* is used in a delexical sense, since it does not add much meaning to the phrase as a whole. In fact, the three-word sequence has a corresponding, stand-alone verb derivable from the noun component of the sequence: *pray*. This makes it possible to analyse *say a prayer* as a Support Verb Construction (SVC) (see Langer, 2005). The collocation in question is compositional, and transparent to a great extent. In contrast, a word sequence like *drink water* would not be considered a collocation since neither of the two elements is used in a figurative, delexical, or technical sense. Instead, the combinatorial potential of these two words is predictable from assigned thematic roles and selectional restrictions.

Arriving at an operational definition of the construct

Having decided on a working definition of collocation, the next step was to decide on how to define collocation *knowledge* operationally. Should I test receptive or productive knowledge? Although learners' production of collocations is indeed an intriguing field of study (see work by Revier and Eyckmans in this volume), I realized that a receptive test format would bring a number of positive effects. Firstly, it would be possible to test a larger number of items in each test session. Secondly, an objective scoring key could be produced for the test. The testing of receptive skills would also have the potential of being transferable to computerized test formats in a way that productive tests would not be to the same extent. For these reasons, I opted for testing receptive collocation knowledge. Based on the theoretical definition of collocation given in Figure 12.1,

I worked from the following definition of receptive collocation knowledge as a construct:

The knowledge necessary for appropriately recognizing that two or more words frequently occur together as conventionalized word combinations in a language, and accessing the meaning of these combinations to some degree.

Figure 12.2 A definition of the construct 'receptive collocation knowledge'

I needed next to determine whether the test task should involve 'recognition' or 'recall' processes. This distinction refers to two different types of cognitive processes on the part of the language user. In a 'recall' process, the form or the meaning of a word is retrieved and supplied when triggered by some sort of prompt stimulus, whereas in a 'recognition' process the form or meaning of a word is recognized from a set of options (Laufer and Goldstein, 2004). A further question was whether I should make use of translation between L1 and L2. The test was intended to be used primarily with Swedish-speaking learners of English, and it would therefore be conceivable to involve both Swedish and English in the test task. Nation (2001) addresses the fact that the use of first language translations in vocabulary tests is often frowned upon, but without a convincing argumentation. As for my test, at some stage of the test development and validation process, I intended to use native speakers of English as a control group. Using explicit translation as part of the task would make this impossible, or at least difficult. In the sense that only words and structures in English would be used, a monolingual task seemed best. I was then left with a receptive recognition task where test takers are presented with items in which they are instructed to choose an existing L2 form from a set of options.

In order to be able to test a large number of items, I chose to use decontextualized items. Certainly, providing some sort of linguistic context around targeted test items makes any task more natural and authentic. However, as pointed out by Cameron (2002), it is reasonable to assume that learners presented with decontextualized test items do not make sense of the tested items in a decontextualized mental void. Rather, she claims, the recognition process may activate recall of previous encounters and their contexts. Also, it is arguable that the more context one adds to a test item, the more the question of what one is really measuring rears its head. More context means that reading comprehension and inferencing skills come into play, and this may lead to what Messick (1995: 742) refers to as 'construct-irrelevant difficulty'.

In terms of collocation types, I needed to concentrate on one type – or at most two – of collocation, since this would make score and test interpretation easier. The more types of structures are brought into a measurement, the more difficult it is to define what it is being measured. Consequently, I decided to primarily concentrate on Verb + Noun Phrase (NP) combinations. This type of combination was chosen first of all because of its frequent occurrence in language (Howarth, 1996; Nesselhauf, 2005; Siepmann, 2005). Moreover, these combinations are reported to be notoriously difficult for learners (Biskup, 1992; Bahns and Eldaw, 1993). Furthermore, Altenberg (1993: 227) claims that they 'tend to form the communicative core of utterances where the most important information is placed'.

Test formats

I decided to construct two test formats. Although this would entail a more cumbersome test development process, it also brought with it a number of advantages. Since very few collocation tests existed, let alone any well-validated ones, having two tests meant that one could be used to find validity support for the other, for example through concurrent validity analyses. Also, if one format did not work as desired, there would still be a chance that the other one would hold promise.

The first format is called COLLEX (collocating lexis). It is a forced-choice format, inspired by a vocabulary size test of single words suggested by Eyckmans (2004). A COLLEX item consists of three word sequences – Verb + NP combinations – juxtaposed horizontally. In each item, there is a frequent and conventionalized English lexical collocation (= 'target collocation') together with two combinations, which are not frequent or conventionalized and which function as distractors (= 'pseudo-collocations'). An example COLLEX item can be seen in Figure 12.3.

The test format works by asking test takers to tick which one of the three word sequences they think is the most common one, and one that would be used by native speakers of English. The underlying assumption of the test format is that one of the three choices is a frequently used, conventionalized word combination in English. Thus, this is a combination that the test takers might have encountered in their

			a	b	c
a. drive a business	b. run a business	c. lead a business	☐	☐	☐

Figure 12.3 An example of a COLLEX item

exposure to the English language. The other word combinations – the pseudo-collocations – are not frequently used or conventionalized word combinations in English, and it is therefore unlikely that the test takers would have been exposed to them in their language input. A straightforward scoring method is used by awarding 1 point for correct choices and 0 points for wrong choices.

The second test format is called COLLMATCH (collocate matching). It was initially a grid format, hence the name, but owing to a number of drawbacks identified during initial trial administrations (see Gyllstad, 2007), I eventually decided to use a more traditional Yes/No format (see Meara and Buxton, 1987; Zimmerman et al., 1977; Anderson and Freebody, 1983). An example of two COLLMATCH items is presented as Figure 12.4.

For each item, informants are asked to decide whether they think the presented sequence is a collocation or not, or rather, if the sequence is a frequently occurring word combination in English or not. The technical term 'collocation' was avoided in the test instructions since it is not a well-known concept to all learners. Just as in COLLEX, informants are rewarded not only for their ability to recognize collocations but also for rejecting pseudo-collocations, but in a slightly different way. In the example, a 'yes' should be chosen for the leftmost item, and a 'no' for the item to the right. In terms of scoring, 1 point is awarded for correct recognitions of collocations and correct rejections of pseudo-collocations, and 0 points are awarded for missed recognitions of collocations and lack of rejections for pseudo-collocations.

The item selection methods used in the different versions of COLLEX and COLLMATCH merits attention. Principally, the item selection was based on a word knowledge framework (Nation, 2001). This is a word-centred approach, as opposed to a more holistic approach (cf. Revier and Eyckmans, this volume), in that single words are used as a point of departure. The underlying assumption is that collocation

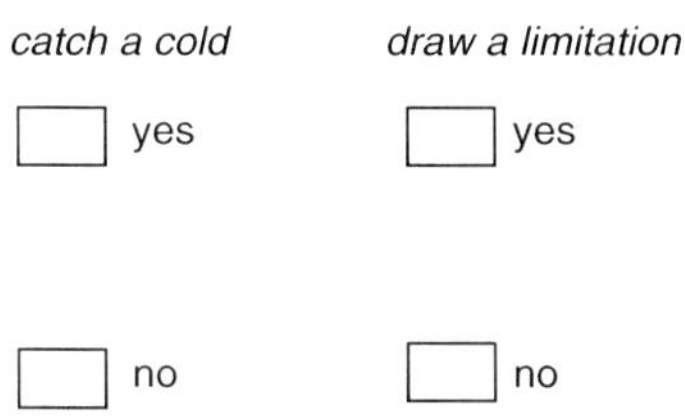

Figure 12.4 Example items from the COLLMATCH test format

knowledge can be measured as a property of single words, that is, that collocation knowledge is based on knowledge of single words in a language, and that these words in turn may be combined with certain other words in that language. For example, in natural language, the delexicalized, high-frequency verb *make* collocates with a large number of object nouns. By sampling some of these object nouns for a test, and asking informants if they recognize the combination of the Verb + NP, I assumed that I could probe the knowledge that those informants have about the combinatory potential of the selected words. By trying to restrict item selection to higher-frequency words that the informants were expected to know minimally in terms of a basic form–meaning mapping, I furthermore assumed that informants' collocational knowledge of these words could be mapped out.

A large-scale test administration of COLLEX and COLLMATCH

Purpose

Previous test administrations prior to the one reported here had shown that COLLEX and COLLMATCH on the whole were reliable and valid measures of receptive collocation knowledge. However, after these early trials, I had introduced a number of modifications that had not been tested with a large population. Therefore, I felt that a large-scale test administration was necessary in order to investigate score reliability and validity more fully for the new test versions. I thought it particularly important to gather validation data from a sizeable group of native speakers of English, since the previous studies had only made use of very small numbers of such informants. Consequently, I will report here on a study in which a total of 307 informants, including both learners of English in Sweden at different levels of study and native speakers of English, were subjected to a test battery consisting of a 50-item COLLEX, a 100-item COLLMATCH, and a 150-item Vocabulary Levels Test (Nation, 2001), in a modified version. The latter was used to be able to compare informants' vocabulary size with their receptive collocation knowledge, and to serve as an indicator of general proficiency level (see Meara and Buxton, 1987; Meara and Jones, 1988).

Item selection

In terms of item selection for COLLEX, care was taken to choose high-frequency words making up the word combinations. This meant using words from the ≤ 5K band. In checking the frequencies of the individual words, the JACET 8000 (Ishikawa et al., 2003) word list, based on the British National Corpus (BNC; Oxford University, 2005), was used. Furthermore, z-scores were checked to ensure that the conventionalized collocations are commonly used and that the distractors are not in frequent use as evidenced through the BNC.

Test items for COLLMATCH were selected in the following way. Verbs from the first 4,000 words of English (1–4K), according to the JACET 8000 list (Ishikawa et al., 2003), were analysed in terms of their noun collocates. Together with two experienced senior lecturers of English, I chose the candidate items. My aim was to use unique words in all items so that a word did not occur twice in the set of test items. In total, 200 words were selected for inclusion in the test. The process resulted in a list of 70 target collocations together with 30 pseudo-collocations. As with COLLEX items, z-scores were retrieved from the BNC to ensure significance for the target collocations and, conversely, lack of significance for the pseudo-collocations.

The test battery also included a vocabulary size measure. The measure used was the Vocabulary Levels Test (VLT) (Nation, 2001) featured in a modified version, here called version VLT M. The 2K band was taken out, and instead more items were added at the 5K and 10K bands. The modified version contained items from VLT version A, published in Schmitt (2000), and also items from VLT version B, published in Nation (2001). The number of items in the modified test was 150 as shown below.

3K	30 items
ACADEMIC	30 items
5K	45 items
10K	45 items
Total	150 items

Research questions

The study was designed to address the following three research questions:

1. Do COLLEX and COLLMATCH produce reliable test scores in terms of internal consistency, and do the test items have a satisfactory discriminatory power?

   In order to answer this question, Classical Test Theory (CTT) reliability values in the form of Cronbach's alpha internal consistency were computed. Furthermore, item facility values and item-total correlation values were calculated to find evidence for the discriminatory power of the test items.

2. Can COLLEX and COLLMATCH discriminate between native speakers of English and Swedish university-level learners of English, and between Swedish learners at different learning levels?

   A test's power to discriminate between groups of individuals at different ability levels is closely connected to the validity of the test. This can be empirically tested through 'a non-equivalent groups design' (Bachman, 2004: 290) based on the division of informants into different *a priori* ability groups. In the present study, the formation of the groups was organized according to level of study as the criterion for Swedish students of English, and for the native speakers of English by virtue of their being native speakers of English and students at university level in Britain. The native speakers were hypothesized to have the highest ability in the measured construct, followed in turn by the highest-level Swedish students. In order to evaluate potential differences, analyses of variances (ANOVAs) were completed.
3. What is the relation between vocabulary size and scores on COLLEX and COLLMATCH?

   It has been suggested that learners with large vocabularies are more proficient in a wide range of language skills than learners with smaller vocabularies (Meara, 1996). This makes it reasonable to assume that this is the case also for collocation knowledge. However, until empirical support is presented, assumptions like these must be treated with caution. In order to evaluate the relationship between the variables, correlation analyses were conducted.

Subjects

The total number of learners taking the test battery was 307. The largest group consisted of Swedish university students of English. Most of them were first-term students (n=163), but sizeable groups of second (n=49) as well as third-term (n=35) students also took the test. The second largest group were native speakers of English (n=34). These individuals were all students of Applied Linguistics at a university in Wales. The third group of learners who took part in the study were upper-secondary school students (n=26) who at the time of testing were in the eleventh grade at a local school in Sweden.

Results

As a first step, descriptive results for all three tests were computed for all 307 test takers. Table 12.1 shows the score distributions on the tests, and Figures 12.5, 12.6, and 12.7 display the frequency distributions. The mean

Table 12.1 Score distributions and test characteristics of VLT M, COLLEX and COLLMATCH for all informants combined (N=307)

Value	VLT M	COLLEX	COLLMATCH
k	150	50	100
MPS	150	50	100
Mean	127.1	41.4	78.0
SD	18.6	6.8	11.1
Range	90	28	48
Minimum	60	22	51
Maximum	150	50	99
Skewness	–.99	–.80	–.06
Kurtosis	.66	–.09	–1.0
Cronbach's α	.96	.89	.89
Mean Item Facility	.85	.83	.78
Mean Item-Total Correlation	.35	.34	.26

k = Number of test items
MPS = Maximum Possible Score

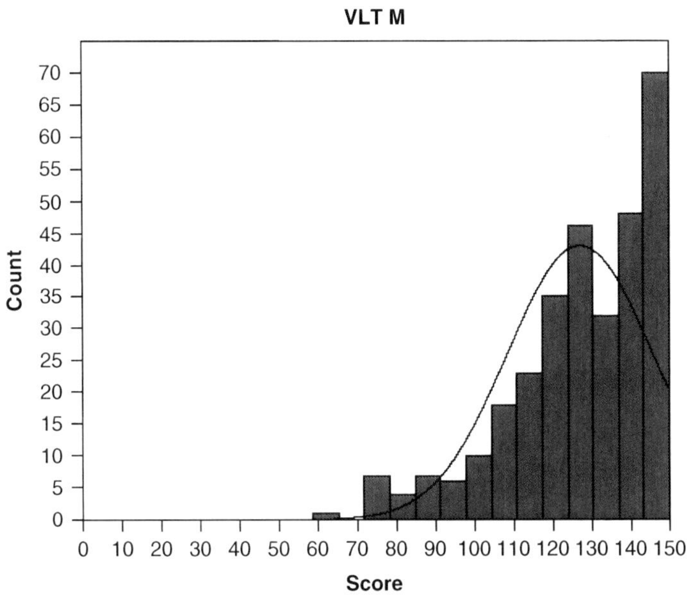

Figure 12.5 Frequency distribution of scores on VLT M (N=307)

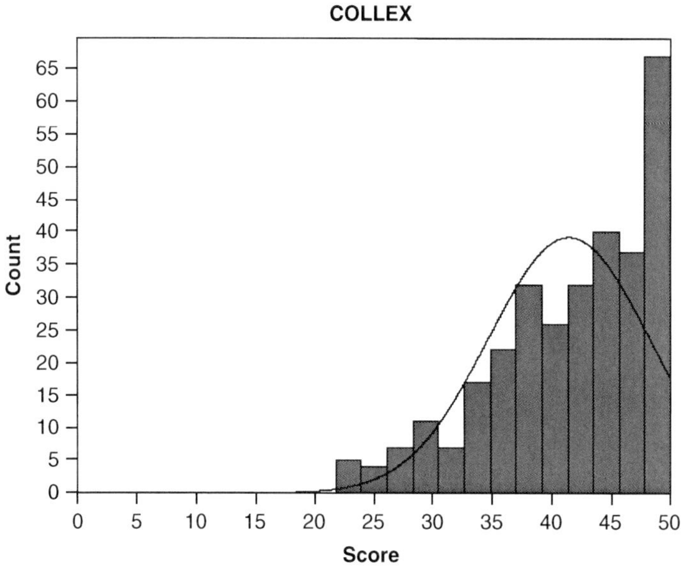

Figure 12.6 Frequency distribution of scores on COLLEX 5 (*N*=307)

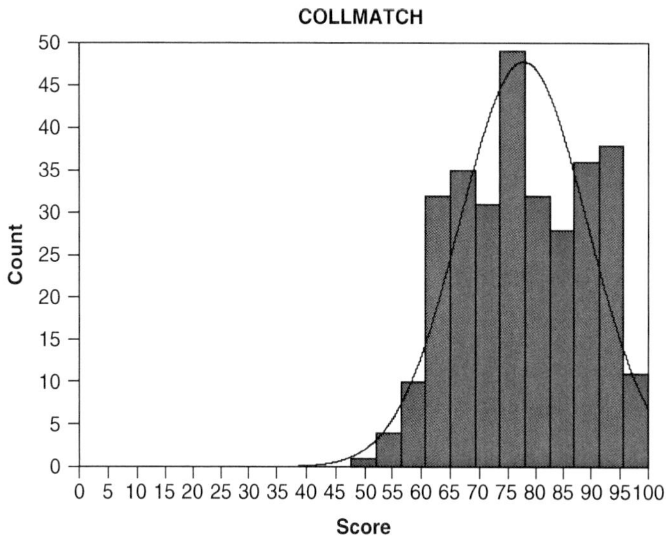

Figure 12.7 Frequency distribution of scores on COLLMATCH 3 (*N*=307)

scores were high on all three tests. This was more or less expected since a great majority of the test takers were university students of English, and the fact that the data for 34 native speakers were included.

On the whole, the values for skewness and kurtosis indicate normality in terms of score distribution (± 2, see Bachman, 2004), even though the distributions on all three tests are more or less negatively skewed, as indicated by the high bars to the right, near maximum score end of the histograms. The scores on VLT M, COLLEX and COLLMATCH were all reliable in terms of internal consistency, with Cronbach's alpha values between .89 and .96.

Reliability estimates at .9 or above are benchmarked as 'excellent' (DeVellis, 1991: 85).

The mean Item Facility values for COLLEX and COLLMATCH were observed at .83, and .78, respectively. These values are fairly high, but the inclusion of the native speaker group must be taken into account. The mean item-total correlation values for COLLEX and COLLMATCH were observed at .34 and .26, respectively. The value for COLLEX is respectable, but the value for COLLMATCH is slightly lower than expected. A separate, follow-up analysis of intended target collocations and pseudo-collocations in COLLMATCH was made. This analysis showed that the former item category, consisting of 70 items, displayed a mean item-total correlation value of .27, whereas the latter item category, consisting of 30 items, displayed a mean item-total correlation value of .22. This means that the target collocations discriminated slightly more effectively between high-scoring and low-scoring informants, respectively, in terms of collocation recognition, than did the pseudo-collocation items.

As a second step, I carried out comparisons of subgroups. Based on the original data presented above, data from a total of 269 informants were singled out for further analyses: all informants who indicated that their L1 was not Swedish were removed from the data set. I did this because I wanted to see how L1 Swedish students performed on the tests, in comparison with a designated group of native speakers of English. As can be seen in Table 12.2, the 139 Swedish first-term students were divided into four subgroups, called SWEuni1A to SWEuni1D. This was done to facilitate subsequent inferential statistic analyses where equal or close to equal group sizes are preferable. The informants were randomly assigned to one of the four subgroups. The Swedish upper-secondary school 11th graders were called SWE 11, the Swedish second-term university students of English were called SWEuni2, the third-term university students of English were called SWEuni3, and, finally, the native speakers of English at university level were called ENGuniNS.

In Figure 12.8, the mean scores for the respective groups are presented in the bars, with standard deviations shown within parentheses.

The overall reliability stayed on the same level as observed with the larger number of informants, viz .89 for both tests. Furthermore, as can be seen in the table, there is a clear progression in scores. Starting with COLLEX, the lowest mean score was observed for the 11th graders, at 28.9. The four first-term groups scored higher but slightly different means, ranging from 40.3 to 41.9. The second-term students scored a mean of 42.5, and the third-term students scored a mean of 45.9. The native speakers, finally, scored a mean of 48.9.

Table 12.2 Mean Item Facility values for items in COLLEX and COLLMATCH by groups

Group	SWE11 (*n*=26)	SWEuni1 (*n*=139)	SWEuni2 (*n*=39)	SWEuni3 (*n*=31)	ENGuniNS (*n*=34)	All SWE groups combined (*n*=235)
COLLEX Mean IF	.58	.82	.85	.92	.98	.81
COLLMATCH Mean IF	.63	.76	.79	.85	.93	.77

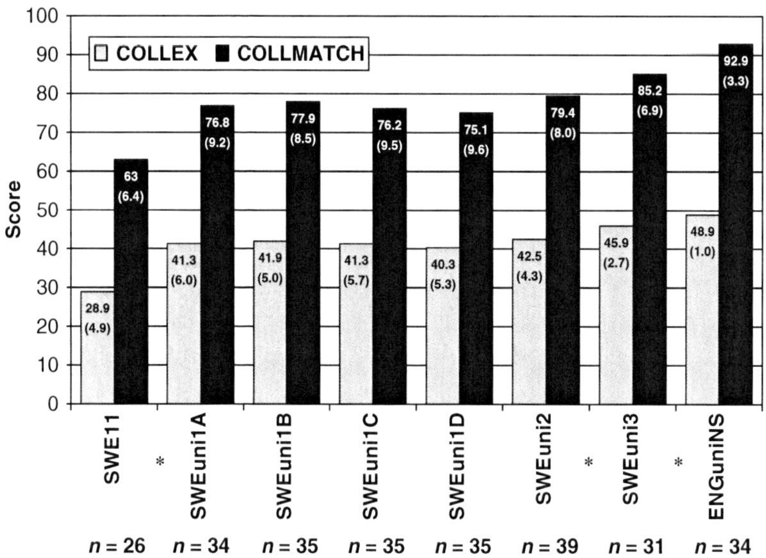

Figure 12.8 Results on COLLEX (k=50, reliability α=.89) and COLLMATCH (k=100, reliability α=.89) by groups

In order to investigate the potential presence of a group effect, I employed a Welch test. The Welch test was used rather than an ANOVA since unequal group sizes existed. More importantly, unequal variance was observed across the groups. The Welch test signalled a significant effect of student group affiliation on test scores, F (7, 102.38) = 96.64, p <.001. A Games-Howell post-hoc test showed that differences between means were significant, except for the differences between any of the four first-term university groups, and the second-term university group. These differences are indicated through asterisks in Figure 12.8. The results for COLLMATCH reflect those for COLLEX. There is a clear progression visible in the COLLMATCH scores. Mean scores increase across study levels, and native speakers scored the highest mean.

A comparison of the eight group means revealed that a group effect existed. A Welch F test indicated significant differences between means, F (7, 107.98) = 86.72, p <.001. In order to find out where these differences lay, I conducted a Games-Howell post-hoc test. The exact same pattern as was found for the COLLEX means was found also for the COLLMATCH means: all means were different from each other except any of the four first-term student means, and the second-term student mean.

When it comes to Item Facility (IF) values, these were computed for the 269 informants and observed at .78 and .83, respectively for COLLEX and COLLMATCH. An analysis of the different subgroups, where the values for the first-term university students were collapsed into one, gave the results shown in Table 12.2.

As expected, the Item Facility means increase by virtue of study level for the Swedish informants, and for the native speakers the value is close to maximum. The very high IF values for the native speakers are positive from a validation point of view.

In order to address Research Question 3, whether there is a relation between vocabulary size and scores on COLLEX and COLLMATCH, a number of correlation analyses were carried out. As a first step, scatterplots were retrieved for the relations between the three variables: VLT M scores, COLLEX scores, and COLLMATCH scores. The scatterplots are shown as Figures 12.9, 12.10, and 12.11 and are based on all groups combined (n=269).

The three scatterplots foreshadow high positive correlations between the variables at hand. They also clearly show the negative skewness of the scores. As a second step, a Pearson Product Moment test was used in order to arrive at correlation coefficients. The obtained correlations are shown in Table 12.3.

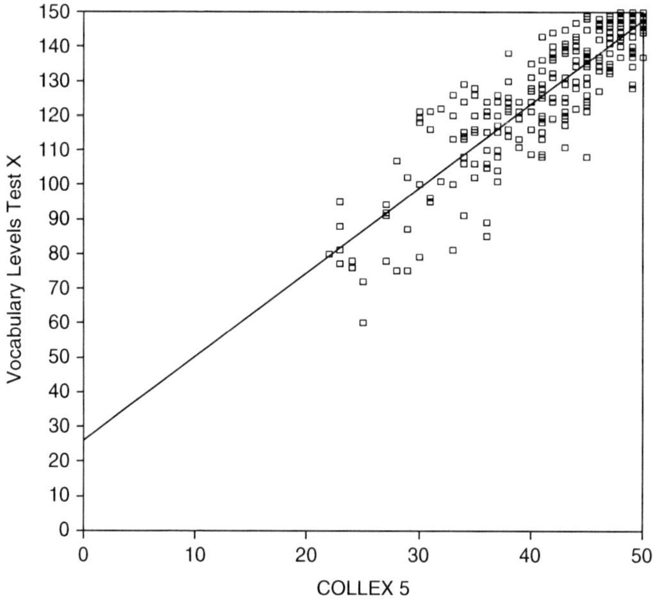

Figure 12.9 Scatterplot of VLT scores against COLLEX scores (n=269)

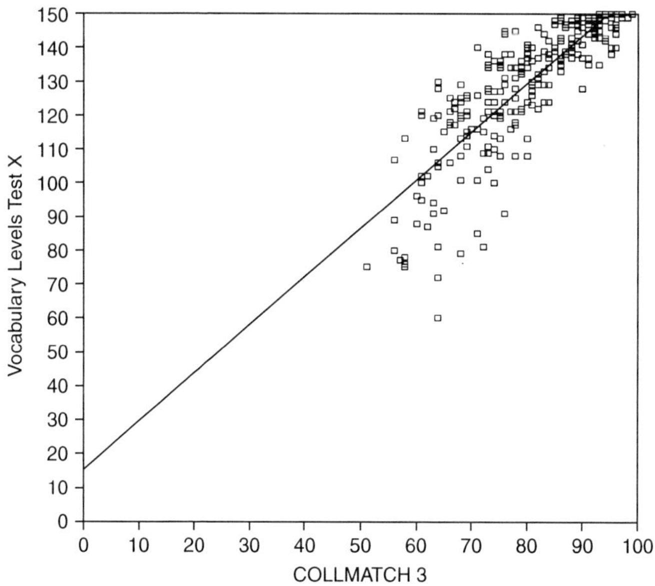

Figure 12.10 Scatterplot of VLT scores against COLLMATCH scores (n=269)

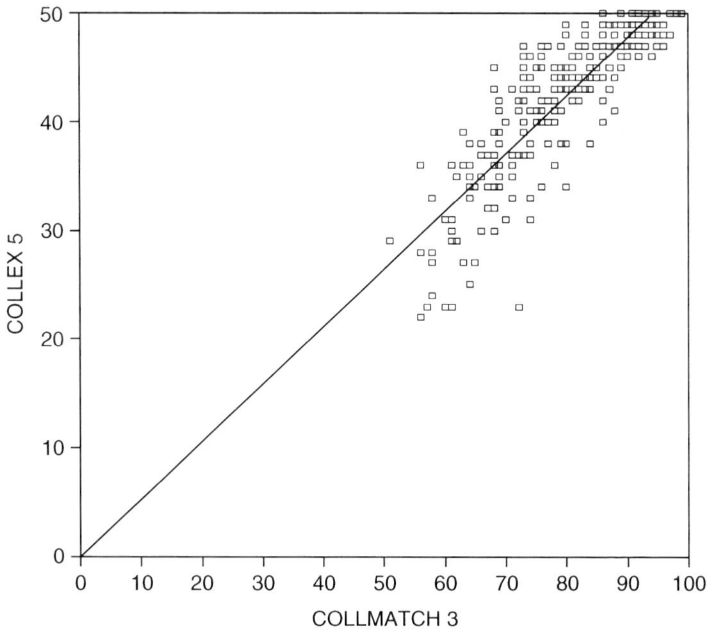

Figure 12.11 Scatterplot of COLLEX scores against COLLMATCH scores (*n*=269)

Table 12.3 Correlations (*r*) between scores on VLT M, COLLEX and COLLMATCH (*n*=269)

Test	VLT M	COLLEX	COLLMATCH
VLT M	—	.88*	.83*
COLLEX	—	—	.86*

* Correlation is significant at p < .01, one-tailed.

As was predicted through the scatterplot visualizations, the test signalled high, positive correlations between all three variables. These indicate that a large receptive vocabulary is beneficial when it comes to recognizing frequent and conventionalized word combinations, that is, collocations, also when word frequencies are controlled for. This raises a number of interesting questions. For example, two widely recognized dimensions of lexical knowledge are 'vocabulary breadth' (also called vocabulary size) and 'vocabulary depth' (see Anderson and Freebody, 1981; Read, 2004). Furthermore, most researchers seem to agree that knowledge of collocation resides in the depth dimension. The results from COLLEX and COLLMATCH could therefore be taken as support of the close relation between the two. However, another way to interpret the findings would be to argue that COLLEX and COLLMATCH are tests of collocation size, that is, a measure of the number of collocations for which a person can recognize the form and assign a basic meaning. Further research on the two tests will need to address these issues.

Concluding remarks

Reliably measured scores are a necessary condition for a valid test. The results of the reported study have shown that the two collocation tests – COLLEX and COLLMATCH – yield reliable scores in terms of internal consistency. However, reliability estimates within Classical Test Theory harbour an unfortunate constraint: the values are intimately linked to the scores produced by the sample of informants on which the tests were trialled. Thus, informant characteristics and test characteristics cannot be separated. A model that does separate between these characteristics is the Item Response model, found within Item Response Theory (IRT; see, for example, Bachman, 2004). A further desirable step in the development of the two tests would be to conduct reliability analyses within the IRT framework (see Barfield, 2009 for an example application).

The validity of COLLEX and COLLMATCH was empirically investigated through a non-equivalent groups design. The results showed that the two tests have an acceptable discriminatory power. However, not all differences between learner groups were statistically significant. It is a moot point whether this stems from the fact that the groups do not come from different populations or whether the tests are not sensitive enough to pick up on existing differences. It could also be the case that collocation knowledge as measured in this study does not develop in a significant way over a period of just six months, which constitutes the difference between the the learning level of each group.

On a final note, I would like to comment on the item selection and its relation to content validity. The item selection method used in the two tests was essentially a word-centred approach, where single words were used as a point of departure. A restriction of this approach is that scores cannot be straightforwardly extrapolated into scores for the target domain, that is, the universe of English collocations consisting of high-frequency Verb + NP combinations. An alternative approach would entail creating a frequency list of all Verb + NP combinations, for example in the 100-million word BNC corpus, and then using a stratified random sampling technique for selecting test items. The advantage of such an approach would be its desirable measurement characteristics. However, it would in all likelihood presuppose a manual analysis of all the word combinations on the frequency list, so that, for example, pure idioms and free combinations could be discarded. This would be an extremely laborious task to undertake. In the absence of such random sampling, then, we are inevitably left with a certain degree of intuition in the development process. This is not necessarily a bad thing, as I hope this chapter has shown.

Note

1. The full research project upon which this chapter is based can be found in Gyllstad (2007).

Acknowledgement

My thanks go to Andy Barfield and Elke Peters for their feedback on earlier drafts of this chapter.

13
Commentary on Part III: Developing and Validating Tests of L2 Collocation Knowledge

John Shillaw

Introduction

The studies in Part III show how the three authors approached the task of developing tests of L2 collocation knowledge. Revier, Eyckmans and Gyllstad face two tasks: firstly, to define and operationalize the construct of collocation, and secondly to demonstrate that the tests actually measure collocational knowledge. However, what may appear to be simple in principle turns out, as the three studies demonstrate, to be very complex in practice. My own experience of validating vocabulary size tests (Shillaw, 1999) taught me how daunting and frustrating it can be working on the development of new lexical measures. The amount of detail and the complexity of the data and analyses can sometimes blur the essentials in a study. In the first section of this commentary I have elected to summarize the three studies. By picking up on some of the central issues in the research, I hope to highlight similarities or differences in the three authors' views about, or approaches to, the testing of L2 collocational knowledge. Then, in the next section, I take a more critical look at some of the issues, particularly those which relate to the validity and reliability of the tests. I end by presenting observations and suggestions for ways that future research might be enhanced.

A summary of the three studies

Construct issues

The issue of transparency is at the heart of Revier's study, and, through the use of semantic criteria, he proposes three classes of collocation, which he defines according to varying degrees of semantic transparency. Significantly, he believes that an awareness and knowledge of the different types of collocation are as psychologically real for EFL learners as they are for native speakers of English – and that this hypothesis can be tested. Revier's primary research goal is to explore the relationship between learners' productive knowledge of collocations and transparency of meaning.

Eyckmans' study is the only one of the three that tries to measure the extent to which L2 collocational competence develops over time. Eyckmans explains that research she and colleagues have been doing into phrasal knowledge and oral production has involved using oral tests that are accurate but time-consuming to administer and score. Her hope is that the Discriminating Collocations Test (DISCO), an easy-to-administer, computer-based test, might prove to be as valid and reliable as the current tests.

Gyllstad's study concentrates some of the crucial issues that researchers face in developing valid and reliable tests of L2 collocational knowledge. As part of the construction and validation of two new tests of English collocation knowledge, Gyllstad sets out to compare the performance of Swedish-speaking learners with native English-speaking students of about the same age. In addition, he also explores the relationship between knowledge of collocations and vocabulary size.

The collocation tests

There are two basic differences in the format of the tests used in the three studies. The first is that Eyckmans and Gyllstad use receptive tests to measure knowledge of verb–object noun collocations, while Revier claims that his CONTRIX test measures productive knowledge of the same type of collocation. The second difference is with the criterion tests that the researchers employ as an integral part of the validation process of the collocation tests. Gyllstad's is interested in the relationship between collocation knowledge and vocabulary size, and so he compares scores from a version of Nation's Levels Test with scores from COLLEX and COLLMATCH. Eyckmans elects to use a test of oral summary skills as the main criterion measure, but she also adds a rational cloze passage as an alternative measure of productive knowledge. Revier does not actually use a criterion test, although he could have chosen to compare the scores from CONTRIX with scores from a vocabulary test that was taken by all of his subjects.

All three researchers use BNC data in their selection of test items, but in different ways. In Revier's study, he begins by selecting possible Verb + Noun combinations directly from the corpus and then narrows the selection to include only those nouns that are of relatively high frequency in the BNC and which meet the semantic criteria related to transparency. The categorization of each Verb + Noun pattern into transparent, semi-transparent or non-transparent is done with the aid of a dictionary, but Revier confesses he has difficulty deciding on the category of some collocations. It is logical to assume that if the test-maker has a problem categorizing some Verb + Noun combinations, then EFL learners are bound to face the same problem. What does this imply about the psychological reality of collocation recognition that Revier believes is shared by native speakers and learners?

Gyllstad and Eyckmans adopted similar approaches to selecting or creating collocation test items in that they both started by choosing candidate words from word lists. The items that Gyllstad selected, both genuine collocations and pseudo-collocations, were checked against the BNC to ensure that their occurrence in the corpus was significant and non-significant respectively. Eyckmans selected her base verbs from the General Service List and then, like Gyllstad, used the BNC to choose Verb + Noun collocations with a high potential of occurrence. She next verified her selection against the Collins COBUILD corpus, calculated the frequency of the collocates in the corpus, and divided them into three bands. Unfortunately, since Eyckmans does not explain the criteria she used to determine the bands, the issue of frequency is rather open to question.

Revier claims CONTRIX is a test of productive skill because learners have to apply syntagmatic and semantic knowledge to complete the sentences that contextualize the target collocation. In contrast, Eyckmans' DISCO and Gyllstad's COLLEX and COLLMATCH seem to test receptive L2 collocations knowledge. The format of DISCO and COLLEX is virtually the same. There are two important differences, however. Firstly, DISCO is made up of 2-word Verb + Noun collocations (e.g. *pay attention*) and requires test-takers to identify the one combination that is <u>not</u> idiomatic in English against two that are conventional collocations. COLLEX, on the other hand, presents a choice of three 3-word combinations, and test-takers must identify the combination that is idiomatic against two that are pseudo-collocations. COLLMATCH uses the well-established checklist format very much like the Yes/No tests developed by Paul Meara and others (Meara and Buxton, 1987; Meara and Jones, 1988).

Test results and validation issues

Before looking at the results of the three studies, it might be useful to consider what evidential support we are looking for to validate the collocation tests, indeed any test. Perhaps the most important thing in this type of research is to establish proof of construct validity, that is, whether the construct is sound (Messick, 1993). Experience suggests that there are a number of methods to do this. Perhaps the most common is to compare scores from the target test with a criterion test (a test of the same or very similar skill), the assumption being that a high and significant correlation coefficient is evidence of construct validity. Eyckmans does this explicitly by comparing scores from DISCO with her speaking and cloze tests. Gyllstad also does this by comparing scores from COLLEX and COLLMATCH. Revier, however, takes a different approach to construct validation. He argues that subjects of different ages will score differentially on CONTRIX because the years of learning English will be reflected in their lexical and collocation knowledge. If this turns out to be the case, then this might be taken as proof that the test is valid.

As well as being valid, a test should also be reliable. The usual way to determine this reliability of a test is through the use of a statistical procedure, such as Cronbach alpha. A detailed analysis of the items themselves is also helpful in determining how well suited an item is to the test and test population, and can suggest how a test can be improved. The issue of reliability is an integral part of the three studies, and item function is one element in the data presented by Revier and Gyllstad.

With an alpha of 0.89, CONTRIX appears to be to be a very reliable test. The analysis of the mean scores of each group on the three subtests shows, firstly, that as Revier anticipated, the scores for all groups decrease as the transparency of a collocation becomes less transparent. ANOVA and post-hoc tests demonstrate the aggregate score differences to be significantly different between the university students and both school grades, but the difference between the 10th and 11th graders is not. Secondly, the results show that the mean score for each subtest increases in line with the number of years spent learning English. The aggregate scores are significant, but the differences within each group are not significant for four of the nine observations.

CONTRIX has very high reliability, but reliability is a measure of the precision of the test instrument, not its accuracy, which is the domain of construct validity. In respect of the test validation, the results of comparing the collocation knowledge of the three groups, especially when using aggregate scores, suggest that there is some merit in Revier's claims that CONTRIX is a valid measure. However, the lack of significant differences on some scores on the subtests suggests that learners' ability to recognize the semantic properties of collocations is not consistent. There also appears to be little to directly support the argument that learners are aware of the psychological reality of collocations. It may be true, as Revier suggests, that lack of significance may reflect stages in the development of knowledge, but with so few subjects such a conclusion may be premature.

Gyllstad has three research questions: Are COLLEX and COLLMATCH reliable tests? Are they valid measures? How do scores from the two tests relate to vocabulary size? Item analysis reveals that COLLEX and COLLMATCH have very high Cronbach alpha coefficients (.89), so both would appear to be reliable. However, the test items are relatively easy for all groups, except the 11th grade students, and this, as well as the lack of significant differences between the more proficient students, suggests that some of the items do not discriminate too well. Gyllstad suggests that this may be because the groups are fundamentally from the same population, or that the tests are not sensitive enough to measure the differences. It is particularly surprising that the mean score from the native English speaker group is only a little higher than the mean score of the third-term university group when one would normally expect a test of collocational knowledge to reveal major differences between native English speakers and a group of EFL learners, no matter how advanced their L2 proficiency is. The fact that the gap is so narrow suggests that the tests are not yet sensitive enough to identify where the differences are between the groups.

If we next consider the results of the correlation analyses, we observe that COLLEX and COLLMATCH have a coefficient of .86, which is high and significant. One might argue that this is fairly strong evidence to show the tests are measuring a similar trait. However, if we go on to examine the relationship between the two tests and the Vocabulary Levels Test, it turns out that the correlation coefficients are almost the same. These figures are high and the correlations are perhaps too strong. From my experience of comparing scores on different kinds of vocabulary tests, I would have anticipated a rather more moderate set of correlations. Gyllstad argues that the results suggest that a large vocabulary is helpful in recognizing word combinations. Possibly, but the strength of the correlations also suggests that the three tests may actually be measuring a completely different trait. At present there is no way to resolve this issue, but the figures pose a fascinating question about the degree to which the size of a learner's L2 lexicon (or the lexicon of a native speaker for that matter) is related to collocational knowledge.

As part of her longitudinal study, Eyckmans uses DISCO and an oral production test as pre- and post-tests to compare developments in the oral ability of a group of advanced learners to their collocation knowledge. The 25 subjects also took a 30-item rational cloze test designed to measure their ability to produce multiword combinations. The reliability of DISCO turns out to be very high at the pre-test stage (.90), which suggests that the items are functioning well. However, the same cannot be said at the post-test stage where a much lower figure (.64) is reported. This decline is accompanied by a significant reduction in the variance of the test, with a standard deviation that is less than half that of the pre-test. Eyckmans notes that the increased mean score is significant and suggests that the lower standard deviation is a result of the group becoming more homogeneous. In fact, I believe there are three possible explanations for such behaviour. The first is, as Eyckmans suggests, that increased homogeneity may be the result of the learners becoming more sensitive to and knowledgeable of phrases as a result of their intensive study. The second explanation is that the reduced variance is a consequence of practice, a problem that is common to all research that employs the same pre- and post-tests. The third explanation is that the pre-test scores may include at least one extreme score – or outlier – and hints at the possibility of the data being skewed. ANOVA requires scores to be normally distributed, or close to it, and variances to be almost equal. Should either of these two assumptions be violated, then the ANOVA results may be invalid and may cast doubt on Eyckmans' claims for the validity of DISCO.

As mentioned earlier, the primary research goal of Eyckmans' study is to demonstrate that DISCO is a viable alternative to the oral tests of phrasal knowledge. Eyckmans believes this to be the case, and the evidence can be summarized as follows. Firstly, after 60 hours of tuition, learners' oral proficiency has improved, and increased phrasal ability results in speech that is significantly more idiomatic. Secondly, results from DISCO show that learners are significantly better at distinguishing between idiomatic and non-idiomatic Verb + Noun combinations, suggesting that phrasal knowledge, including collocation knowledge, has improved. Thirdly, and consequently, Eyckmans suggests that the coincidental improvement of these skills seems to demonstrate that that DISCO has predictive validity with the oral test. However, this claim cannot be substantiated without a direct comparison between the tests, so unfortunately there is no direct evidence at this point for this claim. Eyckmans also reports that the correlation is low between scores from DISCO and scores from the rational cloze test, which might suggest that the relationship between receptive and productive knowledge is actually rather weak.

Final observations

The three chapters in Part III illustrate the complexities and challenges of developing and validating tests of L2 collocation knowledge.

The studies are original in concept, innovative in design and, despite the critical issues I have raised, such high-quality research should encourage others to take up the challenge of developing tests of L2 collocation knowledge, too.

I would like to end with a few general points that I hope might contribute to further research. My first point is that I believe it is essential for researchers to clearly demonstrate that tests that aim to measure L2 collocational knowledge actually do so. With regard to the present studies, I would argue that Revier has made a good case for the construct validity of CONTRIX, but I am not convinced to the same degree when it comes to the construct validity of DISCO, or COLLEX and COLLMATCH. All three tests, I feel, may be measuring something more like a sensitivity to collocational potential, rather than actual knowledge of collocations. My second point is that items for collocation tests need to be carefully selected, in the same way that items are in traditional tests. The authors of the present studies went to great lengths to identify and then select those Verb + Noun combinations they considered to be the most representative from naturally occurring language, but the fact they are representative does not guarantee that the items are well suited for test use. Eyckmans makes this point and suggests that there is a need for researchers to conduct further quantitative studies to validate their tests. For example, as she suggests, exploratory factor analysis would be a very useful method for validating the function of individual items in a test.

My third point is a proposal that future tests should be analysed using Item Response Theory (IRT) models instead of traditional classical test methods, a suggestion made by Gyllstad in the conclusion to his chapter. The advantages of IRT models over classical test models have been demonstrated in recent years (Hambleton and Swaminathan, 1985; McNamara, 1996). My own research (Shillaw, 2009) has shown that using the Rasch model, the simplest of the IRT models, is a valid and practical way of measuring vocabulary size by using the very simplest form of checklist tests.

This leads into the final point I want to make, which is a suggestion that future research into test development needs to go beyond the quantitative model to incorporate qualitative models of validation. The qualitative dimension in different chapters in this volume (Chapters 6–8 and 14–16) demonstrates how helpful it is to consider collocational knowledge from a multiplicity of perspectives, and to look closely at learners' individual evolving perspectives.

Part IV

L2 Collocation Learner Process and Practice Research

14
Collocation Learning through an 'AWARE' Approach: Learner Perspectives and Learning Process

Yang Ying and Marnie O'Neill

Introduction

Collocation[1] is considered an important dimension in language learning as knowing how words combine to make meaning is essential to all language use. Michael Lewis emphasized the importance of collocations in language use by pointing out that both native speakers of a language and successful advanced learners of a foreign language have a high level of 'collocational competence – a sufficiently large and significant phrasal mental lexicon' (Michael Lewis, 2000: 177) that is readily available to them when they use the language. This competence plays an important role in helping them use a language fluently, accurately. and appropriately.

However, most foreign language learners of English at the intermediate level of language proficiency lack this collocational competence, and this insufficiency could lead to three general problems in their language production:

- production of longer phrases and utterances because of a lack of collocations necessary for precise expression (Michael Lewis, 2000);
- production of English that sounds 'odd' and 'foreign' owing to the wrong assumption that word combination in English is the same as that of its translation equivalent in one's mother tongue (Yang and Hendricks, 2004);
- overuse of a few general items resulting in an oversimplified, flat, uninteresting style that lacks 'writing sophistication' (Singleton, 1999: 51).

Difficulties and problems in EFL learners' collocation use, according to Marton (1977) and Biskup (1992), are caused at least partly by the fact that collocations do not generally constitute comprehension problems, and therefore are largely neglected in the process of foreign language teaching and learning. In earlier work that the lead author did with a colleague (Hendricks and Yang, 2002), we became aware that many Chinese students paid more attention to new words (words that they did not know the definitional meaning of) when reading, while frequently ignoring more common and familiar words and how such words are combined to make meaning. The other difficulty in collocation learning arises from the fact that collocations are so pervasive in language input and so numerous that identifying what to learn and learning them effectively seems such a daunting task (Yang and Hendricks, 2004).

Given the important role of collocations in language use, there seems to be a compelling need for foreign language learners to pay more attention to 'the syntagmatic relations of collocation between lexical items' (Gitsaki, 1999: 2) to build their active lexicon. Morgan Lewis (2000) has pointed out that when intermediate-level language learners have learned the grammatical structures of the language and are able to produce such structures correctly, then the only viable way for them to take off again from the intermediate plateau and reach the advanced level of language proficiency is to internalize more collocations rather than 'doing third conditional (grammar) again'. We believe that Lewis has proposed a feasible solution to the problem by urging language teachers to enhance intermediate students' awareness of relatively common words they already know (or half-know) and to point out the words they occur with.

Although the important role of developing foreign language learners' collocational competence has been recognized, it is our view that previous research has been mostly concerned with theoretical discussions of collocational competence and collocation restrictions in the English language (Korosadowicz-Struzynska, 1980; Allerton, 1984; Howarth, 1998a), or examinations of the need for collocation learning (Smadja, 1989; Laufer, 1990; Bahns, 1993; Bahns and Eldaw, 1993; Lennon, 1996) and foreign language learners' use of collocations (Zughoul, 1991; Farghal and Obiedat, 1995). Very little research has been carried out into learners' collocation learning strategies and processes except for two relevant studies: one conducted by Barfield (2006: 269) in which he explored how 'individual learners organize, understand and interpret their own development of lexical and collocation knowledge over time'; and another conducted by Yang with a colleague that examined how students used a Collocation Awareness-Raising (CAR) approach to learn collocations for their writing tasks (Yang and Hendricks, 2004).

In this chapter we present an attempt to address this gap by examining how a group of EFL learners cope with their collocation learning through an 'AWARE' approach. The term 'AWARE' stands for the following steps in a process-oriented learning approach:

A: **A**wareness-raising of important language features, in particular collocations (helping learners notice collocations in the weekly theme-based readings or any other sources of input)
W: **W**hy should we learn collocations? (helping learners see the rationale for/meaning of learning what they learn)
A: **A**cquiring noticed collocations using various strategies (learners making selective use of a repertoire of learning strategies that suit their individual learning style to promote effective learning of collocations)
R: **R**eflection on learning processes and content (learners thinking about their learning processes and making necessary adjustments for better learning)
E: **E**xhibiting what has been learned (learners making a weekly oral report in class on the theme under focus by using as many as possible of the collocations they have noticed and learned).

The AWARE approach and its theoretical underpinnings

One of the key frameworks underlying the AWARE approach is the role of language awareness in learning. Language awareness (LA) has been broadly understood from two quite distinct perspectives: the psycholinguistic, and the educational (Little, 1997). The psycholinguistic perspective views language awareness in terms of levels of awareness (Yang, 2000). Researchers have identified and discussed three different levels of awareness. Noticing – a starting level of awareness of specific features in the target language input (Schmidt, 1992) – is considered a causal factor in learning and a critical first step towards mastering such features. Schmidt and Frota (1986: 317), for example, claim that 'those who notice most learn most.' On the basis of this noticing, learners may develop a second, deeper level of cognitive awareness by employing various cognitive strategies for deep processing of the noticed features in the input, thus having a greater chance of internalizing them. Little (1997: 94) identified a third, higher level of metacognitive awareness when learners 'develop a psychological relation to their learning content and process', and saw this as a critical dimension to learners taking more informed control of their language learning and use.

A broader educational perspective on language awareness brings together the following three dimensions: a simultaneous focus on the learning content, the learning methodology, and the learner in teaching and learning (Gnutzman, 1997). Central to the three dimensions is the role of the learner in the learning process. Learners should see the point in learning what they learn (the learning content), actively involve themselves in the learning process (the role of the learner), make use of suitable cognitive strategies and develop a metacognitive awareness of the learning content and learning process for more effective learning (learning methodology). We believe that increased learner awareness of a process through which something is learned is likely to promote repeated application of this process in their other learning tasks. The metacognitive awareness of their own learning experience may also lead them to learn to become more effective learners through adapting their learning attitudes and behaviors towards those adopted by good language learners (Wright and Bolitho, 1993: 294) and enable them to become more autonomous in their learning in the long run (Yang, 2000; Yang and Jiang, 2003).

Thus, the AWARE approach, a process-oriented learning approach, is based on two central beliefs: One is that learning will be more effective if learners are made aware of language and language learning at three levels: noticing the particular language features that they need to learn, developing an awareness of learning strategies, and a metacognitive awareness of reflecting on their learning process and content. The other central belief is that effective learning is more likely to take place when learners see the significance of learning what they learn and are given opportunities to exhibit what they have learned.

The study

The study described here aims to offer a better understanding of what learners think of the AWARE approach and how they make use of the approach to engage themselves in the collocation learning process. We studied a group of 20 adult students from the People's Republic of China learning English in Singapore, an ESL context. A five-month special English program was conducted for this group of students, who were identified as having achieved an intermediate[2] level of proficiency: they were able to produce grammatically correct sentences in general to express their ideas, albeit in simple limited vocabulary full of unidiomatic expressions that sound 'Chinglish'; lack of collocation competence was a common weakness among the students.

We used a qualitative methodology, aiming to understand selected cases of learners' perspectives on collocation learning and their actual practices in the learning process. As the main researcher, Yang interviewed the students at the beginning and the end of the language program and collected their reflective learning journals for analysis. The interviews were recorded and transcribed. Data from both the interview transcripts and reflective journals were coded so that we could identify major themes in the students' perspectives and practices.

The main research questions addressed were:

1. What are participants' perspectives on each of the five steps in the AWARE approach and how do they make use of each of the steps in their collocation learning process?
2. What difficulties or problems do they encounter during the process and why do they find them difficult?

Findings and discussion

We will present the findings in relation to how students thought of each of the steps of the AWARE approach and what they actually did in the adoption of each step in their collocation learning process. We will also report and discuss students' difficulties and problems in the learning process.

Students' perspectives and practices in relation to collocation 'Awareness-raising'

The students under study were generally positive about the AWARE approach for their collocation learning, referring to it as *'very useful and necessary'*, *'good'*, and *'helpful'*,[3] and most adopted the approach in their collocation learning. Most of the students felt it was on the whole different from the learning approaches they had adopted in their earlier learning, especially in awareness-raising of collocations. Learners confessed that they had little awareness of collocations in their previous learning experience since emphasis then was mainly on learning new and unknown single words as a way to expand the size of their vocabulary. Even when some of the students felt that they learned something similar to what we called collocation, such as phrasal verbs, they generally learned them by following a word/phrasal list offered by the teachers and they were tested on these items. They all reported that they had not been asked to enhance their awareness of word combinations in language input. Some students also pointed out that common word combinations were easily comprehensible, and therefore they did not pay attention to these combinations but focused more on those things that they did not know: they felt that they were learning new things by paying attention to the unknown words. JYF, for example, wrote in her reflective journal that '*before the course, I never heard of collocation*'. HXM also wrote that '*It was not until I attended this course that I got to know about collocation learning.*' HRL said that '*before I started this programme, I did not know the importance of collocation learning, so I did not pay attention to it.*' JL said that she did not know the word collocation before. She learned similar things such as phrases, but basically by remembering the phrases '*teacher gave us*'.

If the language program did not emphasize promoting learners' awareness of collocations, it would not be possible for them to figure out by themselves that they needed to pay attention to this aspect of the language. Now that they were being taught, on their course in Singapore, to be aware of collocations in language input, all of them were able to develop a heightened awareness of collocations, especially through reading. Some students wrote in their journals that, after some time, this '*noticing*' became automatic so that they could not help not noticing the '*good expressions*' when they read, listened to radio broadcasts and watched TV programs. In a word, awareness of collocation was successfully enhanced in all the students taking the program, especially at the level of '*noticing*'.

How students perceived the 'Why' of collocation learning

As to seeing 'why' they need to learn collocations, students all recognized the importance of learning this aspect of the English language. They shared a common belief that learning collocation well could help their use of the language. GJ, for example, wrote in his journal that '*if you master the collocation of a word, you can use it freely*', and he made the analogy that 'what collocation is to a language is what water is to fish'. GRL wrote that '*learning collocations is helpful. It teaches me how to use different words to express a specific meaning, and it makes my language more precise.*' When lacking adequate collocation competence, students found it difficult to express what they wanted to say concisely and they turned to use '*strange*' expressions when they did not know the acceptable expressions in the target language. HHH wrote in his first journal that since he had not paid attention to collocation learning in the past, '*when I wanted to describe something or tell stories, it troubled me a lot to come up with some proper expressions*'. Some students wrote in their journals that '*single words have little power*' and that even if they remembered all the single-word entries in a comprehensive dictionary, they were unlikely to use them well.

Besides the practical use of English, some students also mentioned collocation learning helped their appreciation of the aesthetic value of the language by seeing it as simple but *'colourful'*, *'interesting'*, *'precise'* and *'wonderful'*. GR mentioned the excitement she had when she started to pay attention to collocations in reading, saying that *'It is an excellent feeling. I realize English is marvelous. When reading, it is just like you are exploring and discovering something new all the time.'* Students also linked collocation learning to their overall language improvement. JYF, for example, wrote in her journal that *'I believe collocation learning will help improve my English a lot.'* GR said that collocation learning *'improves our English more quickly'*. JYL wrote that *'As I speak and write more in English, I become increasingly aware of the importance of collocation in English language learning.'*

Students' perspectives and practices in relation to 'Acquiring Strategies'

On 'acquiring strategies' for collocation learning, students felt that the idea of using strategies was not really new since, in China, they had also been taught some language-learning strategies, some of which could be applied to collocation learning as well. The course in Singapore introduced a variety of new strategies to them, and they all believed that having the necessary strategies for collocation learning was important because strategies helped them memorize and learn the collocations and use what they had learned more effectively. Some were apparently aware that different strategies may work differently for different individuals, so they believed it was important to find some strategies that were suitable to themselves.

Most students actively adopted various strategies for their collocation learning selectively to suit their own learning style. For example, HZY used the introduced *'visual learning'* a lot in her collocation learning by imagining a picture of the collocations she noted down whenever possible. Some other students also preferred a visual way of learning, so they watched English movies and tried to notice collocations in the conversations of the movie characters with the help of English subtitles. JXG, for example, said the collocations he could remember clearly were accumulated when he was watching a movie, and *'I could remember the collocations for a very long time and I also know in what circumstances I could use these collocations.'* Some students used self-test as a strategy introduced in a class activity. HF, for example, found this activity interesting and he continued to use it on his own by reading a passage, sorting out the collocations learned, and rewriting the main idea of the passage with blanks to test himself on the missing collocations a few days later. A briefly introduced method of categorizing collocations under themes as a memory-reinforcing strategy was not only adopted, but extended. For example, JYF and GYL wrote in their journals that they figured out a strategy of categorizing different collocations separately; they put '*functional collocations*', transitional expressions and expressions used for particular functions such as '*arguing, persuading*' together, while keeping the content/theme collocations under their respective topics.

Besides the strategies taught, students also searched for and created their own strategies for collocation learning. A common strategy used by all was noting down a selection of collocations met in the reading and reviewing them regularly. One student HF used a computer program that kept all the collocations he noted down and that generated simple tests for him. The program would '*remember*' the collocations he could not produce in the tests and retest him again later. Some students created computer programs to categorize the collocations they noticed under various themes. JYF fondly called her own collection of categorized collocations stored in a file on her computer her own '*collocation dictionary*'; she frequently referred to her personalized dictionary to complete her production tasks. Students also learned to make use of various collocation resources, such as collocation dictionaries and online concordances to help them in their production tasks. Some used a '*key word approach*', which involved the process of identifying the key words they might need to use under a particular topic, checking the dictionary, making a list of the expressions likely to be used and using them in their writing. Another method that some students used was '*revising*' when they underlined some simple and possibly Chinglish expressions they used in their writing assignment, checked the dictionary and tried to replace those expressions with what they found to be better expressions in the dictionary.

Some other strategies employed included:

- using translation to reinforce what they had learned;
- creating stories by using the collocations learned;
- learning with friends where each student read something and tried to memorize the collocations to show to the other students;
- retelling a text or summarizing a text by using the collocations in the original text;

- reviewing what they had learned regularly by making sentences with selected collocations.

In a word, students went beyond the taught strategies to search for various other strategies that they considered effective for their own learning.

Students' perspectives and practices in relation to 'Reflection'

Reflection, which required students to think about their learning process and make necessary adjustments for their future learning, took some time to be accepted by all the students in the group. Although some students with better language proficiency were able to self-initiate a reflective process in learning at an earlier stage, some others, especially those who were weaker in language proficiency, mentioned not understanding what to reflect on because they found it difficult to judge their ability and progress. Some confessed that they just followed what the teachers taught them and did not really reflect on their learning process: the only reflective exercise they did was the learning journals they were required to write. However, after they wrote the reflective journals, they felt they had a better understanding of the effectiveness of their learning, the strategies they had used and the problems and difficulties they had encountered.

There was also an initial trend for students to focus mainly on the cognitive level of reflecting on the learning content, that is, the collocations they noticed and learned, but gradually more students developed a metacognitive level of awareness about the learning processes and the effectiveness of their learning. Once they took time to reflect on their learning processes, they were able to make adjustments in their learning in order to learn better. HHH said '*reflecting on my learning processes can help me find the shortcomings of my learning, so I can try to improve my methods and review what I have learnt*'. Another student, GJ, said that he developed a habit of doing a monthly reflection to self-evaluate his learning process and adopted new strategies when old ones did not prove to be efficient enough. He realized that reflection helped him learn more effectively and said that he would like to continue to reflect regularly on his future learning.

Students' perspectives and practices in relation to 'Exhibiting' what is learned

The last step in the AWARE approach, exhibition, was an attempt to encourage students to '*exhibit*' what they had learned through using the collocations in writing assignments, group activities, and in particular, oral reports. The oral report task required students to make an oral presentation of (exhibit/show) what they had read by trying to make use of some learned collocations. The majority of the students found that the oral report was an effective task for promoting collocation learning, especially when teachers made an explicit requirement for students to use collocations in the task. HRL wrote that *'oral report helps my collocation learning in two ways. Firstly, I read articles about interesting topics and collected and learned collocations while reading. Secondly, I can commit the collected collocations to memory when preparing and presenting an oral report.'* HL (and a few others made the same comments), for example, mentioned that *'what I have used in the oral report becomes my own and I do not forget those collocations I have used'* pointing to the oral report task as an effective reinforcement of what they had learned and a way in promoting *'the use of collocations through using them'*. Some mentioned that the task was only effective when they put in efforts in the preparation process by following a step-by-step process of reading to collect collocations and trying to actually include them in the oral report. Several students joked that they *'hated'* the oral report task as there was so much work involved in order to make a good oral report, but they also considered it *'really effective'* as the task pushed them to learn through the process when they *'notice more collocations, try to select what to use, and try to use them correctly in the right context'*. Students also took the oral report task as a chance for peer learning, so they expected to see quality oral reports from others. FC, for example, expressed resentment when he felt one or two students did not prepare well enough to do a decent job so that it was a waste of time listening to them.

Difficulties and problems encountered

It took some students very long to understand the concept of collocations even after a few training sessions were given to help them pay attention to collocations in reading. One student, HQ, kept thinking collocations meant *'new words'* even after one month of the program. It was not until Yang sat through a reading text with him that he finally understood the concept of paying attention to *'useful expressions'*, not just single words.

Old habits die hard. As the students had been taught to expand their vocabulary through memorizing lists of new words, they felt more secure if they noted down all the new words from a reading text. Paying more attention to word combinations consisting of common words they already knew was understood to be important, but, in actual practice, students still preferred not to miss new words when noting down important vocabulary entries. It was also found that students who were relatively weaker felt that they needed to learn new words first and that they could only be ready to learn collocations when they reached a '*certain standard*'. They felt that collocation learning was for '*better*' students.

The major difficulty that students kept bringing up was the problem of memorizing the collocations noticed. Quite a number of students tended to note down as many collocations as they noticed from their reading textbooks but without much selection, especially in the initial stages of the course. They basically just '*collected*' them without trying to internalize them. They felt frustrated when they faced the big volume of '*messy*' expressions, were unable to recall them when needed and did not know how to put them to use. JYL, for example, wrote that '*even though I have noted down a lot of collocations, I am not able to use them in my oral report or writing assignments flexibly. I rarely spend a lot of time learning what I have noted down.*' Quite a number of students seemed to have an unrealistic expectation that they should be able to remember all the collocations they noted down. When they failed to do so, they considered their collocation learning ineffective. GRL, for one, questioned whether it was a waste of time to notice so many but use so few. This practice of collecting too many and learning too few, however, changed with time as students realized it was not possible to internalize all the collocations they came across. Many started to choose what they believed to be more commonly used expressions and adopted various strategies to '*learn*' them rather than simply '*collecting*' them.

To sum up, the students who took part in this study were positive about collocation learning, considering it an important aspect of English language learning that helps improve their language proficiency, in particular, their use of the language in a more concise and precise way. They found the AWARE approach useful and effective, and most of the students adopted some steps of the AWARE approach in their learning process. All students successfully enhanced their awareness of collocations in language input through instruction at the beginning of the course; most of them learned some strategies and even went beyond to search for other strategies suitable for their own collocation learning. With regard to reflection, most students placed more emphasis on a cognitive level of reflecting on the learning content initially, but they were able to develop a metacognitive level of reflection on the learning processes and made adjustments to promote better learning. Students were able to exhibit their learning, especially in an oral report task, which they found useful in reinforcing the collocations they learned and in helping them learn through use.

Conclusion

This chapter has reported on a study conducted on a group of PRC learners of English and examined their perspectives and their practices in collocation learning through the adoption of an AWARE approach. From the interview data and data from the students' reflective journals, we learned that learners' collocation awareness could be successfully enhanced through pedagogical intervention. The majority of the students, under proper guidance provided at the initial stage of the program, were able to manage their collocation learning independently; they actively sought strategies that suited themselves, made meaningful reflections on the learning content and learning process, and made adjustments to their learning based on what they thought worked well or what did not. The oral report task, an exhibition task of students' collocation learning, was considered effective as learners learned through the process of coping with the task and learned from other peers.

However, at various stages of the learning program, students also encountered different problems such as inability to judge what exactly should be noticed, to decide what and how to reflect on their learning and to find suitable strategies that worked more effectively for them. The majority of the students were able to come to terms with these problems and made necessary changes over time, often independently. Although students admitted that certain problems such as improving recall when collocations are needed for production tasks remained and may not be entirely solved, they were positive about the focus on the learning of collocations and felt that collocation learning was '*of great significance*' for them to improve their language proficiency. We therefore recommend that other English teachers make collocation learning an important element in language programs for students with an intermediate level of proficiency, and explore how to adapt the AWARE approach to help their students learn this aspect of the language more independently and effectively.

Notes

1. A narrow definition of collocation limits it only to co-occurring single words, such as *perform an operation* but not **perform a meeting*, or *hold a meeting* but not **hold an operation*. To define it more broadly, collocation refers to all

combinations of words, including idiomatic phrases. In this study, the broad, more inclusive definition of collocation is adopted (definition following Yang and Hendricks, 2004).

2. Intermediate level of proficiency: the group of students are considered to have reached an intermediate level of proficiency as they have a reasonable level of knowledge of English structures and are able to write grammatically correct sentences. They have a reasonable size of vocabulary and are able to comprehend academic reading texts. They can communicate with others in English, but fluency may be lacking. They are able to express their ideas in writing, but generally in simple words.
3. Words in italics in single quotation marks from this section onwards are original words taken from the students' journals and transcribed interview data.

15
Learning Collocations through Attention-Drawing Techniques: A Qualitative and Quantitative Analysis

Elke Peters

Introduction

When second language (L2) learners read an L2 text, they tend to prioritize text comprehension and text meaning over specific language forms (Peters, 2007a), as a consequence of which many grammatical as well as lexical language features in the input remain unnoticed. Although recent research (Laufer, 2005; Peters, 2007b; Peters et al., 2009) has demonstrated the positive effects of attention-drawing techniques on word learning, it has focused predominantly on recognition and recall of the meaning of individual words. In spite of the growing interest in the use of multiword units by foreign language learners, far fewer studies have been carried out into techniques that may foster the acquisition of these multiword units (Bishop, 2004; Boers et al., 2006). This chapter reports on an exploratory study that aims to examine how an attention-drawing technique may facilitate recall of both individual lexical items and collocations. The technique under investigation is a vocabulary task: a general versus a specific, collocation-oriented task.

Background

L2 learners do not always notice and pick up unknown words when reading a text (Laufer, 2005). This is also true for collocations because L2 learners may understand the meaning of a collocation from the meaning of its parts, even if its form differs from learners' L1 (see Nation, 2001: 325). For example, in Dutch, one would say 'to *do* an effort' (*een inspanning doen*) and not 'to *make* an effort'. As a result, Dutch-speaking L2 learners would run the risk of saying 'he does an effort' instead of 'he makes an effort', although they might not experience any difficulties in understanding the collocation. With the exception of Bishop (2004), Laufer and Girsai (2005) and Boers et al. (2006), there has been little research into how to draw learners' attention to multiword units. In what follows, I first review studies that have dealt with the effect of attention-drawing techniques before presenting my current research.

In a computer-based study, Bishop (2004) found that typographic salience of target items (in red and underlined) resulted in more clicks on formulaic sequences. L2 learners who had read a typographically enhanced text looked up more visually enhanced formulaic sequences than L2 learners who had read the same text but without typographical salience. Unfortunately, Bishop did not report the effect of typographic salience on word learning. Laufer and Girsai (2005) examined the effect of translation tasks after a reading task on L2–L1 and L1–L2 vocabulary learning. They found that the use of translation had a positive effect on students' learning of individual words as well as collocations. Finally, Boers et al. (2006) investigated the effect of the lexical approach on L2 learners' use of formulaic sequences. Two groups were exposed to the same reading and listening materials. One group was asked to focus on word combinations, the other on individual words and grammar. The findings indicated that the experimental group used more formulaic sequences compared to the control group when retelling a story they had just read. In addition, the former group came across as more proficient than the control group, but this difference disappeared in spontaneous speech (conversation/interview).

Aim and research questions

For my own research, I wanted to explore the effect of an attention-drawing technique on recall of the form of individual lexical items and collocations, and address the following research questions:

1. Is there an effect of the attention-drawing technique on the number of target items learned, of the individual target words learned and of the collocations learned?
2. Is there a difference between the number of individual lexical items learned and the number of collocations learned?
3. Is there an interaction between the attention-drawing technique and the type of target item learned (individual target word or collocation)?

Method

Design

The study adopted a between-subject design with one between-subject variable: the attention-drawing technique (a *general* versus *specific, collocation-oriented* task). Participants, assigned to two groups, read an L2 text with marginal glosses and each group carried out a text-related, yet different task. Both groups were allotted 40 minutes; they had the glossed text at their disposal when performing their tasks. One treatment required students to focus on new vocabulary in general when reading the text (= the general vocabulary task), whereas the other treatment required students to focus on both new individual words and collocations (= the specific, collocation-oriented task).

Participants

Fifty-four participants, all advanced EFL students, were recruited from one intact class. They were doing translation and interpreting studies at a Belgian university college, that is, EFL in combination with one other foreign language. The students' L1 was Dutch, except for two students (one bilingual student and one student whose L1 was Bengali). The group consisted of 11 male and 43 female students (19–23 years old). They were assumed to be familiar with the concept of collocation since collocations figure prominently in their vocabulary textbooks.

Materials and data collection instruments

Selection of target words

The 40 target items were taken from the text students had to read (see Table 15.1).First, I made a distinction between individual target words and target collocations. I verified the frequency of the individual words in the *Collins COBUILD English Dictionary for Advanced Learners*, 3rd edn (2001). Only items from the two lowest frequency bands were retained (the four highest frequency bands contain approximately 6,500 words) as these less frequent items were probably not familiar to the participants. I decided to focus on Verb + Noun and Adjective + Noun collocations. The collocations were checked against two different collocation dictionaries. Only collocations that appeared in the *Oxford Collocations Dictionary for Students of English* (OCDSE, 2002) and/or the *BBI Dictionary of English Word Combinations* (Benson, Benson and Ilson, 1997) were selected. The selection procedure led to 19 individual target

Table 15.1 List of target items

Individual words		Collocations	
bluster	trump	harsh criticism	to hold a grudge
cesspit	to applaud	political pundits	to launch a career
credentials	to commemorate	to bend the rules	to lower the (crime) rates
crook	to corner	to carry the headline	to mark the anniversary
devastation	to loathe	to cast doubt on	to raise money
fealty	to rally	to cast one's vote	to run a vendetta
ferocious	to scurry off	to complete a transformation	to run for mayor
notorious	to stride	to deliver a speech	to serve time
spouse		to foster the desire	to take the lead
staunch		to hit the headlines	undisclosed location

words and 21 target collocations being retained, each of which appeared only once in the text.

Text

Learners had to read a slightly adapted 2100-word text, selected from a British newspaper. Seventy-eight words and collocations were underlined and glossed in the margin with an L1 translation, among which were the 40 target items.

Pre-test

The pre-test consisted of 50 test items in Dutch: 40 target items and 10 distractor items that did not appear in the reading text. Participants had to provide the English translation for the 50 test items because I was interested in participants' recall of the form of the target items. To ensure that students would not supply an alternative but correct answer, the first letter(s) of the translation was given.

Post-test

The post-test was identical to the pre-test except that the test items were presented in a different order.

Vocabulary instruction treatment

Two different vocabulary treatments were developed. The first group received a general task instructing them to focus on unfamiliar vocabulary (*pay attention to* ***vocabulary*** *in the text because you will be tested on your knowledge of some words in the text*), whereas the second group were required to devote their attention to unfamiliar individual words as well as collocations (*pay attention to vocabulary (=* ***individual words and collocations****) in the text because ...*). To ensure that participants would indeed focus on vocabulary, they were required to write down new vocabulary[1] on a note sheet. Group 1 (general task) received a note sheet consisting of two pages, on which they could write down unfamiliar vocabulary. Group 2, on the other hand, were given a note sheet that consisted of two pages with each page divided into two columns. In the left-hand column, Group 2 members had to write down unfamiliar individual lexical items, and in the right they had to write down new or unfamiliar collocations. Both groups were told that after having finished the vocabulary task, they would be tested on vocabulary used in the text. In contrast to Group 1, Group 2 were explicitly told that the post-test would contain collocations: *You will have to translate words from Dutch into English ...* (Group 1) versus *You will have to translate individual words and collocations from Dutch into English ...* (Group 2).

Questionnaire

The qualitative data consisted of responses to two short questionnaires about participants' strategy use and their perception of the task and test. Students completed Questionnaire 1 after having completed the vocabulary task, and Questionnaire 2 after the post-tests. Both questionnaires consisted of Likert scale and open questions.

Procedure

The experiment took place during one session. The procedure is presented graphically in Figure 15.1.

1. All participants take the pre-test.
2. Participants are randomly assigned to one of the two experimental groups.
3. They read the instructions pertaining to their specific task (general versus specific, collocation-oriented). They are allotted 40 minutes to complete their task.
4. They perform their task.
5. They fill in Questionnaire 1.
6. All participants take the post-test.
7. They fill in Questionnaire 2.
8. All participants are debriefed about the aim and the procedure of the experiment.

Figure 15.1 Experimental procedure

Scoring and data analysis

The vocabulary pre- and post-test were scored dichotomously. A correct answer received one point, an incorrect one zero points (no or wrong translation). Participants' scores on the post-test were calculated in the light of the total number of target words that were unfamiliar prior to the experimental task. Words that were already known were not considered in the data analysis. As a result, every student received an individual maximum score. For instance, if a student knew five target words prior to the experimental task, his or her maximum score would be 35, that is, 35 out of 40 possible target items. That is the reason why percentages are reported. The test scores were submitted to an ANOVA ($p < .05$). As a measure of effect size, eta-squared ($= \eta^2$) was chosen.[2] Chi-square analyses were employed to analyse the retrospective questions.

Results

First, I present the results of the pre-test and students' performance on the post-test, before dealing with the qualitative analyses.

Quantitative analyses

Pre-test

The results on the pre-test (see Table 15.2) showed that the participants knew approximately one fourth of the target words. They were familiar with more collocations than individual words. Although Group 1 performed slightly better than Group 2, they did not differ significantly.

Research question 1: *Is there a difference between the two groups with respect to the number of target items/individual words/collocations learned?*

Table 15.3 provides the descriptive statistics of the post-test: the total score, the score on the individual words, and the score on the collocations. Surprisingly, participants in Group 1 performed better than participants

Table 15.2 Descriptive statistics for the pre-test

Group	*N*	Total score (Max. = 40)		Individual words (Max. = 19)		Collocations (Max. = 21)	
		Mean	SD	Mean	SD	Mean	SD
Group 1	27	12.7	4.4	4.7	2.2	7.9	2.5
Group 2	27	11.0	4.0	4.0	2.4	7.0	2.4
Both groups	54	11.8	4.2	4.3	2.3	7.5	2.5

Table 15.3 Descriptive statistics (percentages) for the post-test

Group	*N*	Total score		Individual words		Collocations	
		Mean	SD	Mean	SD	Mean	SD
Group 1	27	70.2	20.0	68.3	21.1	72.6	21.2
Group 2	27	60.0	22.1	56.3	25.3	63.7	21.4
Both groups	54	65.0	21.1	62.3	23.9	68.1	21.6

in Group 2 with respect to all target items, the individual words, and the collocations. However, the ANOVA indicated that the difference between the two groups was not significant.

Research question 2: *Is there a difference between the number of individual lexical items learned and the number of collocations learned?*

As can be seen from Table 15.3, participants could recall the form of more collocations compared to individual target items. The ANOVA revealed that the difference between the two types of target item (individual word and collocation) was indeed significant, F (1, 52) = 8.11, $p = .006$, $\eta^2 = .13$. Thus, the second research question can be answered affirmatively.

Research question 3: *Is there an interaction between group and the type of target item learned (individual target words or collocation)?*

Though the difference between the two groups was larger for the individual words (+/– 12 per cent) than for the collocations (+/– 9 per cent), the ANOVA did not reveal any significant interaction between group and type of target item.

Qualitative analysis

Retrospective questions

Students answered seven questions after they had completed the vocabulary task.

Question 1: *The instruction was clear.*

The instruction was clear for most students. Only six students in Group 1 and only one student in Group 2 responded otherwise. The chi-square test revealed that there was no statistically significant difference between the two groups.

Question 2: *The text was interesting.* / **Question 3:** *The text was difficult.*

The vast majority of participants in both groups found the text interesting to read. Most students found the text neither difficult nor easy or not difficult at all. The two groups did not differ from each other in their perception of the text. Because no statistically significant differences were found between the two groups, we can conclude that neither the theme nor the difficulty of the text had an effect on the results.

Question 4: *I liked carrying out the vocabulary task.* / **Question 5:** *I feel that I have learned new vocabulary by performing this task.* / **Question 6:** *The marginal glosses were useful when carrying out the vocabulary task.*

As regards participants' perception of the vocabulary task, more than half of the students in Group 1 claimed to have enjoyed carrying out the vocabulary task, whereas this was only true for one third of the participants in Group 2. Only a few students did not like doing this task (three students in Group 1, six in Group 2). Yet, no statistically significant difference between the two groups was found. Except for one student in Group 2, almost all participants found that they had learned new vocabulary by performing their vocabulary task. A chi-square test indicated that the two groups did not differ from each other. Finally, participants perceived the marginal glosses as helpful for performing the vocabulary task, except for two students in Group 1. Unsurprisingly, no difference was found between the two groups.

Question 7: *How did you proceed? How did you prepare for the vocabulary test? Which strategies did you use? How did you select words? Why did you notice some/certain words?*

Students' answers revealed that there were mainly three selection principles. The majority of students claimed to have selected words because they were new, unfamiliar or difficult (meaning, spelling). Second, participants in both groups indicated that the pre-test had influenced their selection of words because they remembered test items or because they realized they had supplied an incorrect translation for the test items. Third, about 25 per cent of the participants in each group indicated that they had focused predominantly on the vocabulary listed in the marginal glosses when selecting target items. One student in Group 2 thought this disturbing because it predisposed him/her to select only words from the marginal glosses. In general, students' answers remained rather vague and did not reveal many vocabulary learning strategies except writing down or underlining words and repeating them. A few students explicitly mentioned that the use of context facilitated their vocabulary learning.

Students answered the following questions after having taken the vocabulary post-test:

Question 1: *The vocabulary post-test was difficult.* / **Question 2:** *The vocabulary task was a good preparation or the vocabulary post-test.*

Surprisingly, more participants in Group 2 (n=17) perceived the vocabulary post-test as difficult compared to participants in Group 1 (n=10). Twelve students in Group 1 did not find the test difficult or easy in comparison to seven students in Group 2. Only a few students found the test not difficult. The statistical analysis demonstrated that there was indeed a significant difference between the two groups (p = .02). Although the two groups differed in their perception of the test's difficulty, they both stated that the vocabulary task was a good preparation for the vocabulary post-test. Thus, they still perceived their task as useful and beneficial after having finished the test.

Question 3: *I had noticed that many of the glossed words were collocations.* / **Question 4:** *While performing the vocabulary task, I paid special attention to collocations.*

More students in Group 2 (n=23) claimed to have noticed that there were many collocations in the marginal glosses in comparison to Group 1 (n=18). Six students in Group 1 said that they were not aware of this, compared to only one student in Group 2. Unsurprisingly, the analysis showed that the difference between the two groups was significant. With respect to Question 4, both groups stated that they had allocated attentional resources to collocations while performing the vocabulary task. In other words, there was no difference in the way attentional resources were allocated despite the fact that the two groups were set a different task.

Question 5: *How do you assess your preparation in retrospect? Do you find the strategies you used effective? Explain.*

Of the 27 students in Group 1 who answered this question, 17 of them rated their preparation as good. The reasons participants named for being successful in their strategy use were: memorizing target words, writing down target words and repeating them, underlining target words, allocating more attentional resources to vocabulary and collocations, the provision of marginal glosses, and finally the influence of the pre-test, which had helped them select target words. Two participants found that their preparation was not really good, but not bad either. Eight students, however, were not satisfied with the way they had prepared for the post-test. In Group 2, students tended to react similarly, though fewer students perceived the strategies they had used as effective. Fourteen participants claimed that they were well prepared for the post-test. They mentioned that writing down words, the provision of marginal glosses, repeating words, and paying more attention to collocations were useful word learning strategies. Surprisingly, only one student referred to the pre-test, in which the target words were presented for the first time. Two participants found their strategy use not good, but not bad either. Finally, nine participants complained about their strategy use. Some of them said that they had not paid sufficient attention to collocations, while others mentioned that they had been writing down and copying words without being actively engaged in memorizing them.

Question 6: *Did the marginal glosses make you focus on vocabulary in a different or in a specific way? Explain.*

The majority of participants in Group 1 (15) and in Group 2 (13) perceived the marginal glosses as useful because the glosses made them focus on vocabulary in a different way. Because of the marginal glosses, they had paid more attention to collocations or the use of words in context. In addition, the marginal glosses drew their attention to unfamiliar words and collocations they might not have noticed otherwise, or whose meaning could not be inferred from the context. Furthermore, the marginal glosses made the students aware of the precise meaning of unknown words. Several students mentioned again that the marginal glosses influenced their selection of words to be learned. Another benefit was that the marginal glosses made the participants understand the text better. On the other hand, 10 students in Group 1 and eight in Group 2 claimed that the marginal glosses had not changed their approach to unfamiliar vocabulary.

Question 7: *Did the vocabulary task make you focus on vocabulary in a different or specific way? Did it push you in a certain direction? Explain.*

Twelve students in Group 1 claimed that the vocabulary task they were set (= the general vocabulary task) had made a difference in how they had dealt with unfamiliar vocabulary in the text. Seven students mentioned that they had paid more attention to vocabulary, whereas four students explicitly stated that they had devoted more attention to collocations. Some students said that they had paid more attention to the words in context. Students in Group 2, however, received the specific, collocation-oriented task. Fourteen participants stated that their approach was different due to their task. The majority claimed that they had allocated more attentional resources to vocabulary. Surprisingly, only four students said that they had paid more attention to collocations than otherwise. This finding does not differ from Group 1, although the latter had not received the collocation-oriented task. Despite the explicit focus on collocations in the task for Group 2, there were still nine students who claimed that their specific vocabulary task had no effect on how they had dealt with unfamiliar vocabulary.

Participants' notes

Although students wrote down more words, collocations and other formulaic sequences in addition to the target items, the analysis of the notes will be confined to the target items only. As can be seen from Table 15.4, participants in Group 2 wrote down slightly more target items, individual words, and collocations than participants in Group 1, but two-sample t-tests indicated that these differences were not significant.

Table 15.4 also shows that the two groups wrote down more individual target words than collocations. A paired t-test revealed that this difference was statistically significant ($t = 7.75$; df $= 53$; $p < .0001$). This may, among other factors, be attributed to participants' pre-knowledge of the target items as the results of the pre-test showed that they were familiar with more collocations than individual target words.

Though the vast majority of collocations were written down as a whole, there were a few collocations that were noted as individual words. Instead of writing *to hold a grudge*, *to foster the desire*, *an undisclosed location*, *harsh criticism*, and *political pundits*, participants would write *grudge*, *to foster*, *undisclosed*, *harsh*, and *pundits*. That students wrote

Table 15.4 Descriptive statistics for participants' notes

Group	N	All target items			Individual words			Collocations		
		Mean	Sum	SD	Mean	Sum	SD	Mean	Sum	SD
Group 1	27	18.9	510	8.6	11.2	302	4.4	7.6	208	4.6
Group 2	27	20.7	560	9.6	11.5	311	4.7	9.3	219	5.4
Both	54	19.8	1070	9.1	11.4	613	4.5	8.4	427	5.0

down only one word of the collocation can be partially explained by the fact that the adjective–noun collocations occurred as individual words in the marginal glosses.

I also carried out correlation analyses to determine whether there would be a positive relationship between the number of target items written down and participants' score on the post-test. Pearson correlations indicated that there were no significant correlations between the number of target items, individual target words, and collocations written down and participants' scores on the post-test.

A final point I want to comment on is the use of translation. Eleven students in Group 1 and 13 in Group 2 wrote down the target items with their Dutch translation. Slightly more participants in each group copied only the (form of) the target items on their note sheet. I verified whether the variable 'use of translation' might explain differences between students. Although students who did not write down the translation performed slightly better on the post-test (mean = 65.35%; SD = 19.87) than the ones who did (mean = 64.56%; SD = 23.89), two-sample t-tests did not reveal any significant difference between the two groups with respect to their recall of the target items.

Discussion

In this study I wanted to explore the effects of an attention-drawing technique on recall of individual words and collocations by 54 EFL students. Unlike previous research, I did not find positive evidence for the use of an attention-drawing technique for recall of collocations. The findings show that the students who performed the collocation-oriented task did not recall more target items than students who were set the general vocabulary task. Though students in both groups wrote down more individual words than collocations, they still learned more collocations.

One possible explanation for the lack of significant differences might be found in the qualitative data because the retrospective questions, on the one hand, and students' notes, on the other hand, indicated that there were hardly any differences in task approach or strategy use between the two groups. Instead of revealing different attentional priorities, students in both groups exhibited the same strategies and attentional priorities. The retrospective questions showed that students in Group 1 focused partially on collocations as well since, in both groups, collocations were made salient via the pre-test and the marginal glosses. The only differences I found were concerned with students' perception of the post-test, their perception of the strategies they had used, and their noticing of collocations in the marginal glosses. Apart from the questionnaires, students' notes revealed that both groups were engaged in writing down individual words as well as collocations. No differences could be found in students' notes either. In addition, the lack of significant differences could not be explained by the use of translation in participants' notes.

There are, of course, other factors that played a role. Both the pre-test, which contained the target items, and the marginal glosses 'alerted' students to collocations. As has already been mentioned, the pre-test was administered during the same session as the experimental task. Some researchers recommend administering a pre-test at least one week before the experimental treatment (cf. Hulstijn, 2003). Unfortunately, it was not possible to organize the experiment during more than one session for practical reasons. Hence, it cannot be ruled out that the pre-test might have influenced to some degree how students allocated their attentional resources, as was indicated by some students in the retrospective questions (e.g. '*words I didn't know in the pre-test caught my attention*', '*I recognized some words from the pre-test*', '*I wrote down the words for which I could not supply a translation on the pre-test*'). Moreover, Group 1 performed slightly better on the pre-test than Group 2, though the difference was not statistically significant. This could have played a role as well. Another factor might be that the marginal glosses contained collocations because students' answers showed that these glosses were an important selection mechanism: '*I mainly focused on the words in the marginal glosses because they contained the vocabulary I didn't know*', '*the translated words caught my attention*', and '*the unfamiliar words were to be found in the marginal glosses*'. The qualitative data revealed that the marginal glosses made approximately one fifth of the students in Group 1 turn their attention to collocations ('*You'll pay more attention to collocations and the use of words*', '*I focused more on collocations*', '*I devoted more attention to the context in which the words were used*', '*the glosses made you pay attention to the context*', and '*much attention to expressions*'). In other words, the collocations may have been salient for both groups.

One should also bear in mind that the participants in this study were advanced EFL students familiar with the concept of collocation and (probably) aware of its importance in language use. It might be only natural for them to focus on collocations as well, as illustrated in the following comments by students in Group 1: '*It is not only important to pay attention to difficult words but also to collocations*', '*Because of the vocabulary task, I focused mainly on collocations*', '*I wrote down collocations*

I didn't know', and *'I selected words that were used in a new way, e.g. to hit the headlines'*. This raises, of course, the question of whether the findings would be different for less proficient students.

A last issue I would like to address is the combination of quantitative and qualitative data. The quantitative data allowed me to compare students' performance and conduct statistical analyses on which the findings are founded. The retrospective questionnaires and students' notes all helped to refine our understanding of how students had proceeded through the experiment. For instance, the process data showed that both groups focused on collocations. These data were revealing since they provided us with information about what students were actually doing while taking part in the experiment. This may be different from what we as researchers think they are doing. Unfortunately, the information revealed remained rather factual sometimes. But had I not asked students what their approach was, I might still be in the dark about the reasons why the collocation-oriented task did not have an effect on vocabulary learning. Therefore, I would still argue strongly in favour of qualitative research techniques in addition to quantitative ones since they can help us to refine our understanding of the learning activity that is taking place.

At the same time, it needs to be emphasized that this chapter reports on an exploratory study. Thus the results need to be interpreted with care. The main limitation regards the administration of the pre-test during the same session as the experimental tasks. This certainly had an effect on how some students' allocated their attentional resources to collocations. Yet, the lack of a statistically significant difference between the two groups cannot be solely attributed to the pre-test. The fact that the participants in this study were advanced EFL learners who were familiar with the concept and the importance of collocations in language use may have played a major role in the use of similar strategies of the two groups and consequently in the lack of any difference.

Notes

1. Previous research (Peters, 2007a, 2007b; Peters et al., 2009) has shown that *only* telling L2 learners to focus on new vocabulary in a text in preparation for an upcoming vocabulary test has an effect on students' look-up behaviour but not on their recall of target word meaning.
2. Based on Cohen (1992), the values of effect size were interpreted as follows: $\eta^2 > .0099$ (small), $\eta^2 > .0588$ (moderate), and $\eta^2 > .1379$ (large).

16
Following Individuals' L2 Collocation Development over Time

Andy Barfield

Introduction

As a particular feature of language use that sits uneasily at the crossroads between formulaic and novel language (Pawley and Syder, 1983; Sinclair, 1991; Wray, 2002; Hoey, 2005), collocation constrains linguistic choice. This restriction of choice raises not only lexical and psycholinguistic questions, but also important sociocultural issues about how second language (L2) adult learners may differently cope with their L2 collocation development. At the lexical and psycholinguistic levels, Wray (2002: 209–12) proposes that, unlike native speakers, post-childhood L2 learners may break collocations down, at the point of encountering them, into individual lexical units, and are then later faced, at the point of use, with the challenge of relinking such separate items, without knowing what might constitute appropriate pairings. Insofar as that is the case, then we could expect that learners are constantly faced with problems of lexical decision making when they attend to their L2 collocation development. Assuming also that we use language, including collocation, to express individual identity and claim group membership, such decision making may be different for an adult English native speaker and an adult L2 learner, with the result that, for some learners, 'a perfectly nativelike performance may be of relatively little importance' (Wray, 2002: 212). If so, then we can predict that learners' shifting sense of identity within particular contexts and communities of use also impinges on their processes of L2 collocation development.

Previous studies have tended to focus on finished collocation productions by analysing the encodings that learners have already made. This is the major concern of corpus analysis studies (Chi, Wong and Wong, 1994; Gitsaki, 1997; Granger, 1998b; Howarth, 1998b;

Nesselhauf, 2003; Revier and Henriksen, 2006; Hsu, 2007) and translation and/or cloze tests (Biskup, 1992; Bahns and Eldaw, 1993; Farghal and Obiedat, 1995; Bonk, 2000; Huang, 2001; Webb and Kagimoto, 2007). However, very few studies (Yang and Hendricks, 2004; Barfield, 2006; Coxhead, 2008) have attempted to explore the processes of such collocation decision making over time. Although some research has specifically examined the sociocultural dimension in relation to the acquisition of formulaic language (Adolphs and Durow, 2004; Wray and Fitzpatrick, 2008) and collocation (Starfield, 2004), we still know very little about how learners interpret both their collocation practices and their changing sense of who they are in terms of their own *figured worlds* (Holland et al., 1998). A figured world is 'a particular frame of reference, in which persons attribute meaning to their experiences and interpret relationships between people, acts, and resources' (Toohey, 2007: 234). Exploring learners' processes of L2 collocation development and use from within their own figured worlds should help us to reach insights that other more distanced modes of inquiry such as corpus analysis and translation and/or cloze tests have not been able to illuminate.

This chapter presents a longitudinal study of four young adult learners of English as a foreign language within a content-based learning environment and seeks to shed light on their process of L2 collocation development over one academic year. I will first introduce the participants and the structuring of the inquiry, before outlining some of the key processes of development that emerged during the investigation. I will then analyse these processes in greater depth, before concluding with a brief discussion of certain implications of this study.

Participants and context

The four participants in this longitudinal inquiry are Huijuan, Ken, Keiko, and Mayuko (all pseudonyms). At the time of the study, they were third- and fourth-year Politics or International Business and Law majors in the Faculty of Law at Chuo University in Tokyo. For each five-to-six-week project cycle of their elective English course, they conducted research projects through English on human rights and global issues where they chose an issue that they were interested in, and researched it out of class by finding relevant sources, reading, and making notes in English. In class (the class met once a week for 90 minutes over two semesters of 13 weeks), the students used their notes to explain their research to each other, discuss their understanding and build their knowledge further. They also wrote extensive reflections about what and how they were learning. The project cycles culminated in a 15–20 minute poster presentation to a small group of students or completion of an extended written draft for feedback from other students. Huijuan (female) was taking an advanced research and writing course where she worked on two long reports over the year, finishing with a 3000-word paper on poverty in India. Ken (male), Keiko and Mayuko (both females) were in the same advanced research and discussion course, where they investigated topics such as the trafficking of young girls and women in Asia, micro-credit in Bangladesh, and fair trade organic cotton.

In both courses, the students focused each week on building their English collocation knowledge around key ideas in their research notes. This was a required part of each course, and students were asked to make their own collocation notes in their notebooks. The students were shown different ways of making collocation notes so that they could consider the relative strengths and weaknesses of their own way. They also regularly shared with each other and discussed their collocation notes, as well as wrote reflections about how they were recording collocations, so that they could develop over time appropriate practices for themselves.

Longitudinal interview-based inquiry

In order to explore what the students' processes of L2 collocation development were and how they interpreted these processes over time, I conducted a series of out-of-class interviews in English with the four students over the 2007 academic year of two 13-week semesters (mid-April to mid-July/late September to mid-January). The interview approach used can be characterized as 'active' (Holstein and Gubrium, 1995). Rather than working from a narrow set of predetermined interview questions, the active interview approach 'eschews the image of a vessel waiting to be tapped in favour of the notion that the subject's interpretive capabilities must be activated, stimulated and cultivated' (Holstein and Gubrium, 1995: 17). My goal was not to establish objective truths, but rather to 'incite narrative production' (Holstein and Gubrium, 1995: 39) by the students and encourage them both to tell the stories of their L2 collocation development, articulate their own interpretations of their changing collocation processes, and reconsider their individual narratives in light of the stories and interpretations that the other students presented.

I started with three individual interviews with each student, lasting about 45 minutes, but I also wanted to provide the students with spaces to talk directly with each other about their processes of English collocation learning and development in terms of their own figured worlds.

In order to step back from directing every step in the evolving inquiry, the second stage involved each student completing four pair student-to-student interviews, each of which went for 75 minutes or more. For these pair interviews, the students did two interviews with the same partner before switching to a new partner for the last two. As the researcher, I opened and closed each pair interview, but, for long periods of time (for 40 minutes or more in the later pair interviews), I withdrew from the interview so that the students could explain directly to each other significant developments in their practices and understandings of their English collocation learning.

The interviews were audio-recorded and subsequently transcribed, and the students were given a transcript of the previous interview before the next one. Throughout the year, at the end of each interview, the students wrote a 20-minute interview log on what they had noticed and found of interest; they would then use these logs as the principal starting point for the next interview. Other points of triangulation included the transcript of the previous interview, students' course research notes, collocation notes, and in-class written reflections. The inquiry culminated in a final whole-group discussion. The increasingly learner-interactive organization of the inquiry aimed to follow the students' L2 collocation development on their own terms, and open up many spaces for them to articulate their positions and explore similarities and differences in their evolving practices with each other.

Five emerging processes of L2 collocation development

The presentation of key processes in this chapter is organized around specific themes taken up by the students in the final group interview at the end of the 2007 academic year. To prepare for that interview, the four students were asked to look back over their English collocation development during the previous nine months and to map on paper what had been significant for them in their unfolding L2 collocation development. These maps included examples of their collocation notes during the year, with commentaries by the students about changes that they noticed. The students then used these maps as the starting point for the group interview. From these end-of-year reconstructions, I have drawn out five major processes of development:

- understanding and reconfiguring past vocabulary practices;
- interpreting different worlds of everyday use;
- moving from quantity of lexical knowledge to quality of collocation use;

- reconnecting what is known and projecting new identities;
- developing authorship.

I continue by retracing and reinterpreting these processes over prior individual and pair interviews.

Understanding and reconfiguring past vocabulary practices

Throughout 2007, Ken had been critical of the memorization of difficult words that he had been required to do at high school, and, in the group interview in January 2008, he again identified the value of collocation as being connected to his everyday natural use of English. In recounting his English vocabulary history in June 2007, Ken had recalled the competitive edge to memorization in his senior high school days. Practically each day he would talk with his friends about learning English. Ken explains: '*I would ask, "How many words have you remembered now?" And my friends would reply, "Fifty." "Ah that's great!" we would all respond ...*' (Ken, individual interview: 12 June 2007). When Ken finally set foot in university, he couldn't use English at all at the start, and he found this '*pretty shocking*'. What was comforting to him was that his new friends at university had had very similar experiences. Now, three years later, he analysed the effect of learning vocabulary in these terms: '*The reason I couldn't speak English was not that I don't know the words. It's that I didn't know words to say with words. If I know the combination, I can use the nouns that I want to say*' (Ken, individual interview: 5 June 2007). Attributing significance to quantity and difficulty in their vocabulary learning enabled Ken and his friends to make sense of the decontextualized and 'encapsulated learning' (Engeström, 2005) that they were required to do to gain access to higher education. This kind of learning required them to learn about English through Japanese (Smith and Imura, 2004), but not connect their learning to any real-world use of English outside of university entrance exam preparation.

In a different individual interview (4 June 2007), Keiko, a third-year International Business and Law undergraduate, remembers how, at junior high school, she enjoyed memorizing and translating individual words, but felt ashamed of speaking English in class, as speaking was ambivalently valued within this institutional setting. Keiko decided to use a heavy katakana-like[1] pronunciation at school, but, in the private English lessons that she took and on her junior high school trip to New Zealand, she tried to speak naturally. Later, at senior high school, Keiko did translation tests of 30 to 50 English individual words every morning.

This was an early class at 7.30 before the main lessons started. All this effort at memorizing English words for the university entrance exam instilled in Keiko a sense of conflict. English had been her favourite subject at junior high, she reported, but now she came to hate it. She was required to write the same isolated words 20–30 times. Her teacher explained that, if she learnt vocabulary like this, reading would become easier. Keiko didn't find this to be the case. She just thought when she saw a word in a text: *'I know this word, but I can't imagine the meaning.'* Keiko sums up her experience in four words: *'I lost my way.'*

Keiko had opportunities to use English mainly outside of the formal education system through taking conversation school lessons or using English on short school trips abroad. For her, the practices of studying/learning a language and of using a language were strongly differentiated. Her decision to switch her pronunciation allowed her to claim the identity of 'poor speaker' within school and to maintain group membership with her peers and with her teacher. She did not stand out. Outside of school, she invested herself (Norton Pierce, 1995; Norton, 2000) in speaking 'naturally' – in developing the kind of L2 ability (or 'embodied cultural capital' in Bourdieu's terms) that might let her realize her 'right to speech' (Bourdieu, 1977: 648) with other English users. Yet, the separation between these figured worlds of learning and using English was so strong that Keiko ultimately lost her direction.

Certainly, Ken and Keiko had limited chances to engage in 'contextualized, meaning-based tasks' that are necessary 'to develop and strengthen connections among individual lexical items' (Hunt and Beglar, 2005: 28). Before university, they had learnt long lists of isolated words and encoded their English lexical knowledge primarily through word-for-word translation into Japanese. It is clear that a recurrent challenge for them, at later points of language use, was to recombine the atomized elements of their lexical knowledge for the particular communicative purposes they had at hand. These are important lexical and psycholinguistic considerations in understanding their L2 collocation development, but it is equally important to question how their relationship to English (and desire to use English) has been and is 'socially and historically constructed' (Norton, 2000: 10).

Interpreting different worlds of everyday use

The first time that Ken used a collocation dictionary in May 2007 was a transformative experience for him. He decided to look up *offside* and *goal* and discovered that he could create collocations such as *Wayne Rooney was ruled offside* and *Who's in goal for Liverpool?* These were phrases that Ken felt he could '*use and hear in daily life*' (group interview, 14 January 2008). After graduation, he would be working for Nissan where both Japanese and English are used in the workplace, so he imagined that he would often make use of English with other non-native speakers. But it was not just a question of everyday vocabulary: Ken's focus on football collocations was helping him to construct a globalized international identity for his imagined self as a future employee of a transnational Japanese corporation.

Mayuko had a part-time job at a fair trade company where she used English, and she hoped to work in fair trade after graduating. In her part-time job, she also needed to communicate in English without being misunderstood; she felt great pressure on her to be correct, but had been initially uncertain about how to record collocations in a way that would help her use them both inside and outside class. Just as she had had to memorize lists of individual words at school, Mayuko had started by listing many collocations around a given key word. Later, Mayuko questioned the value of doing this: *When I started to learn collocation, I only made list of collocation which used difficult or specialized words. And I felt irritated to use collocation because it took time to remember* (Mayuko, interview log: 12 June 2007). Shortly afterwards, she noted that her engagement with her research was driving her need to explain ideas clearly: *My research in this cycle is getting specialized for future plan and also getting complicated. Now I enjoy researching but I need to explain clearly. Collocation learning will help me a lot* (Mayuko, interview

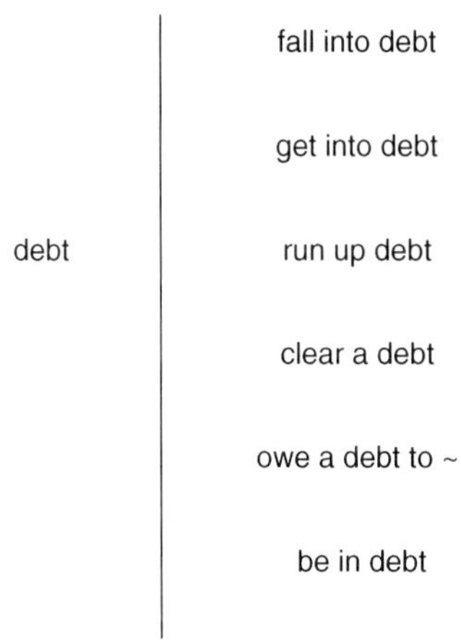

Figure 16.1 An example of Mayuko's collocation notes in April 2007

log: 26 June 2007). Mayuko was reorganizing her ideas and using collocations such as *produce poisonous chemicals* and *dump toxic chemicals* to explain her research area of fair trade organic cotton, but the thought of being misunderstood was troubling her. Where had this need to 'pursue correctness' (Bourdieu, 1977: 656) come from, and how might Mayuko reconcile this with developing her L2 collocation use?

Ken's observations to Mayuko threw some light on the matter. He responded by explaining that he focused on collocating particularly easy words. He showed this example from his notebook.

1. capital	2. accident	3. abolish
• move ~ to ...	• avoid ~	
• establish ~	• cause ~	• ~ formally
• fashion ~	• disastrous ~	

5. personnel	4. hospital
	• build ~
• cut ~	• establish ~
• reduce ~	• psychiatric ~
• government ~	

Figure 16.2 An example of Ken's collocation notes in July 2007

He also explained his collocating as follows:

> I usually choose nouns, especially easy words. People might think I don't have to check the dictionary for accident – it's a very easy word, and everybody knows this word, but I think the easier words have more potential, so I chose accident. I have written down avoid accident and cause accident. And the last one is disastrous accident – this is adjective plus noun. There were a lot of combinations, but I chose these combinations because I thought I can use these combinations in my daily life. ... I also start to work from next April and cut personnel reduce personnel is a very grave matter for me so I chose these words, but I hope I wouldn't use these words in my life.
>
> (Ken, pair interview with Huijuan: 5 July 2007)

Ken's explanation focused on Verb + Noun collocations (or combinations of two lexical items), without any grammatical information (for example, *cause an/the accident*) for encoding them for use. Although he characterized his choices as 'easy', he had chosen *disastrous accident* rather than *serious accident* or *terrible accident,* two collocations that might be more readily identifiable as easy in that both elements of the collocation are highly frequent. Ken seemed concerned with showing Mayuko that he was developing an effective way for recording and using multiword combinations that he judged to be everyday; he also wanted to show that his focus on everyday combinations was helping him break with memorization as the only route to developing his collocation knowledge. He was, he commented, not bothered if he forgot some combinations that he had chosen: *'I wouldn't waste my time checking some difficult words which I will never see again. It's all for my daily life, not academic study.'* By daily life, Ken meant talking with his peers in English here and now, and, as before, with his co-workers in the future – but this imagined future was now partially recast as wielding power over the job security of others.

The issue of selecting collocations for particular worlds of everyday use re-emerged in the first pair interview between Ken and Huijuan later in the year, when they discussed useful collocations for poverty, a common issue in their individual research projects. Huijuan had just explained that she used *absolute poverty, eradicate poverty, eliminate poverty* and *combat poverty* in her term paper, but rejected *alleviate* because it is 'quite a difficult word' (Huijuan, pair interview with Ken: 29 October 2007). They moved next to talking about *eradicate poverty,* a collocation that Ken had noted:

Huijuan:	*You had* ***eradicate***
Ken:	***eradicate*** *yeah because I was very happy when I know when I knew about this collocation*
Huijuan:	*Why*
Ken:	*Well* ***eradicate*** *was the word I remembered in juken*
Huijuan:	*In what*
Ken:	*In juken* [=studying for the university entrance exam]
Huijuan:	*Ahh*
Ken:	*Entrance exam I tried to memorize it* ***eradicate*** *and I couldn't and I met* ***eradicate*** *again so it was kind of revenge*
Huijuan:	*Ahhh mmm*
Ken:	*And I thought makes me look intelligent that's the point*
Huijuan:	*OK*

Ken:	*But I realize when I use the word* ***eradicate*** *my friends can't understand it and I have to explain it again so there's no point using* ***eradicate*** *when you're talking to non-native speaker so maybe it was a mistake to*
Huijuan:	*Choose the word*
Ken:	*Choose the word and try too hard to impress people.*
	(Huijuan and Ken, pair interview: 29 October 2007)

In his here-and-now figured world of using English to explain his research, Ken appears driven by a need to be accepted on equal terms by his peers, and this entails using general everyday collocations. His bitter-sweet recall of his past English vocabulary practices indicates that he could exploit the power of difficult collocations to command his listeners and exert monologic authority (Bourdieu, 1977: 648) over his peers. Ken decides that it makes no sense for him to position himself in such a way: his classmates won't understand him. He prefers to choose collocations that he believes his peers will immediately understand and that he will not have to make the effort to '*explain again*', as he puts it. He thus avoids the risk of communication breakdown, and also circumvents the need for paraphrasing, which some earlier studies (Bahns and Eldaw, 1993; Farghal and Obiedat, 1995) have identified as a coping strategy for learners in dealing with their lack of collocation ability.

A further part of Ken's reasoning is that focusing on 'easy combinations' will help him avoid the need for meaningless memorization: '*All the words which are used often is very easy one and so I don't have to remember very long difficult words*' (Ken, individual interview: 26 June 2007). Investing himself in the everyday use of collocations and avoiding idiomatic but difficult combinations is a major (if not consistent) lexical effect in his collocating. For Ken, it is a cost-effective way of presenting himself as an equal to his peers. Yet, there is a striking contrast between the peer-affirming consequences this practice has now and his sense of the imagined managerial power that might inform his collocation use in the future.

Moving from quantity of lexical knowledge to quality of collocational use

Benson and Lor (1998: 26–8) characterize the shift from quantity to quality in learners' conceptions of learning as a typically important stage in their taking greater overall control of how they are learning and using English. Evidence from the current study suggests that this shift is of specific importance in the development of L2 collocation knowledge, too. An important theme for all four students was the shift from quantity of collocation knowledge to quality of collocation use that they went through in different ways at different times. Huijuan's comment in the group interview about *'not just trying to be native'* (Huijuan, group interview: 14 January 2008) in using collocation directly picked up on the shift away from quantity to quality. Huijuan recalled how she had started the year concerned with recording quantities of collocation: *Focused on variety of words. Tried to get as many as I could for collocation notes. Focused on the meaning of collocations* (Huijuan, end-of-year map: 14 January 2008). The example from her notes given in Figure 16.3 shows how she dealt with collocation variety in practice at the start of the year:

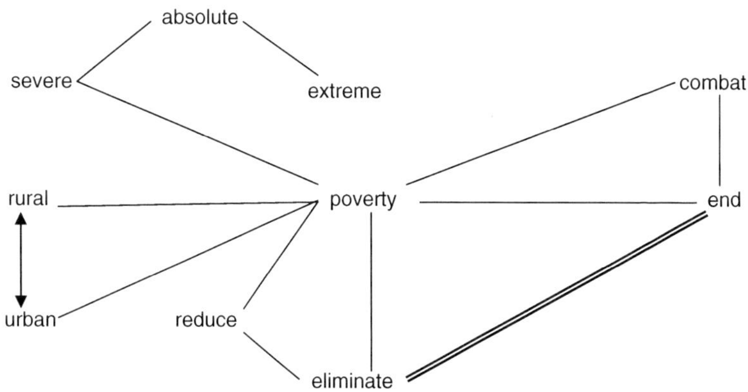

Figure 16.3 An example of Huijuan's collocation notes in May 2007

Looking back over her development during the year, Huijuan felt that she had soon afterwards started to *'reduce the number of collocations'* and *'focus on the order of collocation'* and *'make longer connection of collocations, not just two-word combinations'* (Huijuan, end-of-year map: 14 January 2008), as her research gathered pace and she repeatedly needed to reorganize her ideas in drafting and redrafting the first of her two long term papers for the year. At the same time, Huijuan sometimes rejected everyday collocations in favour of a more academic register: *We also discussed the difference between speaking and writing. Ken said when you present to non-native speaker, you don't choose a difficult collocation like* ***eradicate poverty****, because that will be difficult for listeners to understand. And for* *me, when I do writing, I can choose words by feeling of academic, even if they are difficult* (Huijuan, interview log: 6 December 2007). One instance of this was how she had changed the collocation *big difference* to *enormous difference.* To do this, she had used the *Oxford Collocations Dictionary for Students of English* (2002). By looking at the set of adjectival collocates for *difference* that included *big,* she noticed the ones she often used. She then selected *enormous* as an alternative because it was an adjective she knew and felt others would understand, and *enormous difference* was a collocation that she didn't use that much. Huijuan later noted in her interview log: *I think I choose it for variety and coolness* (Huijuan, interview log: 6 December 2007).

Reconnecting what is known and projecting new identities

The twin themes of variety and coolness had also come up for Keiko and Mayuko in their pair interviews at the end of October, and their interpretation of what these meant for them pointed to processes of development that involved more than just lexical decision making. Mayuko was now researching discrimination against HIV+ women in India, and Keiko media responsibility and victims'/offenders' rights. Keiko went back to the sense of stress that she had experienced in junior and senior high school in memorizing vocabulary: '*to study vocabulary is really stressful before I know collocation*' (Keiko, pair interview with Mayuko: 25 October 2007). She then talked about how making choices between near-equivalent collocations made her feel 'cool': '*to choose words which I want to use is interesting ... sometimes I can find new connection or like I always use* ***protect privacy****, but there is another way to express like* ***preserve privacy*** *or* ***respect privacy****. If I can say a lot of kind of talking expression, I can be more be more native ... cool*' (Keiko, pair interview with Mayuko: 25 October 2007).

However, as Keiko and Mayuko explored this further, it became clear that using collocations was for them not just a question of becoming more nativelike. They also felt they sounded '*less Japanese*' and '*more international*' in that their collocating let them differentiate themselves from '*other average Japanese*', as Mayuko put it, echoing Maher's point that 'Cool is now the main operating principle of cultural hybridity' (Maher, 2005: 89) for different groups of young people in Japan.

In fact, Keiko and Mayuko's collocation choices appeared to be linking into different acts of identity 'in which people reveal both their personal identity and their search for social roles' (Le Page and Tabouret-Keller, 1985: 14). The following extract highlights some critical shifts in the practices and identities that Keiko and Mayuko noticed were becoming prominent for themselves:

Mayuko:	*... before I talk to other people about my research, if I look at this collocation map I can easily remember or know these words. I can use, and then I can use in my conversation with other people.* ***enjoy*** *and* ***get*** *and* ***establish rights*** *are very familiar words to me, so I don't need to remember from the first step, so maybe I can use in my conversation*
Keiko:	*Mmm so so. If it is more difficult words*
Mayuko:	*I can't use in my conversation maybe*
Keiko:	*So are you trying to use more nandaro* [= what do I mean]
Mayuko:	*Simple*
Keiko:	*Simple words*
Mayuko:	*Yes*
Keiko:	*Mmm*
Mayuko:	*As we talked before, simple words sounds more the beginner of English learning, so if I use the word in variety it sounds more not beginner of studying English*
Keiko:	*Eh*
Mayuko:	*These simple words which I chose like* ***right*** *and* ***HIV*** *or* ***discrimination*** *is very simple words, and I can use... everyone can use in their conversation, but not too many people know how to use in variety. But if we know the variety of using these words, we can say in different way, even if I use the same words*
Keiko:	*Mmmm*
Mayuko:	*So I chose more simple words*
Keiko:	*And I think* ***enjoy right*** *is cool* (laughter)
Mayuko:	*I think so too like* ***respect privacy*** *and maybe* ***face discrimination*** *is much cooler than* ***experience discrimination.***

(Keiko and Mayuko, pair interview: 25 October 2007)

Part of their changing sense of identification comes from a desire to appear more adult/sophisticated and less childish/beginner-like in their use of English: *'We learn English for more than nearly 10 years ... it's time to use quality of English'* (Mayuko, pair interview with Keiko: 25 October 2007). Like Huijuan, they don't want to keep repeating the same phrases; but they are also trying to move away, as Ken already had, from difficult collocations towards combinations that are transparent and, at the same time, 'cool' for explaining their research to their peers. At the lexical level, they are becoming more and more able to vary their use of such transparent Verb + Noun collocations. Yet, what they categorize as *'simple words'* appear to be combinations with a personalized salience for explaining their research clearly to others – and part of a wider process in which they reposition themselves as more expert users of the language, as different from their peers, and as diverging from their own former identities as basic language learners.

Developing authorship

The final process to emerge was the gathering sense of authorship that the students' L2 collocation development was enabling them to attain. This came from a more critical awareness of the constraints that they had worked with, both in the current year and in their previous vocabulary learning. Mayuko had started the year by listing new and difficult collocations (as shown in Figure 16.1 earlier), and then struggled to find an appropriate way of organizing her notes for herself. She finally came to see what she called 'collocation packages' as the optimal representation. By collocation package, Mayuko meant a small set of highly usable

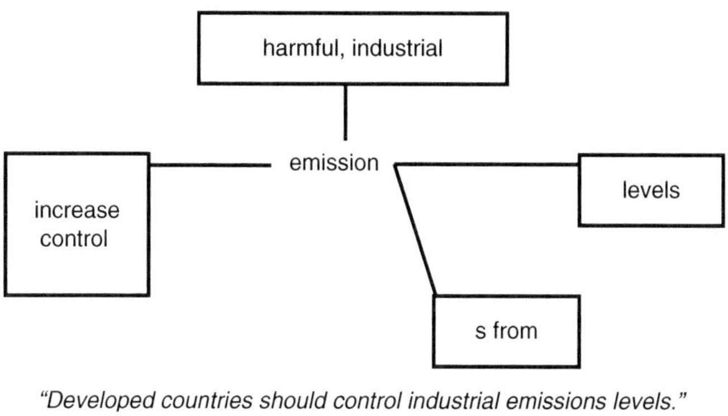

Figure 16.4 Example collocation package (Mayuko) in December 2007

collocate connections around a key idea in her research, together with an example sentence (see Figure 16.4).

Collocation packages literally enabled Mayuko to pack complex information into the noun phrase. This was the tangible lexical effect of her constantly reconstructing key ideas as she worked through multiple texts: the different source webpages and articles she had read, the research notes she had made in extracting important information, and the collocation dictionary she had consulted to help her create the mini-network of collocates around *emission*. Mayuko put her authorship in these terms:

> My research notes is from separate articles and maybe it doesn't have connection each other, but when I research the separated articles, then they get into my brain and then I understand ... and then I put my understanding in the research notes and choose some key words from the research notes and then make the collocation notes, so the collocation notes is from my understanding, so I can explain only looking from collocation notes.
>
> (Mayuko, pair interview with Keiko: 6 December 2007)

Her control of collocation now rested on her being able to include in a collocation package a small compact set of different collocates clustering around the noun and performing different functions (such as collocable verbs, adjectives, and nouns). The final step was to produce an example sentence that she could use as an anchor in moving to spoken explanation of her research to others. Contrary to her previous learning experiences, Mayuko's collocation packages indicated that she no longer believed it important to learn small decontextualized units in order to develop her L2 collocation ability (compare Figures 16.1 and 16.4). Rather, she was now developing collocation packages as a working process that enabled her, at just a moment's glance, to choose and use a highly limited number of collocation choices, and to feel confident, expert and authoritative in encoding and producing them. The packages themselves acted as restricted, but generative, collocation frames for Mayuko.

Concluding comments

One of the risks of analysing learners' finished collocation productions lies in disembodying learners from their learning histories and past practices and interpreting their present performances as free of the constraints of particular social worlds and contexts of use. The benefits of such analyses are that we can arrive at more generalizable statements about L2 collocation performance, but the question remains as to how learners arrive at the moments of performance that are examined. Given the paucity of qualitative studies in L2 collocation research, I chose to use an interview approach that would encourage learners' narration of their L2 collocation development, so that key processes could be explored and reinterpreted over time. The condensed narrative reconstruction of these processes in this chapter reveals there are many factors influencing and constraining learners' L2 collocation development.

What this approach to understanding collocation particularly shows is that, when those processes are tracked, a major dimension of effective collocation learning concerns an ongoing engagement with *lexical and sociocultural reorganization*. More studies on the approaches that different individuals take to handling the challenges and opportunities of such reorganization will enable us, in future, to understand further what learners are doing as they progressively master their L2 collocation development over time.

Note

1. Katakana is a Japanese syllabary that is most often used to transcribe loan words that have become part of everyday Japanese usage. Katakana is sometimes used in textbooks to indicate the Japanese syllabic pronunciation of English words, e.g., *knife* = ナイフ (naifu), *tennis* = テニス (tenisu) and *musical* = ミュージカル (myuujikaru).

Acknowledgement

My thanks go to Huijuan, Ken, Keiko, and Mayuko for taking part in this inquiry, and to Jingyi Jiang, Alison Stewart, Alison Wray, Henrik Gyllstad, John Shillaw, Masuko Miyahara, Mike Nix, Neil Cowie, Steve Brown, Tess Fitzpatrick, and Tin Tin Htun for discussing the research and/or chapter drafts with me at different points.

17
Commentary on Part IV: Processes in the Development of L2 Collocational Knowledge – A Challenge for Language Learners, Researchers and Teachers

Birgit Henriksen and Lars Stenius Stæhr

Introduction

Collocations, that is, frequently recurring lexical patterns, often with specific semantic and syntactic restrictions, can be seen as a subset of formulaic sequences. Mastery of formulaic sequences, including collocations, is a central aspect of communicative competence, enabling the native speaker to process language both fluently and idiomatically (Pawley and Syder, 1983) and to fulfil basic communicative and social needs (Wray, 2002). For the L2 learner, formulaic sequences often function as a gateway to the new language and they may support the process of acquiring more creative language skills. Moreover, the ability to use formulaic sequences, including collocations, is an important element in gaining nativelike competence, and they may play an important role in taking on or rejecting group identity (Wray, 2002). Even though learners in the initial phases of learning may rely on accumulating different types of formulaic sequences, collocational knowledge is, nevertheless, a language phenomenon that is acquired late and often not mastered very well by L2 language learners (see, for example, Arnaud and Savignon, 1997; Revier and Henriksen, 2006). In this chapter, we will focus on the *processes in the development of L2 collocational knowledge*, which is the topic explored in the three research studies in Part IV. We will discuss both the challenges learners are faced with in relation to acquiring collocational knowledge and the challenges researchers are faced with in relation to describing and explaining the acquisition processes involved. Finally, we will briefly address the challenges faced by teachers when they want to focus on L2 collocational knowledge in their teaching practice.

Challenges for learners

It may seem surprising that even fairly advanced learners experience problems in relation to developing L2 collocational knowledge, but as shown in the three studies in Part IV, a number of obvious explanations for this may be found. A recurrent theme in the three studies is the tendency of L2 learners to focus on individual words rather than collocations in input. Learners as well as teachers may not attend to collocations in the input, because these constructions rarely cause comprehension problems. Moreover, learners may simply not be aware of the concept of collocations. Finally, the studies also show that learners often perceive lexical learning as a process of accumulating new language elements rather than as refining and restructuring their existing knowledge, for example, in relation to developing collocational knowledge of already acquired lexical items.

Whereas evidence suggests that adult native speakers notice, process, and store formulaic sequences as whole meaning units (Wray, 2002; Schmitt and Carter, 2004), L2 learners beyond the initial stages of learning primarily attend to separate words. As Barfield (this volume) and Wray (2002) argue, L2 learners will often *focus on individual words* and thus break collocations down into separate units. They are then faced with the challenge of having to recombine these units into collocations in the process of using language. This is supported by Barfield's interview data in which two of the four learners clearly express that the main obstacle to speaking English is not lack of knowledge of individual words, but rather ability to link words together in language use. In the Yang and O'Neill study, learners reported that they did not pay attention to common and easily comprehensible collocations but focused on learning single, unknown words instead. This must be particularly true of the type of collocations where learners can understand the meaning of the collocation by knowing the meaning of the words that constitute the collocation. However, collocations have different degrees of transparency, so learners may be misled by this word-by-word comprehension strategy in their interpretation of less transparent constructions.

Learners who have been exposed to teaching practices that favour decontextualized vocabulary learning may not so readily develop an *awareness of the concept of collocations* and therefore may not feel a need to acquire them. The learners in the Yang and O'Neill study report that they have had little or no previous awareness of collocations and that the new process-oriented learning method they are exposed to in the project draws their attention to larger chunks of language and now makes them notice these. In contrast, Peters observes that both learner groups in her study had some previous awareness of collocations, irrespective of the fact that they may have been exposed to decontextualized teaching techniques. Contrary to previous research findings, Peters did not find an effect for an attention-drawing technique on recall of collocations versus individual words, a result that is partially explained by the fact that both learner groups report that they paid attention to collocations in the input, thus exhibiting awareness of collocational structures.

The difference in learner awareness of the concept of collocation and its importance for language use might be attributed to differences in levels of language proficiency. Whereas the participants in the Yang and O'Neill study were believed to have reached an intermediate level of language proficiency, Peters's informants were advanced EFL students who were well aware of the concept of collocation and who appeared to appreciate the significance of syntagmatic constructions for language use. Yang and O'Neill argue that learners at the borderline between the intermediate and advanced stages of learning need to be made aware of syntagmatic relations and must pay attention to them in input in order to push their language beyond the intermediate stage; they may therefore benefit from an awareness-raising approach.

Learners' growing awareness of the concept of collocations is often characterized by a growing awareness of the differential needs for L2 collocational knowledge. This awareness is accompanied by a shift in learners' understanding of social identity and communicative needs in relation to acquiring and using the new language. This is especially voiced by the learners in the Barfield study, who explain that their incentive to learn collocations is not just driven by a wish to sound more nativelike, but also by the ambition of being able to express individual identity and to claim group membership. The four learners want to attain more precision in their language use and be able to express more complex matters. Moreover, they wish to sound more 'adult-like' (see also Wray, 2002). As the Barfield study shows, learners face potential conflicts between here-and-now social and school-related needs and future, job-related needs. They are thus confronted with questions such as whether they should focus on learning an everyday or academic register – and whether they should focus on correctness or ability for use. Barfield argues that the developmental shifts in practices, identities, and social roles that are captured in the longitudinal self-report data are important for these learners, both in terms of gaining a feeling of being in control of one's own learning process, and in terms of having linguistic choices and being able to function with confidence as a second language user.

Another interesting theme, which pervades the three research studies, is related to the *informants' attitude to learning in general*. The learners seem to focus on expanding their vocabulary in terms of quantity, instead of refining and restructuring the quality of their knowledge of frequent, already acquired words. Some of the learners view difficult, specialized, and low frequent items as an indicator of high language proficiency and thus as a hallmark of learning progress. However, these low frequent items are not necessarily central for creating useful collocations. The learners in the three studies are thus challenged by a need to understand and define their learning requirements in relation to criteria of usefulness. Viewed in terms of frequency-based considerations, more common collocations consisting of frequently occurring lexical items in the target language could be regarded as the most obvious and attainable learning goal. However, this may not correspond with the learners' own perceptions of usefulness, defined in relation to their individual, social, and communicative needs.

In addition to the factors mentioned above, L2 learners are often not exposed to the amount and range of varied input needed for developing nativelike collocational knowledge. Yet, if the input *is* rich enough, learners and teachers are faced with the serious challenge of selection, as the sheer range of possible collocational combinations makes it difficult for them to choose which specific collocations to focus on. Finally, as pointed out by Schmitt and Carter (2004), learners may be cautious about drawing on L1 knowledge of formulaic sequences and therefore tend to avoid positive transfer. It is likely that the same avoidance behaviour limits positive transfer of L1 collocational knowledge.

As mentioned above, collocational knowledge is very important for fluent and idiomatic language use, freeing attentional cognitive resources for higher-order processing. L2 learners with insufficient L2 collocational knowledge may therefore experience problems in language reception and production. If learners are faced with the laborious task of having to combine individual lexical items into idiomatic, nativelike phrases, they will be challenged beyond their abilities in online language production, and if they focus on individual items, comprehension of less transparent constructions may suffer. The lack of easily retrievable language chunks may also have a negative impact on learning. Learners may not have sufficient attentional cognitive resources to notice new language elements in input and to engage in depth of processing (Laufer and Hulstijn, 2001). Problems in developing productive skills may also have serious consequences in relation to the learner's personal identity and in relation to fulfilling social and communicative needs. Lack of confidence and lack of ability to reposition oneself as an individual in the L2 may lead to the feeling of being a 'reduced personality' (Harder, 1980) and could have a serious negative impact on the learners' attitude to the language-learning task and subsequently on their L2 development.

Challenges for researchers

In light of the scarcity of previous process research, researchers wanting to explore processes in the development of L2 collocational knowledge are also faced with a number of serious challenges.

The first major challenge that researchers encounter is the need to be explicit about *theoretical assumptions with regard to acquisition of collocational knowledge*, both in relation to general language-learning theory and in relation to theories of vocabulary acquisition. Unfortunately, the lack of process research on L2 acquisition of collocations and the differences in research procedures and informant groups make it difficult to draw any universal conclusions about developmental processes and to relate findings to assumptions about language learning and vocabulary acquisition. The present studies are based on assumptions about the crucial role of noticing, learner awareness, and depth of processing for L2 collocation development. Moreover, the investigations by Yang and O'Neill and by Barfield draw on theories of social identity and the role of learner autonomy. In terms of theories of vocabulary acquisition, the distinction between contextualized versus decontextualized learning is also raised, and the question of learner development in terms of vocabulary size (acquiring new low-frequent items) versus quality of lexical knowledge is addressed. As demonstrated in the study by Barfield, the development of one of the learners is characterized by a shift towards more limited, but highly usable collocation packages, showing her preference for mini-networks. Moreover, the learners seemed to develop a preference for quality in their word knowledge at the expense of mere word collecting, which reflects a growing awareness of the importance of depth of vocabulary knowledge. However, these findings could have been related more directly to central theories of vocabulary acquisition (e.g. mapping, network building, and processes of word learning in the bilingual lexicon – see, for example, de Groot, 1992; Henriksen, 1999) and to models of lexical competence (e.g. size versus depth; various dimensions of vocabulary knowledge – for an overview, see Read, 2004).

The research field is characterized by a lack of specific models of collocation learning, assumptions about the relationship between learning individual lexical items and learning collocations, and a discussion of whether collocations are different from other types of formulaic sequences with regard to storage, acquisition, and use. Consequently, as Schmitt and Carter (2004: 13) stress, the state of research makes it difficult to describe acquisitional gains and to explain the processes in greater detail. However, Schmitt and Carter (2004) also argue that the acquisition of formulaic sequences fits well with pattern-based, connectionist models of learning. One may assume that some of the same characteristics that have been found for the development of individual lexical items also apply to acquisition of larger lexical chunks; for example, the notion that the process is incremental in nature and is reliant on repeated exposure and use that lead to refinement of knowledge as well as ability for use. Frequency of occurrence will undoubtedly have an effect on collocation acquisition. Moreover, as pointed out by Wray (2002), various other factors may affect learning. The processes employed by very young, teenage or adult learners may vary considerably, for example in their tendency to adopt more holistic or analytic approaches to learning. Dörney, Durow and Zahran (2004) argue that learners' acquisition is affected by learner factors such as language aptitude and learner motivation and, in particular, the degree of sociocultural adaption of the learner – factors that are also highlighted in the research studies on collocation in Part IV.

These contradictory as well as similar findings in studies of formulaic sequences and in studies that focus more narrowly on collocational knowledge highlight the need for a more thorough understanding of the similarities and differences between collocational knowledge and knowledge of other types of formulaic sequences with regard to storage, acquisition, and use. It is still unclear whether collocations are stored as wholes in the mental lexicons of language users and what implications the representation of collocational knowledge may have for language acquisition and use.

The second major challenge that researchers are faced with is addressing the *methodological problems* involved in investigating internal learner processes that cannot be observed and captured directly in product data. Moreover, different research questions require different methodologies. The three studies approach the development of L2 collocational knowledge from different perspectives. Peters investigates acquisition of collocational knowledge by looking at the learners' ability to recall individual lexical items and collocational phrases in a translation task. Pre- and post-test data from the translation task is supplemented with questionnaire data tapping into the learners' strategy use and perception of the tasks. Yang and O'Neill focus on the development in the use of learner strategies through a specific process-oriented learning method. The learners' approach to working with collocations in the learning programme is tracked over time through interviews and reflective learner journals. Barfield explores learners' perceptions of and attitudes towards learning and using collocations by means of in-depth case study interviews and learner–learner discussions collected over time.

The Peters study differs in methodological approach by combining quantitative data with qualitative data, which enables Peters to tap into both the lexical knowledge gained and the processes involved in carrying out the experimental task. However, using data in a one-off, pre-test/post-test design cannot uncover the underlying acquisition processes. Other approaches, for example, introspective methods involving both online and retrospective data employed repeatedly at various stages in the acquisition process, may be needed to capture the actual learning processes involved. The two other studies adopt a qualitative approach both in terms of elicitation methods and data analysis. Interviews, learner–learner discussions and reflective learner reports enable learners to voice their experiences, attitudes, and beliefs as regards the development of their collocational knowledge. Moreover, the longitudinal design provides an insight into the shifts in beliefs, assumptions, attitudes, and expectations over time.

One of the challenges inherent in using qualitative elicitation methods like these is to set up systematic criteria for objectively analysing the data and for selecting representative and recurring themes, enabling the researcher to find consistent patterns in learner responses. Barfield, for example, focuses on five themes that come up in the final group interviews and retraces these throughout his dataset. In all three studies, the researchers identify major themes in the qualitative data collected, but they do not systematically discuss the criteria used for identifying the themes. However, there is no doubt that all three studies benefit from combining different data elicitation methods. A combined approach gives insight into different aspects of the research object, and supplementary qualitative methods may explain data elicited through quantitative methods. For example, Peters is able to explore both knowledge gains and strategy use. The learning journals collected by Yang and O'Neill support the researchers in their analysis of the interview data. Finally, Barfield uses a triangulation approach, eliciting data from multiple sources in order to capture the ongoing shifts in learner attitudes and beliefs in great detail.

Challenges for teachers

The researchers emphasize that their studies are exploratory in nature and that more research is needed to be able to generalize about the processes in the development of L2 collocational knowledge. But, as we have seen, the studies focus on a range of interesting issues that may have implications for teaching. The major challenge for teachers lies in *developing pedagogical tools* for raising learners' awareness of the actual construct of collocations, developing methods for supporting their ability to attend to recurring patterns in the input, and also in developing ways of increasing learners' understanding of the need for consolidating and refining their collocational knowledge of frequently occurring lexical items.

The three studies show how learners may benefit from teaching approaches that heighten learners' awareness of collocations, encouraging the learners to attend more to syntagmatic structures in the input and making learners aware of an actual need for learning and refining their knowledge of lexical patterns. Learners may be guided in their learning in line with the input-processing methodology suggested by Van Patten and Cardierno (1993). The AWARE approach used by Yang and O'Neill outlines a possible method for guiding learners through various steps of awareness-raising. The investigation by Peters also highlights the beneficial role of marginal glosses that include both syntagmatic constructions and individual items. Finally, the Barfield study sheds light on the use of peer–peer reports, written reflective journals and collocation notebooks as potential techniques for guiding learners both in their development of collocational knowledge and in their individual understanding of their own role and identity as L2 language learners. Such techniques may help teachers overcome the difficulty of focusing directly on specific collocations when there is a lack of clear selection criteria and may guide learners in the process of acquiring L2 collocational knowledge.

18
Conclusion: Navigating L2 Collocation Research

Alison Wray

Making a mental map of L2 collocation research

In this concluding chapter, I will reflect on some of the issues, challenges, and opportunities for research into L2 collocation, referring back to the studies in the book and outward to the broader context. My use of the term 'collocation' will be somewhat loose, both so as to capture the range of data types covered in the book, and because there is much to be said that encompasses both word–word collocations and other kinds of multiword (formulaic) strings. More specifically, while it is less than clear that all the features attributed to formulaic language apply to collocations, it is probably true that most of those attributed to collocations also apply to formulaic language. Some costs may ensue from fudging the boundary between the two phenomena, but we would be mistaken if we imagined there is any clearly defined boundary to hold to – and sometimes obscuring one thing is a means of bringing other things to light.

The main function of research is to ask questions and seek answers to them. In the overall context of L2 research, the answers assist our understanding of the nature of language itself, language learning and language knowledge, and contribute to achieving – or helping others achieve – effective approaches to language learning, teaching or testing, and/or associated aspects of communication in the L1–L2 domain. Technological advances, as well as developments in research theory and methodology, continue to offer us new opportunities to address interesting questions. This book reflects several aspects of the research currently being undertaken into L2 knowledge and performance.

Answers do not come easily, though, and our contributions are gently incremental. The questions we really want to ask are far too big to answer in one go. For instance, if we ask *How we can make language learning more effective?*, no single study can tell us – there are too many different types of learner, too many contexts and too many components to the learning process. We gradually assemble answers to the big questions by means of answers to more limited questions, such as *With British school students learning French, is it more effective to teach two hours per week for forty weeks, or a three-week crash course full time?*

In the case of L2 collocation, there are particularly difficult challenges when it comes to mapping out the landscape of different, partial answers to the big general questions, for there will be contributions from studies in many domains, including the linguistic, psychological, pedagogical, and computational. Interpretations of evidence may be founded in socially oriented qualitative analysis, statistical measures or linguistic or psychological theory.

Thus, there are two inherent tensions: between the general and the specific, and between the expectations and assumptions of the different research traditions contributing answers to the same questions. We see exemplified in this book how these tensions are engaged with. Regarding the first, all the research chapters in the book address one or more rather specific research questions, contributing partial answers to much broader questions – see Figure 18.1. The effectiveness of each contribution in making clear the mapping of the specific onto the general may end up determining the extent to which the work is useful to others. This is because each new research report joining the ranks of 'the research literature' provides the basis for hypotheses to be developed by new researchers. It is at the generalized level that connection between two specific studies can be made, allowing appropriate extrapolations and predictions to be made about a new case on the basis of an older one.

Meanwhile, the commentaries on each section of the book also address the relationship between the specific and the general. Nesi (Chapter 9), for instance, finds it 'revealing to compare small, separate and geographically distant studies ... to discover further insights unavailable to the original authors'. Granger, on the other hand, warns us against conceptualizing a generic L2 learner, and argues that we should 'distinguish between different types of L2 learners and L2 learning situations' (Chapter 5). In other words, it is no simple matter to decide just how generalized observations can become without losing their power (Wallace and Wray, 2006: 72–5).

A key function of research is to help determine the extent of valid generalization. Consider, for instance, one clear case in L2 research: the evidence presented over some three decades (perhaps most notably

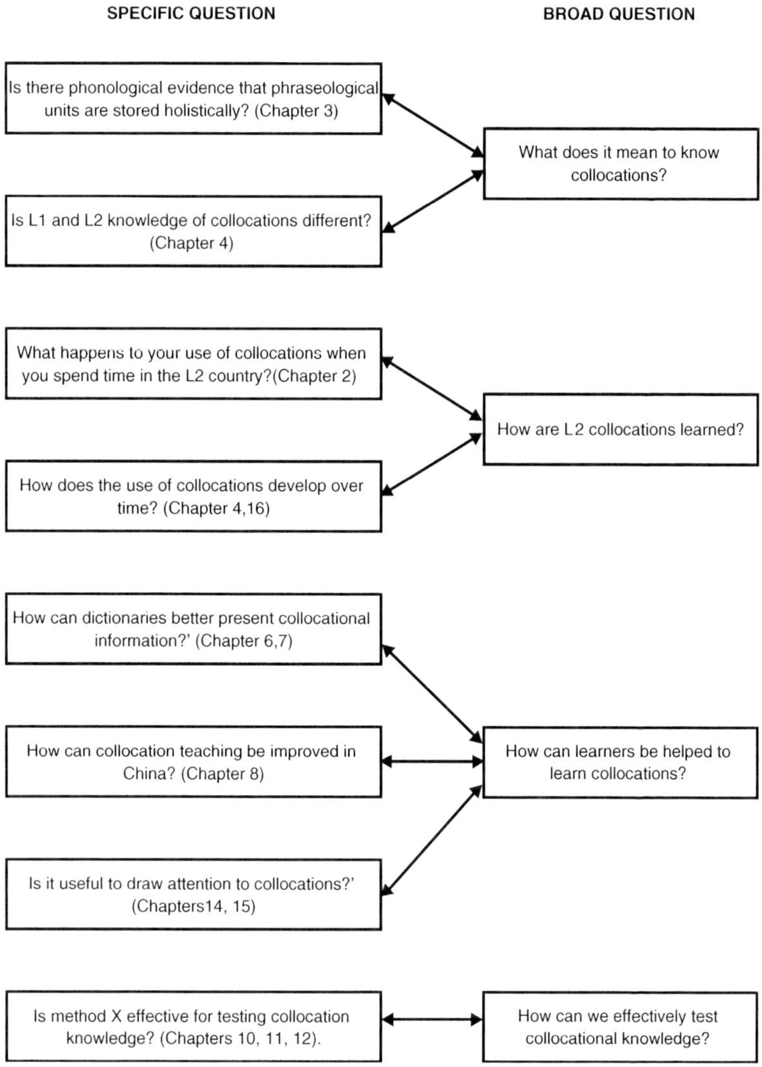

Figure 18.1 Mapping specific investigations in the broader context

by Pienemann, e.g. 1998) that morphological and syntactic features of English are acquired in a particular order by learners, irrespective of *how* they learn or *what input* they receive. The precise parameters of that predictability – in other words, what it takes for a particular learner to buck the trend – are a legitimate and significant focus of research that eventually enables us to evaluate the boundaries of the generalization and understand better the specifics of each case or case type.

So far, research into L2 collocation has not produced such strong and specific claims, but we see tendencies and opportunities in, for example, assumptions about the 'universality' of the adult's atomistic approach to learning as compared with the child's more holistic one (Wray, 2002). This is something that should be examined methodically, establishing how fine-grained our distinctions must be in relation to types of adult learner and the language under examination, if generalizations are to be informative and reliable.

Meanwhile, Shillaw (Chapter 13) brings out the importance of locating studies that use different methods on a single map of the landscape of language learning. He sees equal value in analysing quantitatively the results from large groups of language users and 'look[ing] closely at learners' individual evolving perspectives'. Finally, Henriksen and Stenius Stæhr (Chapter 17) unite the two strands by noting that generalizations cannot be made in the absence of adequate empirical evidence and, particularly, theoretical underpinning.

Keeping in mind the particular cases in this book, and the observations made by the section commentators, I consider below some examples of broad questions that I believe we should keep in mind as we undertake our research, so that we retain the clearest possible view of where our investigations fit with those of others. I will demonstrate how asking the broader questions can lead us to challenge our own assumptions and choose between competing accounts of a phenomenon.

Some questions that define the L2 collocation research landscape

How does research into L2 collocation relate to research into L1 collocation?

To what extent can research from L1 and L2 users be amalgamated? How can findings from one inform the other? The answers are not as straightforward as it might at first appear. There are, naturally, strong pressures on L2 researchers to relate their findings to those from L1 studies. The predominant motivation for L2 linguistic research is the improvement of performance or the measurement of the shortfall between L2 performance and an assumed L1 target of some kind. L2 knowledge is generally perceived as an imperfect version of L1 knowledge. Until corpus-based research became easy to undertake, it was, indeed, common to find that *L2 performance* was being judged as an imperfect version of *L1 knowledge*. Now, at least it is possible to relate L2 performance to L1 performance. However, in the two cases, data may be differently interpreted. In analysing patterns in L1 output, researchers will apply their judgement to exclude items that appear to be random errors (Wray, 2008: 107–8). But many L2 researchers would tend not to view *any* error as random – everything is motivated by the interaction of underlying knowledge and the pressures of performance. The same, of course, could be said of native speakers, but often is not.

How compatible, then, is the full range of evidence from L1 and L2 studies of collocation? In Chapter 1, Barfield and Gyllstad suggest that, compared with L1-focused research, rather little L2-focused research is undertaken in the phraseological tradition – something that would hobble comparison before the first fence. Insofar as they are correct in this assessment, what might be the cause of that difference? It could, of course, be a product simply of the predominant interests of different groups of researchers. Phraseological research has been going on for a very long time, and predates the technological approaches for examining large corpora – perhaps those most engaged in that activity simply had more interest in L1 data. Computational approaches to exploring corpora, on the other hand, seem to appeal equally to those interested in L1 and L2 patterns.

Perhaps there is more to it, though. Some types of phraseological analysis may make assumptions that are difficult to apply to L2 data. For instance, if a phraseological account takes for granted that the producer applies deeply internalized intuitions, then variability in relation to such intuition in L2 user populations would make generalizations difficult. The developing research area of English as a Lingua Franca (e.g. Seidlhofer, Breiteneder and Pitzl, 2006) may bridge the gap somewhat, by raising the status of the L2 pattern beyond that of 'imperfect L1 pattern', so that there is value in investigating the linguistic motivations for forms in their own right.

Where English as a Lingua Franca leads, other aspects of L2 research could follow, to address broader questions such as: *What is intuition and how does it come about? Do L2 learners develop an intuition that is the same as that of native speakers, or different? If the same, how is that achieved, given the very major differences in the learning process? If different, in what cases will these different intuitions result in different judgements or productive behaviours, and how will L1 and L2 users perceive such differences?* These questions generate their own new ones for the more traditional L2 researcher, for instance: *Are L2 learners doomed, because they are trying to use one set of learning tools to master something that is fundamentally defined by its having been created by another set?*

What is collocation anyway?

Processing and access

In a recent paper, Mollet, Wray and Fitzpatrick (in preparation) explore the nature of collocation through the analogy of an academic attending a conference. At any given time, this individual is surrounded by other people. In some cases there is some reason for their proximity to her – one person is a friend and has arranged to have lunch with her; another is a speaker that she has come to listen to. In other cases, there is much less significance to the coincidence of two individuals in the same place at the same time – there was a spare space at the end of the table at lunch, so someone sat there; others attending the same session as our academic are there to hear other speakers, or because they have a quite different interest in the same speaker. Mollet et al. point out that it is through observing the academic over the several days of the conference that one begins to see some patterns. The deliberate ones are reinforced – lunch friends join up for coffee too; the speaker she went to hear now turns up to hear her presentation – while the chance ones fall away as one-offs.

So much is fairly easily mapped onto our conceptualization of word collocations. However, Mollet et al. develop the analogy further. They suggest that one cannot fully appreciate the significance of the company that one individual keeps unless one also knows how the presence of others might influence the behaviour. For instance, suppose our academic were in private negotiation about taking a new job. She would naturally be keen to talk to her contacts at the new institution, but might refrain from doing so when members of her current institution were in the room – the presence of person C can affect how persons A and B interact.

This leads to a proposal to (and a mechanism that can) track 'secondary collocation' in text: fully understanding how words A and B relate entails establishing how the presence or absence of word C influences that relationship. For instance, accomplished prose writing in English (though not necessarily in other languages) is normally characterized by the avoidance of form repetition:

> Consider the sentence 'When the *steamer* had raised *steam* she *steamed* out to sea.' This sentence jars on the ear, and, if only for that reason, is badly written. Synonyms would help us over the difficulty. It is an obvious improvement to say 'When the vessel had raised steam she put out to sea.'
>
> (Joad, 1939: 110)

We may make choices between equivalent grammatical expressions on the same grounds. The sentence in (1) below is accurate, but stylistically less satisfying, perhaps, than (2), where marginal alterations in the structure halve the number of occurrences of the infinitive marker *to*. That is, we cannot fully account for the occurrence of *will* + INF or *of* + PRESENT PARTICIPLE in (2) without noticing how the presence of *to* elsewhere influences the choices made.

(1) The team aims to apply for funding to develop ways to use formulaic language to improve communication in emergency situations.
(2) The team will apply for funding to develop ways of using formulaic language to improve communication in emergency situations.

In some circumstances, the constraints extend to phonological form even when the meaning is different, so that the word *complementary* might be avoided in close proximity to *complimentary*. Most importantly, perhaps, a writer will assist the reader by not using a word that can be interpreted in more than one way in a context that renders it ambiguous. It is for this reason that researchers avoid using the word *significant* to mean 'important' in the context of discussing quantitative research results, where it could be interpreted 'achieving a probability value of less than 0.05'. A British speaker might similarly avoid referring to a *conservative* policy, that is, a reactionary or unimaginative one, in a context where it could be understood to refer a policy of the Conservative party.[1]

Appreciating how one word can determine the presence or absence of a second in relation to a third might contribute to a sophisticated theory of how collocation works. But is it necessary to engage with theory if one only wants to *describe* collocation? It surely is, because one is never really only describing. As soon as we comment on what we have found, predict what might be found next time, or try to locate our findings in the wider body of research, explanation is entailed, even if not explicitly. And that means we should consider just what our underlying assumptions are.

To explore this issue, let us briefly consider the question of how our expectations of collocation patterns and of L2 learners' ability to master them will be different according to the theory we adopt. In different chapters in this book, as in many other published studies, a fundamental discussion, either present or implicit, regards whether collocations should be viewed as 'word + word' or as 'chunk'. Lin and Adolphs (Chapter 3), Reppen (Chapter 4) and Revier (Chapter 10) see collocations predominantly as chunks. In contrast, Groom (Chapter 2),

Eyckmans (Chapter 11), Gyllstad (Chapter 12) and Peters (Chapter 15) approach collocation more from a word + word standpoint. The other research chapters (Handl, Chapter 6; Komuro, Chapter 7; Jiang, Chapter 8; Yang and O'Neill, Chapter 14; Barfield, Chapter 16) shift between the word + word or chunk views, according to the changing position of either the observer or the user. Which way one jumps can determine not only how one interprets one's data but how one analyses it, and indeed what data one selects in the first place.

It is not a matter of us all agreeing on one definition or the other – we are far from being in a position to do that – but there is, I think, value in researchers reflecting on the implications of the definitions they use. Again, it is a matter of stepping back from the specifics of an investigation and asking the bigger questions. For instance, the investigation by Lin and Adolphs in Chapter 3 into the phonological patterns associated with a multiword expression, would make little sense if there were no acknowledgement of other questions, such as *Are multiword expressions holistically stored?* That question in turn will lead us to ask *If they are holistically stored, how does that come about?* and *What determines that one association of words is stored holistically when another is not?* At the same time, one will be asking *Is there any other plausible explanation for apparent evidence of holistic storage?* One such explanation is fast-route assembly – rats get round mazes quicker when they have run them successfully a few times already. So more big questions arise, such as: *What in fact is the difference between fast-route assembly and holistic retrieval, since even in the latter there must be sequential assembly of the phonemes or graphemes?*

To further observe the role of bigger questions, consider Revier's assumptions regarding collocation in Chapter 10:

> First, collocation knowledge can be viewed as an independent construct. Second, collocations constitute lexical items in their own right and, as such, feature formal, semantic, and usage properties similar to those borne by single words. Third, the semantic properties of the constituent words that combine to form collocations are likely to play a role in EFL learners' ability to 'produce' English collocations. Fourth, testing of L2 collocation knowledge needs to focus on the recognition and production of *whole* collocations (this volume).

However, after describing his categorization of collocations as transparent, semi-transparent or non-transparent (this volume), Revier proposes that strings of the first type are probably not holistically processed (this volume) and so, implicitly, fall outside his previous description. His separation out of transparent collocations is not an unreasonable one, and he accounts for it by asserting that 'The *ability to use* transparent collocations ... is more likely [than with the other types] to be dependent on general lexical knowledge and grammatical knowledge' (this volume). He concedes that 'neither transparency nor syntactic regularity necessarily precludes a word combination from being processed holistically' (this volume) but considers that 'the constituents of transparent collocations are much more likely to be learned and processed compositionally (i.e. as separate items) by both foreign language learners and native speakers' (this volume).

While Revier's argument is fine in its own right, it removes a vital piece of the jigsaw. If transparent wordstrings are processed non-holistically, by what mechanism do they become less transparent over time, as many of them evidently do? We know from historical record that non-transparent and irregular multiword strings mostly derive from regular strings. Expressions like *at one fell swoop; woe betide; far be it from me to ...* were once unremarkable. If regular strings are processed anew each time they are used, then why were expressions like this not updated as the language changed?

The solution I have proposed to this conundrum is that holistic processing is not a *result of*, or *reaction to*, non-transparency, but rather a *cause* of it (Wray, 2002: 265–7). That is, perfectly regular, transparent wordstrings rather easily become holistically processed and, by virtue of being so processed, will be protected from changes in the productive language. As for why regular wordstrings can become holistically processed, this relates to the communicative priorities of the native speaker, from first language acquisition onwards. Language acquisition is not an attempt to master the productive capacity of the language code, but rather to achieve functional goals than entail manipulating others to act and think in beneficial ways. By applying the principle of *needs only analysis* (Wray, 2002: 130–2; 2008: 17–20), the child works with the biggest units that can do the job of releasing and creating meaning, and only breaks strings down where there is evidence that doing so will render additional information or permit useful extensions in expression. The overall conservative nature of needs only analysis leaves in place any multiword associations that are consistently associated with a reliable meaning or function. Expressions that are not broken down are less likely to be updated as the language changes over time, so they become increasingly opaque in meaning and/or irregular in form, relative to the changing productive language.

Where does that leave L2 learners? Revier may well be right in his assertion that *they* do not process transparent wordstrings holistically. We can be reasonably confident that adult L2 learners, especially in classroom settings, are strongly oriented towards identifying logical and consistent patterns, and perceive breaches of the patterns as obstacles to efficient learning. It is much easier to explain why this approach results in confusion and error if one does not believe that the system they are trying to learn is fully patterned. In other words, it is Revier's assumption that native speakers do not process transparent collocations holistically that requires further consideration.

What I have tried to demonstrate here is not that Revier is necessarily incorrect, but rather that sometimes rather innocuous-looking assumptions or decisions can have an impact elsewhere. By keeping the bigger questions in mind, one can decide between competing accounts and relate one's own findings and claims to those developed by researchers engaged in producing other parts of the map.

What is being measured?

The dangers of researching what you can measure are well known (this volume, Granger, Chapter 5), and are clearly represented in the notion of the 'lexical bundle', which has a formal definition based on frequency and proximity, not meaning, grammar or pragmatics (Groom, Chapter 2; Reppen, Chapter 4; see Siepmann, 2008: 186ff. for some exploration of the issues associated with definition). Bigger questions that we might keep in view include *Why can meaningful wordstrings not be differentiated from meaningless ones using frequency?*

One answer could be that (some of) the word combinations that corpus linguists discard as meaningless despite being frequent are actually not meaningless at all, but are the fixed parts of larger strings that contain a lot of gaps into which a smaller or larger group of alternates can be inserted.[2] In fact, few researchers would question that it is possible to have a recurrent string that consists of, say, GAP-WORD-GAP-GAP-WORD-WORD-GAP-GAP – it's just that when the start and finish are gaps one can't capture them all that easily. Of course one can search for the fixed words and one can use wild cards, but how is one to establish the nature of the 'gap'? A recurrent string will tend to have not just any old gap but one that admits only a constrained range of words. But even the largest corpora might furnish no more than a half-dozen examples of the basic structure – too few to specify the parameters of the constraints. Recent work by Biber (2008; personal communication) is making headway on capturing the nature of gaps, according to their tendency to be filled by one or many different items, but other aspects of the challenge associated with explaining why both meaningful and meaningless wordstrings are turned up by frequency counts remain to be addressed.

Terminology

At the start of this chapter I noted that my use of the term 'collocation' would be deliberately loose, and suggested that there can be advantages to taking this approach, even though, overall, clear definitions are essential for good research (Wray, 2009). Researchers into formulaic language and collocation are very familiar with the problem of how terminology can waver in focus and coverage. Granger raises this matter in her commentary on the learner corpus-based studies (Chapters 2–4), and Shillaw argues that in the assessment of L2 collocation knowledge (e.g. Chapters 10–12) the parameters of collocation must be very tightly defined. But why is it difficult to keep the terminology straight? Is it because people tend to pick up someone else's term rather than coin their own? Is it because there is a limit to how many terms we can coin? Is it ignorance and laziness in not checking what the previous definitions of terms have been, and/or in clearly specifying one's own? Is it that people genuinely think they are talking about the same thing as someone else, and it takes a third person to point out that they are not?

It may be that our struggle with terminology is fundamental to the nature of our pursuit. Even if we start with something secure and known – use the terminology as others have – we will probably end up muddying the waters. That is because our aim in research is to step from the known into the unknown. We take something we know and we ask questions about it. We want to discover properties previously not recognized or fully understood, and these properties are not, of course, part of the existing definition. Subsequent researchers may ignore those properties, build them in or take issue with them. The result will inevitably be several different 'meanings' for one term.

What does learning collocations entail?

According to Henriksen and Stenius Stæhr (Chapter 17):

> Even though learners in the initial phases of learning may rely on accumulating different types of formulaic sequences, collocational knowledge is, nevertheless, a language phenomenon that is acquired late and often not mastered very well by L2 language learners.
>
> (this volume)

Is this inevitable, or is poor collocation learning down to mistaken teaching methods? Earlier, I described a theoretical model according to which languages, being predominantly determined by the processing that children do, have only a limited amount of consistent patterning. It was noted that, if this account is correct, then post-childhood L2 learners might be bringing the wrong set of tools to the job, considering how languages achieve their form.

Specifically, teaching materials will, give or take the odd useful phrase, tend to introduce the regular patterns before noting the exceptions. As a result, learners are primed to assume transparency and logicality, and will naturally develop the idea that language can be learned word by word. They may, as a result, see no importance in noticing collocational patterns, because they fail to see the subtle *irregularity* that resides in the preferential association of two perfectly ordinary-looking words.

To what extent would L2 learners be assisted, then, by earlier exposure to irregularity and opacity, with no requirement to understand why the forms are the way they are, only to accept them? The approach has been tried many times over the centuries and around the world, but opinions have differed as to its effectiveness. New technological capacities, however, offer better opportunities to examine the effects of different approaches to learning. Coupled with a sophisticated understanding of the dual importance of accuracy in expressing new ideas and idiomaticity, it may be increasingly possible in the future to establish when and how collocations are best introduced to different types of learner.

Meanwhile, another factor may need taking into account when evaluating the nature and extent of a learner's success: the effect of the difference between receptive and productive knowledge. One of the challenges for classroom learners is that they judge their own knowledge on the basis of not only – indeed perhaps not so much – what they can say, but also what they understand when they read texts and listen in the classroom, and what they can produce when they have the leisure to draft and craft their (written) work. This may lead to an underestimation of the difference between their receptive and productive knowledge.

This difference may be a way of explaining some of the errors that learners make. Wray and Fitzpatrick (2008; see also Wray, 2008: 251–7) explore the incidence of errors in wordstrings memorized for verbatim repetition, and propose that learners consistently overestimate their ability to produce material they have encountered before, because they don't realize the shortfall between what seems familiar and comprehensible when they see it, and what they have productive command of.

In the context of L2 collocations, it would mean that associations taken for granted as part of receptive knowledge were not adequately internalized to produce the same associations reliably in output. If what characterizes 'errors' in the output of relatively competent L2 users is actually a representation of the difference between receptive and productive knowledge, we have a useful basis for supporting learning. We can avoid simply re-presenting information the learners already have, and direct efforts instead towards narrowing the gap between what they know and what they can do.

Conclusion

Much of what I have said in this chapter reinforces Henriksen and Stenius Stæhr's observation regarding the 'need to be explicit about *theoretical assumptions with regard to acquisition of collocational knowledge,* both in relation to general language learning theory and in relation to theories of vocabulary acquisition' (this volume). Like them, I have suggested that the local research endeavour needs to be clearly anchored in broader questions that can unite many studies of different types. In turn, the broader questions will be gradually refined, as the boundaries of useful generalization are increasingly established.

Across all research domains there is now considerable interest in developing effective means to answer big questions – how to save endangered species, halt climate change, manage cultural division, cure cancers, etc. The prevailing trend is to seek joint answers from multidisciplinary teams. More quietly, and with rather less funding, researchers into L2 collocation are engaged in a similarly multidisciplinary pursuit. This volume exemplifies some of the lines of enquiry and methods, but others also exist – including those associated with artificial intelligence, communication disorders, and variation across discourse function. If we agree that big questions are best answered by examining them from many different viewpoints, then, provided we continue to embrace the challenge, research into the development and nature of collocational knowledge and performance in a second language has a bright and productive future.

Notes

1. Speakers also solve this problem by referring to 'conservative with a small c' and 'conservative with a large c'.
2. Others may be the final item of one string and the first of another with which it often co-occurs – the observation only making sense when the gaps in each string are taken into account.

References

Adolphs, S. and Durow, V. (2004). 'Social-Cultural Integration and the Development of Formulaic Sequences', in N. Schmitt (ed.), *Formulaic Sequences: Acquisition, Processing and Use* (107–26). Amsterdam: John Benjamins.

Aijmer, K. (1996). *Conversational Routines in English.* London: Longman.

Aisenstadt, E. (1979). 'Collocability Restrictions in Dictionaries', in R. R. K. Hartmann (ed.), *Dictionaries and their Users* (71–4). Exeter: Exeter University.

Aisenstadt, E. (1981). 'Restricted Collocations in English Lexicology and Lexicography', *ITL (Instituut voor Toegepaste Linguistiek) Review of Applied Linguistics* 53: 53–61.

Aitchison, J. (2003). *Words in the Mind: An Introduction to the Mental Lexicon.* Oxford: Blackwell.

Alderson, C., Clapham, C. and Wall, D. (1995). *Language Test Construction and Evaluation.* Cambridge: Cambridge University Press.

Alexander, L. G. (1967). *New Concept English.* London: Longman.

Alexander, L. G. and He, Q. (1997). *New Concept English.* Beijing: Longman and Foreign Language Teaching and Research Press.

Allerton, D. (1984). 'Three or Four Levels of Word Co-Occurrence Restriction', *Lingua* 63/1: 17–40.

Altenberg, B. (1993). 'Recurrent Verb-Complement Constructions in the London-Lund Corpus', in J. Aarts, P. de Haan and N. Oostdijk (eds), *English Language Corpora: Design, Analysis and Exploitation* (227–45). Amsterdam: Rodopi.

Altenberg, B. (1998). 'On thc Phraseology of Spoken English: The Evidence of Recurrent Word-Combinations', in A. P. Cowie (ed.), *Phraseology: Theory, Analysis, and Applications* (101–22). Oxford: Oxford University Press.

Anderson, R. C. and Freebody, P. (1981). 'Vocabulary Knowledge', in J. T. Guthrie (ed.), *Comprehension and Teaching: Research Reviews* (77–117). Newark, DE: International Reading Association.

Anderson, R. C. and Freebody, P. (1983). 'Reading Comprehension and the Assessment and Acquisition of Word Knowledge', in B. Hunston (ed.), *Advances in Reading/Language Research Volume 2* (231–56). Greenwich: JAI Press.

Anthony, L. (2006). *AntConc* v3.2.1. Available at: http://www.antlab.sci.waseda.ac.jp/software.html.

Appleby, R. (2000). 'Review of: 'The BBI Dictionary of English Word Combinations', 'Dictionary of Selected Collocations' and 'Longman Idioms Dictionary', *ELT Journal* 54/1: 89–91.

Arnaud, P. J. L. and Béjoint, H. (eds) (1992). *Vocabulary and Applied Linguistics.* London: Macmillan.

Arnaud, P. J. L. and Savignon, S. J. (1997). 'Rare Words, Complex Lexical Units and the Advanced Learner', in J. Coady and T. Huckin (eds), *Second Language Vocabulary Acquisition* (157–73). Cambridge: Cambridge University Press.

Atkins, B. T. S. and Varantola, K. (1997). 'Monitoring Dictionary Use', *International Journal of Lexicography* 10/1: 1–45.

Axelsson, M. W. (2003). *The Uppsala Student English Corpus Manual.* Uppsala University, Department of English: Sweden.

Bachman, L. F. (1990). *Fundamental Considerations in Language Testing*. Oxford: Oxford University Press.
Bachman, L. F. (2004). *Statistical Analysis for Language Assessment*. Cambridge: Cambridge University Press.
Bachman, L. F. and Palmer, A. (1996). *Language Testing in Practice*. Oxford: Oxford University Press.
Bahns, J. (1993). 'Lexical Collocations: A Contrastive View', *ELT Journal* 47/1: 56–63.
Bahns, J. and Eldaw, M. (1993). 'Should We Teach EFL Students Collocations?', *System* 21/1: 101–14.
Baigent, M. (1999). 'Teaching in Chunks: Integrating a Lexical Approach', *Modern English Teacher* 8/1: 51–4.
Barfield, A. (2001). 'Review of M. Lewis (ed.) (2000): "Teaching Collocation: Further Developments in the Lexical Approach"', *ELT Journal* 55/4: 413–15.
Barfield, A. (2006). 'An Exploration of Second Language Collocation Knowledge and Development', *Unpublished PhD Thesis*. University of Wales, Swansea.
Barfield, A. (2009). 'Exploring Productive L2 Collocation Knowledge', in T. Fitzpatrick and A. Barfield (eds), *Lexical Processing in Language Learners: Papers and Perspectives in Honour of Paul Meara* (95–110). Clevedon: Multilingual Matters.
Barlow, M. (2004). *Collocate 1.0: Locating collocations and terminology*. Software Program. Houston, TX. Distributor: Athelstan.
Barnbrook, G. (1996). *Language and Computers*. Edinburgh: Edinburgh University Press.
Barnbrook, G. (2007). 'Sinclair on Collocation', *International Journal of Corpus Linguistics* 12/2: 183–99.
Béjoint, H. (1981). 'The Foreign Student's Use of Monolingual English Dictionaries: A Study of Language Needs and Reference Skills', *Applied Linguistics* 2/3: 207–22.
Béjoint, H. (1994). *Tradition and Innovation in Modern English Dictionaries*. Oxford: Clarendon Press.
Béjoint, H. (2000). *Modern Lexicography: An Introduction*. Oxford: Oxford University Press.
Belz, J. A. and Vyatkina, N. (2008). 'The Pedagogical Mediation of a Developmental Learner Corpus for Classroom-Based Language Instruction', *Language Learning and Technology* 12/3: 33–52.
Benner, P. A. (1997). *Breakthroughs in Critical Reading*. New York: Jamestown Publishers.
Benson, M. (1985). 'Collocations and Idioms', in R. Ilson (ed.), *Dictionaries, Lexicography and Language Learning* (61–8). Oxford: Pergamon Press and The British Council.
Benson, M. (1989). 'The Structure of the Collocational Dictionary', *International Journal of Lexicography* 2/1: 1–14.
Benson, M., Benson, E. and Ilson, R. (1986a). *Lexicographic Description of English*. Amsterdam: John Benjamins.
Benson, M., Benson, E. and Ilson, R. (1986b). *The BBI Combinatory Dictionary of English*. Amsterdam: John Benjamins.
Benson, M., Benson, E. and Ilson, R. (1997). *The BBI Dictionary of English Word Combinations*. Amsterdam: John Benjamins.
Benson, P. and Lor, W. (1998). *Making Sense of Autonomous Language Learning: Conceptions of Learning and Readiness for Autonomy*. English Centre Monograph, No. 2. Hong Kong: University of Hong Kong.

Biber, D. (2004). 'Lexical Bundles in Academic Speech and Writing', in B. Lewandowska-Tomaszczyk (ed.), *Practical Applications in Language and Computers* (165–78). Frankfurt: Peter Lang.

Biber, D. (2006). *University Language: A Corpus-based Study of Spoken and Written Registers*. Amsterdam: John Benjamins.

Biber, D. (2008). 'Frequency-Based Approaches to Formulaic Language in English: Extending the Construct of Lexical Bundle'. *Paper presented at Kings College*, London, 8 December 2008.

Biber, D. and Barbieri, F. (2007). 'Lexical Bundles in University Spoken and Written Registers', *English for Specific Purposes* 26/3: 263–86.

Biber, D. and Conrad, S. (1999). 'Lexical Bundles in Conversation and Academic Prose', in H. Hasselgard and S. Oksefjell (eds), *Out of Corpora: Studies in Honour of Stig Johansson* (181–9). Amsterdam: Rodopi.

Biber, D., Conrad, S. and Cortes, V. (2003). 'Lexical Bundles in Speech and Writing: An Initial Taxonomy', in A. Wilson, P. Rayson and T. McEnery (eds), *Corpus Linguistics by the Lune: A Festschrift for Geoffrey Leech* (71–92). Frankfurt: Peter Lang.

Biber, D., Conrad, S. and Cortes, V. (2004). 'If you Look at ...: Lexical Bundles in University Teaching and Textbooks', *Applied Linguistics* 25/3: 371–405.

Biber, D., Conrad, S. and Reppen, R. (1998). *Corpus Linguistics: Investigating Language Structure and Use*. Cambridge: Cambridge University Press.

Biber, D., Johansson, S., Leech, G., Conrad, S. and Finegan, E. (1999a). 'Lexical Expressions in Speech and Writing', in *Longman Grammar of Spoken and Written English* (988–1036). Harlow, Essex: Longman.

Biber, D., Johansson, S., Leech, G., Conrad, S. and Finegan, E. (1999b). *Longman Grammar of Spoken and Written English*. Harlow: Pearson ESL.

Bishop, H. (2004). 'The Effect of Typographic Salience on the Look Up and Comprehension of Unknown Formulaic Sequences', in N. Schmitt (ed.), *Formulaic Sequences: Acquisition, Processing and Use* (227–48). Amsterdam: John Benjamins.

Biskup, D. (1992). 'L1 Influence on Learners' Renderings of English Collocations: A Polish/German Empirical Study', in P. J. L. Arnaud and H. Béjoint (eds), *Vocabulary and Applied Linguistics* (85–93). London: Macmillan.

Boers, F. and Lindstromberg, S. (2008). *Cognitive Linguistic Approaches to Teaching Vocabulary and Phraseology*. Berlin: Mouton de Gruyter.

Boers, F., Eyckmans, J. and Stengers, H. (2006). 'Motivating Multiword Units: Rationale, Mnemonic Benefits, and Cognitive Style Variables', in S. H. Foster-Cohen, M. Medved Krajnovic and J. Mihaljević Djigunović (eds), *EUROSLA Yearbook 6* (169–90). Amsterdam: John Benjamins.

Boers, F., Eyckmans, J., Kappel, J., Stengers, H. and Demecheleer, M. (2006). 'Formulaic Sequences and Perceived Oral Proficiency: Putting a Lexical Approach to the Test', *Language Teaching Research* 10/3: 245–61.

Boersma, P. (2001). 'Praat, a System for Doing Phonetics by Computer', *Glot International* 5:9/10: 341–5.

Bogaards, P. (1990). 'Où cherche-t-on dans le dictionnaire?', *International Journal of Lexicography* 3/2: 79–102.

Bogaards, P. and Laufer, B. (eds) (2004). *Vocabulary in a Second Language*. Amsterdam: John Benjamins.

Bolinger, D. (1976). 'Meaning and Memory', *Forum Linguisticum* 1: 1–14.

Bonk, W. J. (2000). 'Testing ESL Learners' Knowledge of Collocations', *Educational Resources Information Center Research Report ED 442309*.

Bonk, W. J. (2001). 'Testing ESL Learners' Knowledge of Collocations', in T. Hudson and J. D. Brown (eds), *A Focus on Language Test Development: Expanding the Language Proficiency Construct Across a Variety of Tests* (113–42). Honolulu, HI: University of Hawai'i, Second Language Teaching and Curriculum Center.

Boonmoh, A. and Nesi, H. (2007). 'A Survey of Dictionary Use by Thai University Staff and Students, with Special Reference to Pocket Electronic Dictionaries', *Horizontes de Lingüística Aplicada* 6/2: 79–90.

Bourdieu, P. (1977). 'The Economics of Linguistic Exchanges', *Social Science Information* 16/6: 645–68.

Cameron, L. (2002). 'Measuring Vocabulary Size in English as an Additional Language', *Language Teaching Research* 6/2: 145–73.

Carter, R. (1998). *Vocabulary: Applied Linguistic Perspectives*. London: Allen & Unwin.

Channell, J. (1981). 'Applying Semantic Theory to Vocabulary Teaching', *ELT Journal* 35/2: 115–22.

Chapelle, C. (1998). 'Construct Definition and Validity Inquiry in SLA Research', in L. F. Bachman and A. D. Cohen (eds), *Interfaces Between Second Language Acquisition and Language Testing Research* (32–70). Cambridge: Cambridge University Press.

Cheng, W., Greaves, C. and Warren, M. (2006). 'From n-gram to skipgram to concgram', *International Journal of Corpus Linguistics* 11/4: 411–33.

Chi, M., Wong, P. and Wong, C. (1994). 'Collocational Problems Amongst ESL Learners: A Corpus-Based Study', in L. Flowerdew and A. K. K. Tong (eds), *Entering Text* (157–63). Hong Kong: Hong Kong University of Science and Technology Language Centre.

Christiansen, M. and Chater, N. (2001). 'Connectionist Psycholinguistics: Capturing the Empirical Data', *Trends in Cognitive Sciences* 5/2: 82–8.

Clear, J. (1993). 'From Firth Principles: Computational Tools for the Study of Collocation', in M. Baker, G. Francis and E. Tognini-Bonelli (eds), *Text and Technology: In Honour of John Sinclair* (271–92). Amsterdam: John Benjamins.

Coady, J. and Huckin, T. (eds) (1997). *Second Language Vocabulary Acquisition*. Cambridge: Cambridge University Press.

Cobb, T. (2003). 'Analyzing Late Interlanguage with Learner Corpora: Québec Replications of Three European Studies', *The Canadian Modern Language Review/La Revue canadienne des langues vivantes* 59/3: 393–423.

Cobb, T. (2006). 'Review of Nadja Nesselhauf (2005): "Collocations in a learner corpus"', *The Canadian Modern Language Review* 63/2: 293–5.

Cobb, T. (2006). *Web VocabProfile BNC-20* v3.2. Available at: http://www.lextutor.ca/vp/bnc/.

COBUILD English Collocations on CD-ROM (1995). London and New York: HarperCollins.

Cohen, J. (1992). 'A Power Primer', *Psychological Bulletin* 112/1: 155–9.

Collins COBUILD English Dictionary for Advanced Learners, 3rd edition (2001). Glasgow: HarperCollins.

Colson, J. P. (2003). 'Corpus Linguistics and Phraseological Statistics: A Few Hypotheses and Examples', in H. Burger, A. Häcki Buhofer and G. Gréciano (eds), *Flut von Texten – Vielfalt der Kulturen/Ascona 2001 zur Methodologie und Kulturspezifik der Phraseologie* (47–59). Baltmannsweiler: Schneider Verlag Hohengehren.

Colson, J. P. (2008). 'Cross-Linguistic Phraseological Studies: An Overview', in S. Granger and F. Meunier (eds), *Phraseology: An Interdisciplinary Perspective* (191–206). Amsterdam: John Benjamins.

Conklin, C. and Schmitt, N. (2007). 'Formulaic Sequences: Are they Processed More Quickly than Nonformulaic Language by Native and Nonnative Speakers?', *Applied Linguistics* 29/1: 72–89.

Conrad, S. (2001). 'Variation among Disciplinary Texts: A Comparison of Textbooks and Journal Articles in Biology and History', in S. Conrad and D. Biber (eds), *Variation in English: Multi-dimensional Studies* (94–107). Harlow: Longman.

Cortes, V. (2004). 'Lexical Bundles in Published and Student Writing in History and Biology', *English for Specific Purposes* 23/4: 397–423.

Coseriu, E. (1973). *Probleme der strukturellen Semantik*. Tübingen: Narr.

Coulmas, F. (1979). 'Idiomaticity as a Problem of Pragmatics', in H. Parret, M. Sbísa and J. Verschueren (eds), *Possibilities and Limitations of Pragmatics: Proceedings of the Conference on Pragmatics, Urbino, Italy, July 8–14, 1979* (139–51). Amsterdam: John Benjamins.

Council of Europe (2001). *Common European Framework of Reference for Languages: Learning, Teaching, Assessment*. Cambridge: Cambridge University Press.

Cowie, A. P. (1981). 'The Treatment of Collocations and Idioms in Learners' Dictionaries', *Applied Linguistics* 2/3: 223–35.

Cowie, A. P. (1988). 'Stable and Creative Aspects of Vocabulary Use', in R. Carter and M. McCarthy (eds), *Vocabulary and Language Teaching* (126–39). London: Longman.

Cowie, A. P. (1991). 'Multiword Units in Newspaper Language', in S. Granger (ed.), *Perspectives on the English Lexicon: A Tribute to Jaques van Roey* (101–16). Louvain-la-Neuve: Cahiers de l'Institut de Linguistique de Louvain.

Cowie, A. P. (1994). 'Phraseology', in R. E. Asher (ed.), *The Encyclopedia of Language and Linguistics* (3168–71). Oxford: Pergamon.

Cowie, A. P. (1998a). 'Introduction', in A. P. Cowie (ed.), *Phraseology: Theory, Analysis, and Applications* (1–20). Oxford: Oxford University Press.

Cowie, A. P. (1998b). 'Phraseological Dictionaries: Some East-West Comparisons', in A. P. Cowie (ed.), *Phraseology: Theory, Analysis, and Applications* (209–28). Oxford: Oxford University Press.

Cowie, A. P. (ed.) (1998c). *Phraseology: Theory, Analysis, and Applications*. Oxford: Oxford University Press.

Cowie, A. P. (1999). *English Dictionaries for Foreign Learners*. Oxford: Oxford University Press.

Cowie, A. P. and Howarth, P. (1996). 'Phraseological Competence and Written Proficiency', in G. M. Blue and R. Mitchell (eds), *Language and Education: British Studies in Applied Linguistics 11* (80–93). Clevedon: Multilingual Matters.

Coxhead, A. (2008). 'Phraseology and English for Academic Purposes: Challenges and Opportunities', in F. Meunier and S. Granger (eds), *Phraseology in Foreign Language Learning and Teaching* (149–61). Amsterdam: John Benjamins.

Cruttenden, A. (1997). *Intonation*, 2nd edition. Cambridge: Cambridge University Press.

Cueto, N. R. (1998). 'Review of J. Hill and M. Lewis (eds) (1997): "Dictionary of Selected Collocations"', *TESL-EJ* 3/3 (R-11): 1–3.

Dahlmann, I. and Adolphs, S. (2007). 'Pauses as an Indicator of Psycholinguistically Valid Multi-Word Expressions (MWEs)?', in N. Gregoire, S. Evert and S. N. Kim (eds), *Proceedings of the ACL Workshop on A Broader Perspective on Multiword Expressions* (49–56). Prague: Association of Computational Linguistics.

Daller, H., Milton, J. and Treffers-Daller, J. (2007). *Modelling and Assessing Vocabulary Knowledge*. Cambridge: Cambridge University Press.

De Cock, S. (1998). 'A Recurrent Word Combination Approach to the Study of Formulae in the Speech of Native and Non-Native Speakers of English', *International Journal of Corpus Linguistics* 3/1: 59–80.

De Cock, S. (2000). 'Repetitive Phrasal Chunkiness and Advanced EFL Speech and Writing', in C. Mair and M. Hundt (eds), *Corpus Linguistics and Linguistic Theory* (51–68). Amsterdam: Rodopi.

De Cock, S. (2004). 'Preferred Sequences of Words in NS and NNS Speech', *Belgian Journal of English Language and Literatures (BELL)* New Series 2: 225–46.

De Cock, S., Granger, S., Leech, G. and McEnery, T. (1998). 'An Automated Approach to the Phrasicon of EFL Learners', in S. Granger (ed.), *Learner English on Computer* (67–79). Harlow: Longman.

Dechert, H. W. (1983). 'How a Story is Done in a Second Language', in C. Faerch and G. Kasper (eds), *Strategies in Interlanguage Communication* (175–95). London: Longman.

Dechert, H. W. and Lennon, P. (1989). 'Collocational Blends of Advanced Learners: A Preliminary Analysis', in W. Olesky (ed.), *Contrastive Pragmatics* (131–68). Amsterdam: John Benjamins.

De Groot, A. M. B. (1992). 'Determinants of Word Translation', *Journal of Experimental Psychology: Learning, Memory, and Cognition* 18/5: 1001–18.

Deng, Y. P. (2005). 'A Survey of College Students' Skills and Strategies of Dictionary Use in English Learning', *CELEA Journal* 28/4: 73–7.

Department of Higher Education, Ministry of Education of the People's Republic of China, (2004). *College English Curriculum Requirements*. Available at: http://www.bac.edu.cn/tdeparts/waiyubu/english/CollegeEnglish.asp.

DeVellis, R. F. (1991). *Scale Development*. Newbury Park, NJ: Sage Publications.

Dörnyei, Z., Durow, V. and Zahran, K. (2004). 'Individual Differences and their Effects on Formulaic Sequence Acquisition', in N. Schmitt (ed.), *Formulaic Sequences: Acquisition, Processing and Use* (55–86). Amsterdam: John Benjamins.

Ellis, N. C. (1997). 'Vocabulary Acquisition: Word Structure, Collocation, Word-Class, and Meaning', in N. Schmitt and M. McCarthy (eds), *Vocabulary: Description, Acquisition and Pedagogy* (122–39). Cambridge: Cambridge University Press.

Ellis, N. C. (1998). 'Emergentism, Connectionism and Language Learning', *Language Learning* 48/4: 631–64.

Ellis, N. C. (2002). 'Frequency Effects in Language Processing. A Review with Implications for Theories of Implicit and Explicit Language Acquisition', *Studies in Second Language Acquisition* 24/2: 143–88.

Ellis, N. C. (2003). 'Constructions, Chunking and Connectionism: The Emergence of Second Language Structure', in C. Doughty and M. Long (eds), *The Handbook of Second Language Acquisition* (63–103). Oxford: Blackwell.

Ellis, N. C. (2008). 'Phraseology: The Periphery and the Heart of Language', in F. Meunier and S. Granger (eds), *Phraseology in Language Learning and Teaching* (1–13). Amsterdam: John Benjamins.

Engeström, Y. (2005). '*Non scolae sed vitae discimus*: Toward Overcoming the Encapsulation of School Learning', in H. Daniels (ed.), *An Introduction to Vygotsky* (157–76). London: Routledge.

Erman, B. (2007). 'Cognitive Processes as Evidence of the Idiom Principle', *International Journal of Corpus Linguistics* 12/1: 25–53.

Eyckmans, J. (2004). *Measuring Receptive Vocabulary Size: Reliability and Validity of the Yes/No Vocabulary Test.* Utrecht: LOT.

Eyckmans, J. (2007). 'Taking SLA Research to Interpreting: Does Knowledge of Phrases Foster Fluency?', in F. Boers, J. Darquennes and R. Temmerman (eds), *Multilingualism and Applied Comparative Linguistics Volume 1: Pedagogical Perspectives* (89–105). Cambridge: Cambridge Scholars Publishing.

Eyckmans, J., Boers, F. and Demecheleer, M. (2004). 'The Deleted-Essentials Test: An Effective Affective Compromise', *Humanising Language Teaching* 6/4. Available at: www.hltmag.co.uk/nov04/mart04.rtf.

Eyckmans, J., Boers, F. and Stengers, H. (2006). 'The Discriminating Collocations Test: A Corpus-Based Measure of Phrasal Knowledge'. *Paper presented at EUROSLA 16*, Antalya, Turkey, 13–16 September 2006.

Eyckmans, J., Boers, F. and Stengers, H. (2007). 'Identifying Chunks: Who Can See the Wood for the Trees?', *Language Forum* 33/2: 85–100.

Eyckmans, J., Stengers, H. and Boers, F. (2007a). 'Making Sense of Multiword Units', in *Actas del XX Simposio Internacional de Comunicación Social* (719–21). Santiago de Cuba: Centro de Lingüística Aplicada.

Eyckmans, J., Stengers, H. and Boers, F. (2007b). 'Measuring Phrasal Knowledge in the L2'. *Paper presented at the 29th Annual Language Testing Research Colloquium*, University of Barcelona, Spain, 9–11 June 2007.

Eyckmans, J., Van de Velde, H., Van Hout, R. and Boers, F. (2007). 'Learners' Response Behaviour in Yes/No Vocabulary Tests', in H. Daller, J. Milton and J. Treffers-Daller (eds), *Modelling and Assessing Vocabulary Knowledge* (59–76). Cambridge: Cambridge University Press.

Farghal, M. and Obiedat, H. (1995). 'Collocations: A Neglected Variable in EFL', *International Review of Applied Linguistics* 33/4: 315–31.

Fayez-Hussein, R. (1990). 'Collocations: The Missing Link in Vocabulary Acquisition Amongst EFL Learners', in J. Fisiak (ed.), *Papers and Studies in Contrastive Linguistics: The Polish English Contrastive Project Volume 26* (123–36). Poznań: Adam Mickiewicz University.

Firth, J. R. (1952/3). 'Linguistic Analysis as a Study of Meaning', in F. R. Palmer (ed.), *Selected Papers of J.R. Firth 1952-59* (12–26). London: Longmans.

Firth, J. R. (1956). 'Descriptive Linguistics and the Study of English', in F. R. Palmer (ed.), *Selected Papers of J.R. Firth 1952-59* (96–113). London: Longmans.

Firth, J. R. (1957a). 'A Synopsis of Linguistic Theory, 1930–55', in F. R. Palmer (ed.), *Selected Papers of J. R. Firth 1952–59* (168–205). London: Longmans.

Firth, J. R. (1957b). 'Modes of Meaning', in *Papers in Linguistics 1934–1951* (190–215). London: Oxford University Press.

Firth, J. R. (1957c). *Papers in Linguistics 1934–1951*. London: Oxford University Press.

Fitzpatrick, T. and Barfield, A. (eds) (2009). *Lexical Processing in Language Learners: Papers and Perspectives in Honour of Paul Meara*. Clevedon: Multilingual Matters.

Fletcher, W. (2003). *Phrases in English* (PIE). Available at: http://www.kwicfinder.com/BNC/.

Fontenelle, T. (1998). 'Discovering Significant Lexical Functions in Dictionary Entries', in A. P. Cowie (ed.), *Phraseology: Theory, Analysis, and Applications* (189–207). Oxford: Oxford University Press.

Francis, G., Manning, E. and Hunston, S. (1996). *Collins COBUILD Grammar Patterns 1: Verbs*. London: HarperCollins.
Francis, G., Manning, E. and Hunston, S. (1998). *Collins COBUILD Grammar Patterns 2: Nouns and adjectives*. London: HarperCollins.
Frankenberg-Garcia, A. (2005). 'A Peek Into What Today's Language Learners as Researchers Actually Do', *International Journal of Lexicography* 18/3: 335–55.
Fraser, S. A. (2001). 'A Statistical Analysis of the Vocabulary of Medical Research Articles (3): Technical and Subtechnical Vocabulary', *Integrated Studies in Nursing Science* 4/2: 27–45.
Frath, P. and Gledhill, C. (2005). 'Free-Range Clusters or Frozen Chunks? Reference as a Defining Criterion for Linguistic Units', *Recherches Anglaises et Nord-américaines* 38: 25–44.
Gass, S. (1997). *Input, Interaction, and the Second Language Learner*. Mahwah, NJ: Lawrence Erlbaum.
Gilquin, G., Granger, S. and Paquot, M. (2007). 'Learner Corpora: The Missing Link in EAP Pedagogy', in P. Thompson (ed.), *Corpus-based EAP Pedagogy*. Special issue of *Journal of English for Academic Purposes* 6/4: 319–35.
Gilquin, G. and Granger, S. (forthcoming). 'From EFL to ESL: Evidence from the International Corpus of Learner English', in J. Mukherjee and M. Hundt (eds), *Exploring Second-language Varieties of English and Learner Englishes: Bridging a Paradigm Gap*. Amsterdam: John Benjamins.
Gitsaki, C. (1997). 'Patterns in the Development of English Collocational Knowledge: Some Pedagogical Implications', *Journal of Communication and International Studies* 1/4: 43–54.
Gitsaki, C. (1999). *Second Language Lexical Acquisition: A Study of the Development of Collocational Knowledge*. San Francisco: International Scholars Publications.
Gledhill, C. (2000). *Collocations in Science Writing*. Tübingen: Gunter Narr.
Gnutzman, C. (1997). 'Language Awareness: Progress in Language Learning and Language Education, or Reformulation of Old Ideas?', *Language Awareness* 6/2: 65–74.
Gold, D. L. (1988). 'Review of M. Benson, E. Benson and R. Ilson (eds) (1986): "The BBI Combinatory Dictionary of English: A Guide to Word Combinations"', *International Journal of Lexicography* 1/1: 56–9.
Goldberg, A. (2006). *Constructions at Work: The Nature of Generalization in Language*. Oxford: Oxford University Press.
Grabe, W. and Kaplan, R. (1996). *Theory and Practice of Writing*. Harlow: Longman.
Granger, S. (1998a). *Learner English on Computer*. London: Longman.
Granger, S. (1998b). 'Prefabricated Patterns in Advanced EFL Writing: Collocations and Formulae', in A. P. Cowie (ed.), *Phraseology: Theory, Analysis and Applications* (145–60). Oxford: Oxford University Press.
Granger, S. (2003). 'The International Corpus of Learner English: A New Resource for Foreign Language Learning and Teaching and Second Language Acquisition Research', *TESOL Quarterly* 37/3: 538–46.
Granger, S. (2009). 'The Contribution of Learner Corpora to Second Language Acquisition and Foreign Language Teaching: A Critical Evaluation', in K. Aijmer (ed.), *Corpora and Language Teaching* (13–32). Amsterdam: John Benjamins.
Granger, S. (in press). 'From Phraseology to Pedagogy: Challenges and Prospects', in T. Herbst, P. Uhrig and S. Schüller (eds), *Chunks in the Description of Language: A Tribute to John Sinclair*. Berlin: Mouton de Gruyter.

Granger, S. and Meunier, F. (eds) (2008). *Phraseology: An Interdisciplinary Perspective*. Amsterdam: John Benjamins.

Granger, S. and Paquot, M. (2008). 'Disentangling the Phraseological Web', in S. Granger and F. Meunier (eds), *Phraseology: An Interdisciplinary Perspective* (27–49). Amsterdam: John Benjamins.

Granger, S. and Paquot, M. (2009). 'Lexical Verbs in Academic Discourse: A Corpus-Driven Study of Learner Use', in M. Charles, S. Hunston and D. Pecorari (eds), *At the Interface of Corpus and Discourse: Analysing Academic Discourses*. London: Continuum.

Granger, S. and Rayson, P. (1998). 'Automatic Profiling of Learner Texts', in S. Granger (ed.), *Learner English on Computer* (119–31). New York: Addison Wesley Longman.

Granger, S., Dagneaux, E., Meunier, F. and Paquot, M. (2009). *The International Corpus of Learner English. Version 2. Handbook and CD-ROM*. Louvain-la-Neuve: Presses Universitaires de Louvain.

Guan, B. and Zheng, S. (2005). 'Recurrent Word Combinations in English Essays of Chinese College Students', *Modern Foreign Languages* 28/3: 288–96.

Gui, S. (2005). 'A Survey of Preposition Usage of Chinese English Learners', in H. Z. Yang, S. Gui and D. Yang (eds), *Corpus-Based Analysis of Chinese Learner English* (226–45). Shanghai: Shanghai Foreign Language Education Press.

Gui, S. and Yang, H. (2003). *Chinese Learner English Corpus*. Shanghai: Shanghai Foreign Language Education Press.

Gyllstad, H. (2004). 'Testing L2 Vocabulary: Current Test Formats in English as a L2 Used at Swedish Universities', in F. Heinat and S. Manninen (eds), *The Department of English in Lund: Working Papers in Linguistics* 4: 21–40. Lund: Lund University.

Gyllstad, H. (2005). 'The Word Doctor', in *Essential Teacher, Compleat Links* 2/3. Available at: http://www.tesol.org/s_tesol/secetdoc.asp?CID=963&DID=4245.

Gyllstad, H. (2007). *Testing English Collocations: Developing Receptive Tests for Use with Advanced Swedish Learners*. Lund: Lund University.

Haastrup, K. and Henriksen, B. (2000). 'Vocabulary Acquisition: Acquiring Depth of Knowledge through Network Building', *International Journal of Applied Linguistics* 10/2: 221–40.

Halliday, M. A. K. (1961). 'Categories of the Theory of Grammar', *Word* 17/3: 241–92.

Halliday, M. A. K. (1966). 'Lexis as a Linguistic Level', in C. E. Bazell, C. Catford, M. A. K. Halliday and R. H. Robbins (eds), *In Memory of J. R. Firth* (148–62). London: Longmans.

Hambleton, R. K. and Swaminathan, H. (1985). *Item Response Theory: Principles and Applications*. Boston: Kluwer.

Handl, S. (2008). 'Essential Collocations for Learners of English: The Role of Collocational Direction and Weight', in S. Granger and F. Meunier (eds), *Phraseology in Foreign Language Learning and Teaching* (43–65). Amsterdam: John Benjamins.

Handl, S. and Graf, E. (2009). 'Collocation, Anchoring and the Mental Lexicon – An Ontogenetic Perspective', in H-J Schmid and S. Handl (eds), *Cognitive Foundations of Linguistic Usage Patterns*. Berlin: Mouton de Gruyter.

Handl, S. (in preparation). *Collocation – Convenience Food for the Learner: A Corpus-based EFL-oriented Study of Habitual Syntagmatic Relations*.

Harder, P. (1980). 'Discourse as Self-Expression: On the Reduced Personality of the Second Language Learner', *Applied Linguistics* 1/3: 262–70.

HarperCollins (2007). *Bank of English*. Available at: http://www.collins.co.uk/books.aspx?group=153.

Hartmann, R. R. K. (2001). *Teaching and Researching Lexicography*. London: Longman.

Hausmann, F. J. (1979). 'Un dictionnaire des collocations est-il possible?', *Travaux de linguistique et de littérature* 17/1: 187–95.

Hausmann, F. J. (1984). 'Wortschatzlernen ist Kollokationslernen: Zum Lehren und Lernen französischer Wortverbindungen', *Praxis des neusprachlichen Unterricht* 31: 395–406.

Hendricks, A. E., and Yang, Y. (2002). 'Lexical Collocations and Transferability', *Paper presented at the 7th English in South East Asia Conference*, Hong Kong Baptist University, Hong Kong, 6–8 December 2002.

Henning, G. (1987). *A Guide to Language Testing: Development, Evaluation, and Research*. New York: Newbury House.

Henriksen, B. (1999). 'Three Dimensions of Vocabulary Development', *Studies in Second Language Acquisition* 21/2: 303–17.

Herbst, T. (1988). 'Review of M. Benson, E. Benson and R. Ilson (eds) (1986): "The BBI Combinatory Dictionary of English: A Guide to Word Combinations"', *System* 16/3: 380–4.

Herbst, T. (1996). 'What are Collocations: Sandy Beaches or False Teeth?', *English Studies* 77/4: 379–93.

Heuberger, R. (2000). *Monolingual Dictionaries for Foreign Learners of English: A Constructive Evaluation of the State-of-the-Art Reference Works in Book Form and on CD-Rom*. Wien: Braumüller.

Heyer, G., Läuter, M., Quasthoff, U., Wittig, T. and Wolff, C. (2001). 'Learning Relations Using Collocations', in *Proceedings of the International Joint Conference on Artificial Intelligence (IJCAI) 2001 Workshop on Ontology Learning* (19–24). Available at: http://explorer.csse.uwa.edu.au/reference/paper/233281602.pdf.

Hickey, T. (1993). 'Identifying Formulas in First Language Acquisition', *Journal of Child Language* 20/1: 27–41.

Hill, J. and Lewis, M. (eds) (1997). *Dictionary of Selected Collocations*. Hove, UK: Language Teaching Publications.

Hoey, M. (2005). *Lexical Priming: A New Theory of Words and Language*. London: Routledge.

Holland, D., Lachicott, W., Skinner, D. and Cain, C. (1998). *Identity and Agency in Cultural Worlds*. Cambridge, MA: Harvard University Press.

Holstein, J. A. and Gubrium, J. F. (1995). *The Active Interview*. London: Sage.

Hornby, A. S., Gatenby, E. V. and Wakefield, H. (1942). *Idiomatic and Syntactic English Dictionary*. Tokyo: Kaitakusha.

Hornby, A. S., Gatenby, E. V. and Wakefield, H. (1948). *A Learner's Dictionary of Current English*. Retitled in 1952 as *The Advanced Learner's Dictionary of Current English*. Oxford: Oxford University Press.

Howarth, P. (1996). *Phraseology in English Academic Writing: Some Implications for Language Learning and Dictionary Making*. Tübingen: Max Niemeyer.

Howarth, P. (1998a). 'Phraseology and Second Language Proficiency', *Applied Linguistics* 19/1: 24–44.

Howarth, P. (1998b). 'The Phraseology of Learners' Academic Writing', in A. P. Cowie (ed.), *Phraseology: Theory, Analysis and Applications* (161–86). Oxford: Oxford University Press.

Howarth, P. (2000). 'Review of M. Benson, E. Benson and R. Ilson (eds) (1997): "The BBI Dictionary of English Word Combinations"', *International Journal of Lexicography* 13/1: 50–4.

Hsu, J. (2007). 'Lexical Collocations and their Relation to the Online Writing of Taiwanese College English Majors and Non-English Majors', *Electronic Journal of Foreign Language Teaching* 4/2: 192–209. Available at: http://eflt.nus.edu.sg/v4n22007/hsu.pdf.

Huang, L. (2001). 'Knowledge of English Collocations: An Analysis of Taiwanese EFL Learners', in C. Luke and R. Rubrecht (eds), *Texas Papers in Foreign Language Education: Selected Proceedings from the Texas Foreign Language Education Conference 2001*. Educational Resources Information Center Document ED465 228.

Hulstijn, J. H. (2003). 'Incidental and Intentional Learning', in C. Doughty and M.H. Long (eds), *Handbook of Second Language Acquisition* (349–81). Malden, MA: Blackwell.

Hundt, M., Sand, S., and Siemund, R. (1998). *Manual of Information to Accompany the Freiburg-LOB Corpus of British English ('FLOB')*. Germany: Englisches Seminar, Albert-Ludwigs-Universität Freiburg. Available at: http://khnt.hit.uib.no/icame/manuals/flob/INDEX.HTM.

Hunston, S. (2002). *Corpora in Applied Linguistics*. Cambridge: Cambridge University Press.

Hunston, S. (2006). Starting with the Small Words: Patterns, Lexis and Semantic Sequences. *Paper presented at Exploring the Lexis-Grammar Interface*, University of Hannover, Germany, 5–7 October 2006.

Hunston, S. and Francis, G. (2000). *Pattern Grammar: A Corpus-driven Approach to the Lexical Grammar of English*. Amsterdam: John Benjamins.

Hunt, A. and Beglar, D. (2005). 'A Framework for Developing EFL Reading Vocabulary', *Reading in a Foreign Language* 17/1: 23–59.

Hyland, K. (2008). 'As Can be Seen: Lexical Bundles and Disciplinary Variation', *English for Specific Purposes* 27/1: 4–21.

Iannucci, J. (1987). 'Review of M. Benson, M. Benson and R. Ilson (eds) (1986): *"The BBI Combinatory Dictionary of English: A Guide to Word Combinations"*', *Dictionaries* 9: 272–5.

Ishikawa, S., Uemura, T., Kaneda, M., Shimizu, S., Sugimori, N. and Tono, Y. (2003). *JACET 8000: JACET List of 8000 Basic Words*. Tokyo: JACET.

Jehle, G. (2007). *The Advanced Foreign Learner's Mental Lexicon: Storage and Retrieval of Verb-Noun Collocations like 'to embezzle money'*. München: Dr. Kovac.

Jenkins, J. and Seidlhofer, B. (2001). 'Teaching English as a Lingua Franca for Europe', *Guardian Weekly*, 18 April 2001.

Jiang, N., and Nekrasova, T. M. (2007). 'The Processing of Formulaic Sequences by Second Language Speakers', *The Modern Language Journal*, 91/3: 433–45.

Joad, C. E. M (ed.) (1939). *How to Write, Think and Speak Correctly*. London: Odhams Press.

Jones, S. and Sinclair, J. (1974). 'English Lexical Collocations: A Study in Computational Linguistics', *Cahiers de Lexicologie* 24/1: 15–61.

Kaye, A. and McDaniel, K. (1989). 'Review of M. Benson, E. Benson and R. Ilson (eds) (1986): "The BBI Combinatory Dictionary of English: A Guide to Word Combinations"', *Lingua* 77: 375–77.

Keshavarz, M. H. and Salimi, H. (2007). 'Collocational Competence and Cloze Test Performance: A Study of Iranian EFL Learners', *International Journal of Applied Linguistics* 17/1: 81–92.

Klotz, M. (2000). *Grammatik und Lexik. Studien zur Syntagmatik englischer Verben.* Tübingen: Stauffenburg.

Klotz, M. (2003). 'Review of "Oxford Collocations Dictionary for Students of English"', *International Journal of Lexicography* 16/1: 57–61.

Knowles, F. (1993). 'Review of C. D. Kozlowska (1991): "English Adverbial Collocations"', *International Journal of Lexicography* 6/4: 300–4.

Komuro, Y. (2004). 'An analysis of the *Oxford Collocations Dictionary for Students of English*', *Lexicon* 34: 1–29.

Korosadowicz-Struzynska, M. (1980). 'Word Collocations in FL Vocabulary Instruction', *Studia Anglica Posnaniensia Poznan* 12: 109–20.

Kozlowska, D. and Dzieržanowska, H. (1982). *Selected English Collocations.* Warszawa: PWN.

Krishnamurthy, R. (ed.) (2004). *English Collocation Studies: The OSTI Report.* London: Continuum.

Kucera, H. and Francis, W. N. (1967). *Computational Analysis of Present-day American English.* Providence: Brown University Press.

Langer, S. (2005). 'A Linguistic Test Battery for Support Verb Constructions', *Linguisticae Investigationes* 27/2: 171–84.

Laufer, B. (1990). 'Why are Some Words More Difficult Than Others? Some Intralexical Factors that Affect the Learning of Words', *International Review of Applied Linguistics* 28/4: 293–307.

Laufer, B. (2005). 'Focus on Form in Second Language Vocabulary Learning', in S. H. Foster-Cohen, M. P. Garcia-Mayo and J. Cenoz (eds), *EUROSLA Yearbook: Volume 5* (223–50). Amsterdam: John Benjamins.

Laufer, B. and Girsai, N. (2005). 'Vocabulary Acquisition through Text-Based Translation Tasks'. *Paper presented at EUROSLA 15*, Dubrovnik, Croatia, 14–17 September 2005.

Laufer, B. and Girsai, N. (2008). 'Form-Focused Instruction in Second Language Vocabulary Learning: A Case for Contrastive Analysis and Translation', *Applied Linguistics* 29/4: 694–716.

Laufer, B. and Goldstein, Z. (2004). 'Testing Vocabulary Knowledge: Size, Strength, and Computer Adaptiveness', *Language Learning* 54/3: 399–436.

Laufer, B. and Hulstijn, J. (2001). 'Incidental Vocabulary Acquisition in a Second Language: The Construct of Task-Induced Involvement', *Applied Linguistics* 22/1: 1–26.

Laufer, B. and Kimmel, M. (1997). 'Bilingualised Dictionaries. How Learners Really Use Them', *System* 25/3: 361–9.

Le Page, R. B. and Tabouret-Keller, A. (1985). *Acts of Identity. Creole-based Approaches to Language and Ethnicity.* Cambridge: Cambridge University Press.

Lea, D. and Runcie, M. (2002). 'Blunt Instruments and Fine Distinctions: A Collocations Dictionary for Students of English', in A. Braasch and C. Povisen (eds), *Proceedings of the Tenth EURALEX International Congress EURALEX 2002* (819–29). Copenhagen: Center for Sprogteknologi.

Leech, G., Rayson, P. and Wilson, A. (2001). *Word Frequencies in Written and Spoken English*. Harlow: Pearson Education.

Lehiste, I. (1973). 'Phonetic Disambiguation of Syntactic Ambiguity', *Glossa* 7/2: 103–22.

Leńko-Szymańska, A. (2008). 'Formulaic Sequences in Apprentice Writing – Does More Mean Better?' *Paper presented at The Eighth Teaching and Language Corpora*, Lisbon, Portugal, 3–6 July 2008.

Lennon, P. (1996). 'Getting "Easy" Verbs Wrong at the Advanced Level', *International Review of Applied Linguistics* 34/1: 23–36.

Lewis, M. (1993). *The Lexical Approach: The State of ELT and a Way Forward*. Hove: Language Teaching Publications.

Lewis, M. (1997). *Implementing the Lexical Approach: Putting Theory into Practice*. Hove: Language Teaching Publications.

Lewis, M. (2000). *Teaching Collocation: Further Developments in the Lexical Approach*. Hove: Language Teaching Publications.

Lewis, Michael (2000). 'Learning in the Lexical Approach', in M. Lewis (ed.), *Teaching Collocation: Further Developments in the Lexical Approach* (155–85). Hove: Language Teaching Publications.

Lewis, Morgan (2000). 'There is Nothing as Practical as a Good Theory', in M. Lewis (ed.), *Teaching Collocation: Further Developments in the Lexical Approach* (10–27). Hove: England: Language Teaching Publications.

Lindstromberg, S. and Boers, F. (2008). *Teaching Chunks of Language: From Noticing to Remembering*. Brighton: Helbling Languages.

Little, D. (1997). 'Language Awareness and the Autonomous Language Learner', *Language Awareness* 6/2 and 3: 93–104.

Longman Dictionary of Contemporary English, 3rd edition (1995). Harlow: Longman.

The Longman Dictionary of Contemporary English, 4th edition (2005). Harlow: Pearson Education Longman.

Longman Language Activator (1993). Harlow: Longman.

Macmillan English Dictionary for Advanced Learners (2002). Oxford: Macmillan Education.

Maher, J. C. (2005). 'Metroethnicity, Language, and the Principle of Cool', *International Journal of the Sociology of Language* 175/6: 83–102.

Mair, C. (1997). 'Parallel Corpora: A Real-Time Approach to Language Change in Progress', in M. Ljung (ed.), *Corpus-Based Studies in English: Papers from the Seventeenth International Conference on English-Language Research Based on Computerized Corpora (ICAME 17)* (195–209). Amsterdam: Rodopi

Manning, C. and Schütze, H. (1999). *Foundations of Statistical Natural Language Processing*. Cambridge, MA: MIT Press.

Marks, J. (2003). 'Review of "The Oxford Collocations Dictionary for Students of English"' (2002), *Modern English Teaching* 12/2: 75–6.

Marton, W. (1977). 'Foreign Vocabulary Learning as Problem No.1 of Language Teaching at the Advanced Level', *Interlanguage Studies Bulletin* 2/1: 33–57.

McCarthy, M. and O'Dell, F. (2005). *English Collocations in Use*. Cambridge: Cambridge University Press.

McNamara, T. (2000). *Language Testing*. Oxford: Oxford University Press.

McNamara, T. F. (1996). *Measuring Second Language Performance*. London: Longman.

Meara, P. M. (1990). 'A Note on Passive Vocabulary', *Second Language Research* 6/2: 150–4.
Meara, P. M. (1992). 'Network Structures and Vocabulary Acquisition in a Foreign Language', in P. J. L. Arnaud and H. Bejoint (eds), *Vocabulary and Applied Linguistics* (62–70). London: Macmillan.
Meara, P. M. (1996). 'The Dimensions of Lexical Competence', in G. Brown, K. Malmkjaer and J. Williams (eds), *Performance and Competence in Second Language Acquisition* (35–53). Cambridge: Cambridge University Press.
Meara, P. M. and Buxton, B. (1987). 'An Alternative to Multiple Choice Vocabulary Tests', *Language Testing* 4/2: 142–54.
Meara, P. M. and Jones, G. (1988). 'Vocabulary Size as a Placement Indicator', in P. Grunwell (ed.), *Applied Linguistics in Society* (80–7). London: CILT.
Meara, P. M. and Wolter, B. (2004). 'V_Links: Beyond Vocabulary Depth', *Angles on the English Speaking World* 4: 85–97.
Mel'čuk, I. (1998). 'Collocations and Lexical Functions', in A. P. Cowie (ed.) *Phraseology: Theory, Analysis, and Applications* (24–53). Oxford: Oxford University Press.
Messick, S. (1993). 'Validity', in R. L. Linn (ed.), *Educational Measurement*, 3rd edition (13–103). New York: American Council of Education.
Messick, S. (1995). 'Validity of Psychological Assessment', *American Psychologist* 50/9: 741–9.
Meunier, F. and Granger, S. (eds) (2008). *Phraseology in Foreign Language Learning and Teaching*. Amsterdam: John Benjamins.
Miao, H. and Sun, L. (2005). 'The Chunking Effect of Delexicalized High-Frequency Verb Collocations: A Corpus-Based Study', *Journal of PLA University of Foreign Languages* 28/3: 40–54.
Midlane, V. (2005). 'Students' Use of Portable Electronic Dictionaries in the EFL/ESL Classroom: A Survey of Teacher Attitudes', *M.Ed. Dissertation*. Faculty of Education, University of Manchester. Available at: http://www.bankgatetutors.co.uk/PEDs.htm.
Milton, J. (1998). 'Exploiting L1 and Interlanguage Corpora in the Design of an Electronic Language Learning and Production Environment', in S. Granger (ed.), *Learner English on Computer* (186–98). Harlow: Longman.
Mochizuki, M. (2002). 'Exploration of Two Aspects of Vocabulary Knowledge: Paradigmatic and Collocational', *Annual Review of English Language Education in Japan* 13: 121–9.
Mollet, E., Wray, A. and Fitzpatrick, T. (in preparation). 'Accessing Second-Order Collocation through Lexical Co-Occurrence Networks'.
Moon, R. (1987). 'The Analysis of Meaning', in J. Sinclair (ed.), *Looking Up: An Account of the COBUILD Project in Lexical Computing* (86–103). London: Collins ELT.
Moon, R. (1997). 'Vocabulary Connections: Multiword-Items in English', in N. Schmitt and M. McCarthy (eds), *Vocabulary: Description, Acquisition and Pedagogy* (40–63). Cambridge: Cambridge University Press.
Moon, R. (1998). *Fixed Expressions and Idioms in English: A Corpus-based Approach*. Oxford: Clarendon Press.
Moreno Jaén, M. (2007) 'A Corpus-Driven Design of a Test for Assessing the ESL Collocational Competence of University Students', *International Journal of English Studies* 7/2: 127–47.

Nation, I. S. P. (1990). *Teaching and Learning Vocabulary.* Boston, MA: Heinle & Heinle.

Nation, I. S. P. (2001). *Learning Vocabulary in Another Language.* Cambridge: Cambridge University Press.

Nattinger, J. and DeCarrico, J. (1992). *Lexical Phrases and Language Teaching.* Oxford: Oxford University Press.

Nesselhauf, N. (2003). 'The Use of Collocations by Advanced Learners of English and Some Implications for Teaching', *Applied Linguistics* 24/2: 223–42.

Nesselhauf, N. (2004). 'What are Collocations?', in D. J. Allerton, N. Nesselhauf and P. Skandera (eds), *Phraseological Units: Basic Concepts and Their Application* (1–21). Basel: Schwabe.

Nesselhauf, N. (2005). *Collocations in a Learner Corpus.* Amsterdam: John Benjamins.

Nesselhauf, N. (2006). 'Researching L2 Production with ICLE', in S. Braun, K. Kohn, and J. Mukherjee (eds), *Corpus Technology and Language Pedagogy* (141–56). Frankfurt: Peter Lang.

Norton Pierce, B. (1995). 'Social Identity, Investment, and Language Learning', *TESOL Quarterly* 29/1: 9–31.

Norton, B. (2000). *Identity and Language Learning: Gender, Ethnicity and Educational Change.* Harlow: Longman.

Nuccorini, S. (2003). 'Towards an "ideal" Dictionary of English Collocations', in P. van Sterkenburg (ed.), *A Practical Guide to Lexicography* (366–87). Amsterdam: John Benjamins.

Oakes, M. (1998). *Statistics in Corpus Linguistics.* Edinburgh: Edinburgh University Press.

Oakey, D. J. (2002). 'Lexical Phrases for Teaching Academic Writing in English: Corpus Evidence', in S. Nuccorini (ed.), *Phrases and Phraseology: Data and Descriptions* (85–105). Bern: Peter Lang.

Oxford Advanced Learner's Dictionary, 7th edition (2005). Oxford: Oxford University Press.

Oxford Collocations Dictionary for Students of English (2002). Oxford: Oxford University Press.

Oxford University (2005). *British National Corpus.* Available at: http://www.natcorp.ox.ac.uk/.

Paikeday, T. (1989). 'Revolutionizing Dictionaries', *American Speech* 64/4: 354–62.

Palmer, F. R. (ed.) (1957). *Selected Papers of J. R. Firth 1952–59.* London: Longmans.

Palmer, H. (1930). *Interim Report on Vocabulary Selection submitted to the Seventh Annual Conference of English Teachers under the auspices of the Institute for Research in English Teaching.* Tokyo: IRET. [Reprinted in *The Selected Writings of Harold E. Palmer, Volume 9: Vocabulary.* Tokyo: Honnotomosha (1995).]

Palmer, H. (1931). *Second Interim Report on Vocabulary Selection.* Tokyo: Kaitakusha.

Palmer, H. (1933a). 'Our Research on Collocations', *The Bulletin of the Institute for Research in English Teaching* 95: 1–2.

Palmer, H. (1933b). *Second Interim Report on English Collocations.* Tokyo: Kaitakusha. Reprinted 1966.

Palmer, H. (1934). 'Director's Report', *The Bulletin of the Institute for Research in English Teaching* 108: 16–24.

Park, J. S. Y. (2002). 'Cognitive and Interactional Motivations for the Intonation Unit', *Studies in Language* 26/3: 637–80.

Partington, A. (1998). *Patterns and Meanings: Using Corpora for English Language Research and Teaching*. Amsterdam: John Benjamins.

Pawley, A. and Syder, F. H. (1983). 'Two Puzzles for Linguistic Theory: Nativelike Selection and Nativelike Fluency', in J. C. Richards and R. W. Schmidt (eds), *Language and Communication* (191–226). London: Longman.

Pecman, M. (2008). 'Compilation, Formalisation and Presentation of Bilingual Phraseology: Problems and Possible Solutions', in F. Meunier and S. Granger (eds), *Phraseology in Foreign Language Learning and Teaching* (203–22). Amsterdam: John Benjamins.

Peters, A. M. (1983). *The Units of Language Acquisition*. Cambridge: Cambridge University Press.

Peters, E. (2007a). 'The Influence of Task Instruction on Vocabulary Acquisition and Reading Comprehension', in M.P. Garcia-Mayo (ed.), *Investigating Tasks in Formal Language Learning* (178–98). Clevedon: Multilingual Matters.

Peters, E. (2007b). 'Manipulating L2 Learners' Online Dictionary Use and its Effect on L2 Word Retention', *Language, Learning & Technology* 11/2: 36–58.

Peters, E., Hulstijn, J. H., Sercu, L. and Lutjeharms M. (2009). 'Learning L2 Vocabulary Through Reading: The Effect of Three Enhancement Techniques Compared', *Language Learning* 59/1: 113–51

Philip, G. (2008). 'Reassessing the Cannon: "Fixed" Phrases in General Reference Corpora', in S. Granger and F. Meunier (eds), *Phraseology: An Interdisciplinary Perspective* (95–108). Amsterdam: John Benjamins.

Piennemann, M. (1998). *Language Processing and Second Language Development: Processability Theory*. Amsterdam: John Benjamins.

Piotrowski, T. (1987). 'Review of M. Benson, E. Benson and R. Ilson (1986): *"Lexicographic Description of English"* and *"The BBI Combinatory Dictionary of English: A Guide to Word Combinations"*', *International Review of Applied Linguistics* 25/2: 173–5.

Poirier, E. (2003). 'Conséquences didactiques et théoriques du caractère conventionnel et arbitraire de la traduction des unités phraséologiques', *Meta* 48/3: 402–10.

Price, P. J., Ostendorf, M., Shattuck-Hufnagel, S. and Fong, C. (1991). 'The Use of Prosody in Syntactic Disambiguation', *Journal of the Acoustical Society of America* 90/6: 2956–70.

Princeton University (undated). *Visuwords*™. Available at: http://www.visuwords.com/.

Pulverness, A. (2007). 'Review of M. McCarthy and F. O'Dell (2005): "English Collocations in Use"', *ELT Journal* 61/2: 182–5.

Randall, M. (2007). *Memory, Psychology and Second Language Learning*. Amsterdam: John Benjamins.

Read, J. (2000). *Assessing Vocabulary*. Cambridge: Cambridge University Press.

Read, J. (2004). 'Plumbing the Depths: How Should the Construct of Vocabulary Knowledge be Defined?', in P. Bogaards and B. Laufer (eds), *Vocabulary in a Second Language* (209–27). Amsterdam: John Benjamins.

Read, J. and Nation, P. (2004). 'Measurement of Formulaic Sequences', in N. Schmitt (ed.), *Formulaic Sequences: Acquisition, Processing and Use* (23–35). Amsterdam: John Benjamins.

Renouf, A. (1987). 'Moving on', in J. Sinclair (ed.), *Looking Up: An Account of the COBUILD Project in Lexical Computing* (167–78). London: Collins ELT.

Reppen, R. (2001). 'Register Variation in Student and Adult Speech and Writing', in S. Conrad and D. Biber (eds), *Variation in English: Multi-dimensional Studies* (187–99). London: Longman.

Reppen, R. (2007). 'L1 and L2 Writing Development of Elementary Students: Two Perspectives', in Y. Kawaguchi, T. Takagaki, N. Tomimori, and Y. Tsurgura (eds), *Corpus-Based Perspectives in Linguistics* (147–67). Amsterdam: John Benjamins.

Reppen, R. and Vásquez, C. (2007). 'Using Corpus Linguistics to Investigate the Language of Teacher Training', in J. Walinski, K. Kredens and S. Gozdz-Roszkowski (eds), *Corpora and ICT in Language Studies* (13–29). Frankfurt: Peter Lang.

Revier, R. L. and Henriksen, B. (2006). 'Teaching Collocations: Pedagogical Implications Based on a Cross-Sectional Study of Danish EFL Learners' Written Production of English Collocations', in M. Bendtsen, M. Björklund, C. Fant and L. Forsman (eds), *Språk, lärande och utbildning i sikte — Festskrift tillägnad professor Kaj Sjöholm*. Rapport nr 20. (173–89). Vasa: Pedagogiska fakulteten vid Åbo Akademi.

Richard, J. C. (2006). 'Materials Development and Research: Making the Connection', *RELC Journal* 37/1: 5–26.

Richards, J. C. (1976). 'The Role of Vocabulary Teaching', *TESOL Quarterly* 10/1: 77–84.

Rundell, M. (1999). 'Dictionary Use in Production', *International Journal of Lexicography* 12/1: 35–53.

Saito, H. (1915). *Jukugo-Honi-Eiwa-Chu-Jiten* [*Saito's Idiomological English-Japanese Dictionary*]. Tokyo: Nichieisha.

Schafer, A. J., Warren, P., Speer, S. R., White, S. D. and Sokol, S. (2000). 'Prosodic Disambiguation in Ambiguous and Unambiguous Situations'. *Paper presented at the Annual Meeting of the Linguistic Society of America*, Chicago, 6–9 January 2000.

Schmid, H.-J. (2003). 'Collocation: Hard to Pin Down, But Bloody Useful', *Zeitschrift für Anglistik und Amerikanistik* 51/3: 235–58.

Schmidt, R. (1990). 'The Role of Consciousness in Second Language Learning', *Applied Linguistics* 11/2: 129–58.

Schmidt, R. (1992). 'Awareness in Second Language Acquisition', *Annual Review of Applied Linguistics* 13: 206–26.

Schmidt, R. and Frota, S. (1986). 'Developing Basic Conversational Ability in a Second Language: A Case Study of an Adult Learner of Portuguese', in R.R. Day (ed.), *Talking to Learn: Conversation in Second Language Acquisition* (237–326). Rowley, MA: Newbury House.

Schmitt, N. (1998). 'Measuring Collocational Knowledge: Key Issues and an Experimental Assessment Procedure', *ITL Review of Applied Linguistics* 119–120: 27–47.

Schmitt, N. (1999). 'The Relationship Between TOEFL Vocabulary Items and Meaning, Association, Collocations and Word-Class Knowledge', *Language Testing* 16/2: 189–216.

Schmitt, N. (2000). *Vocabulary in Language Teaching*. Cambridge: Cambridge University Press.

Schmitt, N. (ed.) (2004). *Formulaic Sequences: Acquisition, Processing and Use*. Amsterdam: John Benjamins.

Schmitt, N. and Carter, R. (2004). 'Formulaic Sequences in Action: An Introduction', in N. Schmitt (ed.), *Formulaic Sequences: Acquisition, Processing and Use* (1–22). Amsterdam: John Benjamins.

Schmitt, N. and McCarthy, M. (eds) (1997). *Vocabulary Description, Acquisition and Pedagogy*. Cambridge: Cambridge University Press.

Schmitt, N. and Underwood, G. (2004). 'Exploring the Processing of Formulaic Sequences Through a Self-Paced Reading Task', in N. Schmitt (ed.), *Formulaic Sequences: Acquisition, Processing and Use* (173–90). Amsterdam; Philadelphia: John Benjamins.

Scott, M. (2001). 'Comparing Corpora and Identifying Key Words, Collocations and Frequency Distributions Through the WordSmith Tools Suite of Computer Software', in M. Ghadessy, A. Henry and R. Roseberry (eds), *Small Corpus Studies and ELT* (47–67). Amsterdam: John Benjamins.

Scott, M. (2008). *WordSmith Tools* v4. Oxford: Oxford University Press. Available at: http://www.lexically.net/wordsmith/index.html.

Scott, M. and Tribble, C. (2006). *Textual Patterns: Key Words and Corpus Analysis in Language Education*. Amsterdam: John Benjamins.

Seidlhofer, B. (2005). 'English as a Lingua Franca', *ELT Journal* 59/4: 339–41.

Seidlhofer, B. (2007). 'Common Property: English as a Lingua Franca in Europe', in J. Cummins and C. Davison (eds), *International Handbook of English Language Teaching* (137–53). New York: Springer.

Seidlhofer, B. and Jenkins, J. (2003). 'English as a Lingua Franca and the Politics of Property', in C. Mair (ed.), *The Politics of English as a World Language* (139–54). Amsterdam: Rodopi.

Seidlhofer, B., Breiteneder, A. and Pitzl, M-L. (2006). 'English as a Lingua Franca in Europe: Challenges for Applied Linguistics', *Annual Review of Applied Linguistics* 26: 3–34.

Shillaw, J. (1999). 'The Application of the Rasch Model to Yes/No Vocabulary Tests'. *Unpublished PhD Thesis*. University of Wales, Swansea.

Shillaw, J. (2009). 'Putting Yes/No Tests in Context', in T. Fitzpatrick and A. Barfield (eds), *Lexical Processing in Language Learners: Papers and Perspectives in Honour of Paul Meara*. Clevedon: Multilingual Matters.

Siepmann, D. (2005). 'Collocation, Colligation and Encoding Dictionaries. Part I: Lexicological Aspects', *International Journal of Lexicography* 18/4: 409–43.

Siepmann, D. (2006). 'Collocation, Colligation and Encoding Dictionaries. Part II: Lexicographical Aspects', *International Journal of Lexicography* 19/1: 1–39.

Siepmann, D. (2008). 'Phraseology in Learners' Dictionaries: What, Where and How?', in F. Meunier and S. Granger, S. (eds), *Phraseology in Foreign Language Learning and Teaching* (101–19). Amsterdam: John Benjamins.

Sinclair, J. (1966). 'Beginning the Study of Lexis', in C. E. Bazell, C. Catford, M. A. K. Halliday and R. H. Robbins (eds), *In Memory of J. R. Firth* (410–30). London: Longmans.

Sinclair, J. (1987a). 'Collocation: A Progress Report', in R. Steele and T. Threadgold (eds), *Language Topics: Essays in Honour of Michael Halliday* (319–31). Amsterdam: John Benjamins.

Sinclair, J. (1987b). 'The Nature of the Evidence', in J. Sinclair (ed.), *Looking Up: An Account of the COBUILD Project in Lexical Computing* (150–9). London: Collins ELT.

Sinclair, J. (1991). *Corpus, Concordance and Collocation.* Oxford: Oxford University Press.
Sinclair, J. (1996). 'The Search for Units of Meaning', *Textus* 9: 75–106.
Sinclair, J. (2001). 'Review of D. Biber, S. Johansson, G. Leech, S. Conrad and E. Finegan (1999): "The Longman Grammar of Spoken and Written English"', *International Journal of Corpus Linguistics* 6/2: 339–59.
Sinclair, J. (2003). *Reading Concordances.* Harlow: Pearson Longman.
Sinclair, J. (2004). *Trust the Text: Language, Corpus and Discourse.* London: Routledge.
Sinclair, J. and Renouf, A. (1988). 'A Lexical Syllabus for Language Learning', in R. Carter and M. J. McCarthy (eds), *Vocabulary and Language Teaching* (140–58). London: Longman.
Sinclair, J., Jones, S. and Daley, R. (1970). 'English Lexical Studies: Report to OSTI on Project C/LP/08', in R. Krishnamurthy (ed.), *English Collocation Studies: The OSTI Report* (2–204). London: Continuum.
Singleton, D. (1999). *Exploring the Second Language Mental Lexicon.* Cambridge: Cambridge University Press.
Siyanova, A. and Schmitt, N. (2008). 'L2 Learner Production and Processing of Collocation: A Multi-Study Perspective', *The Canadian Modern Language Review/La Revue canadienne des langues vivantes* 64/3: 429–58.
Smadja, F. A. (1989). 'Lexical Co-Occurrence: The Missing Link', *Literary and Linguistic Computing* 4/3: 163–8.
Smith, R. C. (1998). 'The Palmer-Hornby Contribution to English Teaching in Japan', *International Journal of Lexicography* 11/4: 269–91.
Smith, R. C. (1999). *The Writings of Harold E. Palmer: An Overview.* Tokyo: Hon-no-Tomosha. Available at: www.warwick.ac.uk/~elsdr/WritingsofH.E.Palmer.pdf.
Smith, R. C. and Imura, M. (2004). 'Lessons from the Past: Traditions and Reforms', in V. Makarova and T. Rodgers (eds), *English Language Teaching: The Case of Japan* (29–48). Munich: Lincom Europa.
Starfield, S. (2004). '"Why does this Feel Empowering?" Thesis Writing, Concordancing, and the Corporatizing University', in B. Norton and K. Toohey (eds), *Critical Pedagogies and Language Learning* (138–57). Cambridge: Cambridge University Press.
Stein, G. (2004). 'Monolingual Dictionaries for Foreign Learners of English: A Constructive Evaluation of the State-of-the-Art Reference Works in Book Form and on CD-Rom', *International Journal of Lexicography* 17/1: 95–7.
Stengers, H. (2007). 'Is English Exceptionally Idiomatic? Testing the Waters for a Lexical Approach to Spanish', in F. Boers, J. Darquennes and R. Temmerman (eds), *Multilingualism and Applied Comparative Linguistics* (107–26). Newcastle: Cambridge Scholars Publishing.
Stubbs, M. (2002). *Words and Phrases: Corpus Studies of Lexical Semantics.* Oxford: Blackwell.
Stubbs, M. (2003). 'Two Quantitative Methods of Studying Phraseology in English', *International Journal of Corpus Linguistics* 7/2: 215–44.
Stubbs, M. (2004). 'A Quantitative Approach to Collocations', in D. J. Allerton, N. Nesselhauf and P. Skandera (eds), *Phraseological Units: Basic Concepts and Their Application* (107–19). Basel: Schwabe.
Stubbs, M. and Barth, I. (2003). 'Using Recurrent Phrases as Text-Type Discriminators: A Quantitative Method and Some Findings', *Functions of Language* 10/1: 61–104.

Swain, M. (1995). 'Three Functions of Output in Second Language Learning', in G. Cook and B. Seidlhofer (eds), *Principle and Practice in Applied Linguistics: Studies in Honor of H. G. Widdowson* (97–114). Oxford: Oxford University Press.

Thinkmap, Inc. (undated). *The Visual Thesaurus®* Version 3. Available at: http://www.visualthesaurus.com.

Thornbury, S. (1998). 'The Lexical Approach: A Journey without Maps?', *Modern English Teacher* 7/4: 7–13.

Tirkkonen-Condit, S. (2002). 'Translationese – A Myth or an Empirical Fact?', *Target* 14/2: 207–20.

Tognini-Bonelli, H. (2001). *Corpus Linguistics at Work*. Amsterdam: John Benjamins.

Toohey, K. (2007). 'Autonomy/Agency through Socio-Cultural Lenses', in A. Barfield and S. Brown (eds), *Reconstructing Autonomy in Language Education: Inquiry and Innovation* (231–42). Basingstoke: Palgrave Macmillan.

Underwood, G., Schmitt, N. and Galpin, A. (2004). 'The Eyes Have It: An Eye-Movement Study into the Processing of Formulaic Sequences', in N. Schmitt (ed.), *Formulaic Sequences: Acquisition, Processing and Use* (153–72). Amsterdam: John Benjamins.

Van Patten, B. and Cardierno, T. (1993). 'Explicit Instruction and Input Processing', *Studies in Second Language Acquisition* 15/2: 225–41.

Vermeer, A. (2001). 'Breadth and Depth of Vocabulary in Relation to Acquisition and Frequency of Input', *Applied Psycholinguistics* 22/2: 217–34.

Walker, C. (2008). 'Factors which Influence the Process of Collocation', in F. Boers, and S. Lindstromberg (eds), *Cognitive Linguistic Approaches to Teaching Vocabulary and Phraseology* (291–308). Berlin: Mouton De Gruyter.

Wallace, M. and Wray, A. (2006). *Critical Reading and Writing for Postgraduates*. London: Sage.

Warren, B. (2005). 'A Model of Idiomaticity', *Nordic Journal of English Studies* 4/1: 35–54.

Warren, P., Schafer, A. J., Speer, S. R. and White, S. D. (2000). 'Prosodic Resolution of Prepositional Phrase Ambiguity in Ambiguous and Unambiguous Situations', *UCLA Working Papers in Phonetics*, 99: 5–33.

Webb, S. and Kagimoto, E. (2007). 'Teaching and Learning Collocation'. *Paper presented at the 33rd Japan Association for Language Teaching Conference*, Tokyo, 22–25 November 2007.

Wei, N. (2002a). 'A Corpus-Driven Study of Semantic Prosodies in Specialized Texts', *Modern Foreign Languages* 25/2: 165–75.

Wei, N. (2002b). 'Corpus-Based and Corpus-Driven Approaches to the Study of Collocation', *Contemporary Linguistics* 4/2: 101–14.

West, M. (1953). *A General Service List of English Words*. London: Longman.

Wichmann, A. (2000). *Intonation in Text and Discourse*. Harlow: Longman.

Wilks, C. and Meara, P. M. (2007). 'Implementing Graph Theory Approaches to the Exploration of Density and Structure an L1 and L2 Word Association Networks', in H. Daller, J. Milton and J. Treffers-Daller (eds), *Modelling and Assessing Vocabulary Knowledge* (167–82). Cambridge: Cambridge University Press.

Willis, D. (2003). *Rules, Patterns and Words*. Cambridge: Cambridge University Press.

Wolter, B. (2006). 'Lexical Network Structures and L2 Vocabulary Acquisition: The Role of L1 Lexical/Conceptual Knowledge', *Applied Linguistics* 27/4: 741–7.

Wray, A. (2002). *Formulaic Language and the Lexicon*. Cambridge: Cambridge University Press.

Wray, A. (2004). '"Here's one I prepared earlier": Formulaic Language Learning on Television', in N. Schmitt (ed.), *Formulaic Sequences: Acquisition, Processing and Use* (249–68). Amsterdam: John Benjamins.

Wray, A. (2008). *Formulaic Language: Pushing the Boundaries*. Oxford: Oxford University Press.

Wray, A. (2009). 'Identifying Formulaic Language: Persistent Challenges and New Opportunities', in R. L. Corrigan, E. A. Moravcsik, H. Oulali and K. M. Wheatley (eds), *Formulaic Language: Volume 1, Distribution and Historical Change*. Typological Studies in Language (27–51). Amsterdam: John Benjamins.

Wray, A. and Fitzpatrick, T. (2008). 'Why Can't you Just Leave it Alone? Deviations from Memorized Language as a Gauge of Nativelike Competence', in F. Meunier and S. Granger (eds), *Phraseology in Foreign Language Learning and Teaching* (123–48). Amsterdam: John Benjamins.

Wright, T. and Bolitho, R. (1993). 'Language Awareness: A Missing Link in Language Teacher Education?', *ELT Journal* 47/4: 292–304.

Yang, D. (1999). 'Interlanguage Errors and Cross-Linguistic Influence: A Corpus-Based Approach to Chinese EFL Learners' Written Production'. *Unpublished PhD Thesis*. People's Republic of China: Guangdong University of Foreign Studies, Guangzhou.

Yang, Y. (2000). 'Grammar and Beyond Grammar in the Chinese Tertiary EFL Classroom: A Language Awareness Perspective'. *Unpublished M.Phil. Thesis*. Chinese University of Hong Kong.

Yang, Y. and Hendricks, A. (2004). 'Collocation Awareness in the Writing Process', *Journal of Reflections on English Language Teaching* 3: 51–78.

Yang, Y. and Jiang, J. Y. (2003). 'Awareness of Collocations in English Language Teaching and Learning', *Foreign Languages and Culture: Researches and Achievements* 1/1: 196–203.

Yorio, C. A. (1989). 'Idiomaticity as an Indicator of Second Language Proficiency', in K. Hyltenstam and L. K. Obler (eds), *Bilingualism Across the Lifespan: Aspects of Acquisition, Maturity, and Loss* (55–72). Cambridge: Cambridge University Press.

Zhang, X. (1993). 'English Collocations and their Effect on the Writing of Native and Non-Native College Freshmen'. *Unpublished PhD Thesis*. Indiana University of Pennsylvania.

Zhao, W. (2005). 'Erroneous V + N Collocations: L1 Transfer and L2 Acquisition', in H. Z. Yang, S. Gui and D. Yang (eds), *Corpus-Based Analysis of Chinese Learner English* (275–88). Shanghai: Shanghai Foreign Language Education Press.

Zimmerman, J., Broder, P., Shaugnessy, J. and Underwood, B. (1977). 'A Recognition Test of Vocabulary Using Signal-Detection Measures and Some Correlates of Word and Non Word Recognition', *Intelligence* 1: 5–13.

Zughoul, M. R. (1991). 'Lexical Choice: Towards Writing Problematic Word Lists', *International Review of Applied Linguistics* 29/1: 45–60.

Index